"David Heywood's book is timely. The effect of Covid on theological education is to move the teaching and learning online, like many other educational institutions. Online learning is potentially more flexible and makes geography irrelevant (even national boundaries). Why be fixed on a primary model of a residential (quasi monastic) community and a secondary one that tries to do a scaled down version of this? The cracks in the system and its effectiveness, let alone its cost are showing. At this point David Heywood's book speaks to many issues: the need to make theological reflection a core discipline and practice, training together of lay and people for licensed ministries, the danger of training an elite, centring on Christian practices rather than intellectual subjects, questioning the efficacy of frontloading of education, training as timely rather than all at the beginning. These are some of the issues delved into and examined in the book. As such it opens up a rather closed debate about the current provision of theological education and suggests a new path for the future. There is much to be considered here."

Phillip Tovey, Principal, Oxford Local Ministry Pathway

"As someone who has worked in the field of ministerial formation, predominantly with lay people, for over thirty five years I welcome David's timely and prescient contribution to the debate. In the challenging climate we face as we seek to reframe ministry and mission with the opportunities and constraints that exist, the four key principles that David outlines in this book of ministerial formation as a life long, collaborative, experiential learning and reflective practice focused for a varied and diverse ministry seem apt. This is a well researched book which draws on a wide range of contexts to root the discussion in practice and the footnotes show the breadth and depth of sources engaged with allowing follow up for those who wish to delve more deeply into particular aspects. I particularly appreciate the suggestion of incorporating emotional intelligence competencies into the formation curriculum and the associated grade descriptors, equipping emotionally intelligent ministers (using that term inclusively) would help make much of the current work in formation more explicit and measurable. I commend this book to anyone wanting to reflect on formation and training for mission, ministry and whole life discipleship."

Sally Nash, Director, Insitute for Children, Youth and Mission

"This book raises vital questions about collaborative ministry and what needs to be addressed, not least in how the formation of clergy needs to be strongly focused from the outset on enabling all baptised followers of Christ of every age to be formed and transformed as everyday disciples, Sunday to Saturday. The question of how to address the destructive and pervasive ethos of clericalism is highlighted. I found this book refreshing and heartening, yet it is not for the faint-hearted or those who do not want to participate in kingdom-shaped transformation in the Church, rather than reorganisation which simply focuses on rearranging the chairs on the deck with a few tweaks to the way clergy are trained and deployed."

Rachel Treweek, Bishop of Gloucester, UK

"David Heywood unfolds with lucidity and wisdom a new paradigm for ministerial formation. In doing so he provides a clear and informed assessment of the current situation and problems associated with the prevailing academic and skills-based approach to theological education. Heywood offers a more integrative, practical and mission focussed approach to formation for the local church. His emphasis is on life-long learning and a collaborative ethos. In Heywood's account discipleship and ministry are interrelated and lay and ordained ministries are properly integrated. Heywood is surely right when he notes that 'at heart' formation is about the 'redirection of the affections .... in the company of others'. Heywood's concrete proposals for ministry formation nudge the Church deeper into the new paradigm. This book will be of immense value for those involved in the development of ministry formation programs and all who seek to serve the mission of God as disciples of Christ. This is an important and timely book from a seasoned theologian full of practical wisdom."

Stephen Pickard, Executive Director, Australian Centre for Christianity and Culture

"I have long believed, with David Heywood that ministerial formation in the Church of England (and by extension much more widely) is not fit for purpose. I hope this book, drawing as it does on years of experience, real world research and extensive literature, will act like a 'good virus' to infect our Churches with a vision of what is possible in the formation of the whole people of God so that they can participate in the mission of God. I trust that it will be read, reflected and acted on by Church leaders and theological educators right across this land and many others."

Nigel Rooms, Leader, Partnership for Missional Church

"A central part of David's calling is to help the Church think through the interwoven questions of discipleship and ministry and the relationship between lay and ordained in the Body of Christ. Kingdom Learning is another powerful contribution to that process. David's deep, clear and incisive reflections will, I hope, be a vital resource to the whole Church as we seek fruitful ways forward in the midst of and beyond the COVID pandemic."

Stephen Croft, Bishop of Oxford, UK

"I welcome David Heywood's vision of a new theoretical and practical paradigm for ministerial formation. There can be few authors as well qualified to write on this topic, not only by the depth of their study and reflection, but also through their practical experience of teaching and ministry. David's book deserves to be taken seriously by all those in the churches who are concerned with 'theological education', with reuniting discipleship and ministry, or with the connection that lies at the heart of true Christian learning between our human experience and the resources of the gospel."

Jeff Astley, Alister Hardy Professor of Religious and Spiritual Experience, Bishop Grosseteste University, UK

"In this excellent and challenging book, David Heywood builds on his earlier studies that examined how ministry might be reimagined and shaped by the learning dynamic of the Kingdom of God. *Reimagining Ministerial Formation* offers hope in its call for a life-long holistic engagement with reflective learning. It doesn't just offer the Church hope, it has potential to transform the landscape of higher education too and a richer dialogue between these and diverse sectors of society. Wide-ranging, rich in its Scriptural and historical interaction, and up-to-date in its referencing of the changing landscape of COVID_19 RMF is a thoughtful and accessible study that can help each of us create and curate the space to grow our collaborative and diverse ministries for the 21st century and beyond".

Helen-Ann Hartley, Bishop of Ripon

"How do we organise formation so that the whole of a disciple is permeable to every learning opportunity in every area of their life, able to become mature in Christ and encourage and equip others to do the same? In this book David presents a vision of ministerial formation that makes my heart sing. It is, as he states, already emerging: aimed at the discipling of the whole church in a variety of ministries for the sake of God's kingdom, and following the missio Dei, it is local, contextual, accessible to all, holistic, non-hierarchical, and gloriously every-day. With a cornerstone of theological reflection, collaborative and individual, and keeping the goal of emotionally intelligent, pastorally imaginative and wise practitioners in mind, his vision presents a coherent argument and a compelling call to all involved in shaping the future of learning in the church. As an accidental training provider for missioners across a diocese, I will be regularly referring to this as an inspiration, checklist and guide."

Tina Hodgett, Evangelism and Pioneer Team Leader, Diocese of Bath and Wells

"David has written a wise, nuanced and thoughtful book which will enrich the debate about ministerial formation in the next season of the life of the Church of England. His deep analysis of the current reality should provoke radical heart searching among those who have responsibility for the design and funding of ministerial formation, particularly as it involves the priesthood of all believers. This should be the blue print for the future of ministerial education!"

Mandy Ford, Dean of Bristol

"If we are to shape a future for flourishing communities of faith engaged in the mission of God then reframing ministry roles as gifts that enable the mission and ministry of the whole people of God is an urgent task. Built on the firm foundation of decades of teaching and research this book identifies barriers and blocks to formation of the whole people of God and offers generative solutions for transforming our paradigm and practices in this. I thoroughly recommend it to all who are concerned with being a church of missionary disciples."

Nick Shepherd, Programme Director, "Setting God's People Free"

Reimagining Ministerial Formation

David Heywood

scm press

© David Heywood 2021
Published in 2021 by SCM Press
Editorial office
3rd Floor, Invicta House,
108–114 Golden Lane,
London EC1Y 0TG, UK
www.scmpress.co.uk

SCM Press is an imprint of Hymns Ancient & Modern Ltd
(a registered charity)

Hymns Ancient & Modern® is a registered trademark of
Hymns Ancient & Modern Ltd
13A Hellesdon Park Road, Norwich,
Norfolk NR6 5DR, UK

Unless otherwise indicated, the Scripture quotations contained herein
are from The New Revised Standard Version of the Bible,
Anglicized Edition, copyright © 1989, 1995 by the Division of Christian
Education of the National Council of the churches of Christ in the United States
of America, and are used by permission. All rights reserved.

British Library Cataloguing in Publication data

A catalogue record for this book is available
from the British Library

978-0-334-06042-0

Typeset by Regent Typesetting
Printed and bound by
CPI Group (UK) Ltd

Contents

Preface   ix

Introduction: Ministerial Formation for the Whole Church   1
1 An Emerging New Paradigm   19
2 Moving on from the Academic Model   38
3 Adopting the New Paradigm   88
4 A Different World   131

Appendices   147
Index   177

Preface

In many ways, *Reimagining Ministerial Formation* is the third in a series. It builds directly on two of my previous books, *Reimagining Ministry* (2011) and *Kingdom Learning* (2017).[1]

Over the last 30 years or more, the Holy Spirit has been calling the church in Britain to a renewed emphasis on mission as an integral part of its life. In a variety of ways, the policies of the Churches at national level and the life of the churches locally are being shaped by mission. In *Reimagining Ministry*, I explored the ways in which the church's understanding and practice of ministry might respond to its changing understanding and practice of mission. I suggested that it is possible to discern a number of stages by which mission has gradually taken root in the church's life and that each strategic step has laid a foundation for the next, not only in the church's practice but in its 'operant' or 'enacted' theology. I joined many other writers in suggesting that the theological heart of our redis-covery of mission lies in a vision of the *missio Dei* or mission of God and of God's coming rule or kingdom. I explored the idea of the church as *koinonia* or communion, a 'foretaste' of the kingdom, and concluded that the pattern of ministry that best serves God's mission is collaborative, rooted in loving relationship. In practical terms, this means that, instead of understanding ordained ministry as the standard form of ministry and all other forms as auxiliary optional extras, the standard form of ministry is collaborative local ministry. The function of ordained ministry is to 'animate' the ministry of the whole people of God, to enable, equip and connect local ministry.[2]

In a church shaped for mission, which understands 'ministry' as the ministry of the whole church, discipleship becomes a vital element. It requires local churches to become learning communities, where God's people grow in discipleship and are equipped for ministry. *Kingdom Learning* grew out of my conviction that two elements are required to make this a reality: good practice in adult education and skills of theo-logical reflection. Since theological reflection is grounded in the cycle of experiential learning, these two requirements are closely related. As I write later in this book, theological reflection is good pedagogy and good pedagogy is reflective. *Kingdom Learning* is an exploration of theological reflection and its role in learning for discipleship and ministry. It draws on an earlier book, *Divine Revelation and Human Learning*, the fruit of my doctoral thesis, in which, by charting the connections between the psychology of learning and the theology of revelation, I endeavoured to show how the natural ways in which people learn play an integral part in the transforming work of the Holy Spirit.[3] Since *Kingdom Learning* sets out the foundation of a theory of learning to resource discipleship and ministry, *Reimagining Ministerial Formation* repeats a few sections of the earlier book. I hope that readers of both will not find this overly tedious. On the other hand, some aspects of the argument of this book are dealt with in greater detail in *Kingdom Learning*. In particular, it includes a fuller account of good practice in adult education, which I take to be essential to ministerial formation.

In *Reimagining Ministry*, I expressed the hope that the next significant step forward in the church's practice of mission and ministry would be the recognition and encouragement of 'whole-life discipleship', now coming to be called 'everyday faith'. As *Kingdom Learning* was in publication, the Church of England published a report entitled 'Setting God's People Free' calling for exactly that. Although by no means the first report urging the Church of England to put into practice its theoretical commitment to the ministry of the whole church, 'Setting God's People Free' went further in at least three respects:

- It pointed out that the ministry of lay people and their leadership in the life of the Church required a foundation in 'whole-life discipleship': 'fruitful, faithful mission and ministry, influence, leadership and, most importantly, vibrant relationship with Jesus Christ in all of life'.[4]
- It challenged the Church to accept a process through which to change its structures to enable whole-life discipleship.
- It named 'clericalism' as a key factor preventing the Church from embracing the discipleship and ministry of all.

Since I too believe that ministry arises from discipleship and is an integral part of it, 'everyday faith' occupies an important place in this study of ministerial formation. In the first place, in the life-long learning model of formation that I advocate everyday faith is the indispensable foundation. Second, because the enabling of whole-life discipleship and the building of communities where God's people learn together are vital tasks of church leadership.

However, as Peter Senge writes, 'New insights fail to get put into practice because they conflict with deeply held internal images of how the world works, images that limit us to familiar ways of thinking and acting.'[5] 'Setting God's People Free' also calls attention to the 'deeply held internal image', entrenched for centuries in the church's theology and structures of power, which has prevented it from recognizing the vital importance of lay discipleship. At the heart of clericalism lies the assumption that ministry is the prerogative of the clergy, so that ministry comes to be defined as 'what the clergy do'. As I noted in *Kingdom Learning*, the consequences of clericalism are many:

- many clergy are reluctant to devolve responsibility and involve others in ministry
- many congregations are reluctant to share in ministry with the clergy
- the church devotes a disproportionate share of its resources to the training of the clergy, to the relative neglect of formation for lay discipleship and ministry
- because of their training the clergy come to be thought of as an elite, while the laity come to believe that 'they are not academic enough to handle theology' nor 'ordained enough' to be theologians[6]
- when it does take place, lay ministry is often seen as 'helping the clergy'
- rather than arising from the distinctive shape of lay ministry, training courses for lay people often reproduce the shape of training designed for the clergy
- schemes of pastoral reorganization concentrate on the deployment of the clergy rather than the mission of the whole church
- clergy, upon whom the responsibility for mission and ministry is seen to fall, become burned out attempting to fulfil an impossible task
- ordained ministry consumes the overwhelming proportion of the Church's financial resources, time and energy.

In summary, clericalism denies the truth that laity and clergy are 'equal in worth and status, complementary in gifting and vocation, mutually accountable in discipleship and equal partners in mission'.[7]

As a deeply embedded shared mindset with spiritual consequences, clericalism is one of the 'principalities and powers' referred to in the New Testament, whose effects are to blind people to the truth and imprison them in false and dehumanizing ways of understanding.[8] My fear is that, since unconsciously held shared assumptions lie at the heart of any human system, the church will be unable to respond to the call of the Holy Spirit unless it consciously and intentionally renounces clericalism. This would require an act of repentance in the full sense of the word: not only a *metanoia*, or change of mindset, but a recognition that clericalism is not simply an unfortunate mistake but a grievous sin deeply entrenched for centuries in the church's structures of power and a determination to turn away from it wherever it may be found. Accordingly, in the final chapter of this book, which takes the form of a retrospect, a public act of repentance is seen as a vital step in the church's ability to reform itself.

In previous generations, training for ordained ministry was known as 'theological education' and the providers of such training are still known as 'Theological Education Institutions'. However, since at least 2003, with the publication of the report *Formation for Ministry within a Learning Church*, 'formation' has become the preferred language of the Church of England.[9] The term 'ministerial formation' reflects the welcome recognition that learning for ministry involves the whole person. Whereas 'education' may place the focus on growth in knowledge and 'training' on acquiring skills, 'formation', rightly used, encompasses the whole process.[10]

Nevertheless, the Church's adoption of the language of 'formation' has not been accompanied by any kind of precision as to what formation involves.[11] Words such as 'learning', 'education' and 'training' tend to be used interchangeably in descriptions of formation, and in the following pages I have often used these terms in ways that overlap. Behind this usage lies a definition of formation 'in its widest sense' offered by Jeff Astley:

> *All* the processes of teaching and/or learning that help to shape a learner in a tradition and its beliefs, experiences and practices, in a way that leads to the learner's acceptance of that tradition in her thinking, valuing, feeling and perceiving, and her dispositions to act and experience, *together with her appraisal of the tradition's merits and faults.*[12]

Implicit in Astley's definition is the assumption that underlies this book, namely that formation is not something reserved for those aspiring to ordination or licensed ministry but is for all Christians. Since ministry arises from and is an aspect of discipleship, formation for ministry is continuous with formation for discipleship. It also makes explicit that there is a critical element within the formative process through which the

Christian disciple learns to inhabit the living tradition of Christian faith, that formation may involve wrestling with elements of the tradition in order to inhabit them in an intelligent and responsible way.

What, then, is the outcome of those processes of learning? How are we to understand the goal of Christian formation?

- At its heart, formation is a redirection of the affections. Jesus taught his followers to pray daily, 'Our Father in heaven, hallowed be your name. Your kingdom come; your will be done on earth as in heaven.' Inhabiting the Christian tradition means that God the holy Trinity becomes the object of our devotion, Jesus Christ our only reference point and the coming of his kingdom on earth our chief longing.
- Next, formation takes place in company with others. In the words of Paul, we are 'called into the *koinonia*' [or 'fellowship'] of Jesus Christ (1 Corinthians 1.9). To be 'members' of Christ's Body means more than simply becoming part of both a local congregation and the worldwide family of God's people. It means developing formative relationships with other Christians and offering our God-given gifts for the building up of the whole Body.
- Intellectually, formation involves coming to 'see' the whole of life from the perspective of the Christian tradition: the world as the creation of a good and wise Creator; ourselves and others as loved and cherished; the world as marred by sin both personal and structural but redeemed by Jesus' death and resurrection; God as present and active in the world through his Spirit; the future as determined by God's purpose for the final coming of his kingdom. In formation, these, among other insights, come to make up the 'ordinary theology' of every Christian.

  By 'ordinary theology' we mean the theology of 'ordinary' Christians who have had no formal theological training. This should not be taken as denigrating such theology as second-rate. Rather, 'ordinary' should be taken as 'an honourable word connoting what is "regular", "normal", "usual", "prevalent" and "common"'.[13] In a recent piece of research, Elizabeth Jordan demonstrates the ways in which the 'ordinary theology' of church members who understood the local church as 'family' was, in some ways, more sophisticated and more faithful to scripture than that of the clergy whose academic study had caused them to be sceptical about such a view.[14] Ordinary theology, then, ought not to be understood as an imperfect grasp of the field of academic theology but rather as the believer's perspective on the whole of life, shaped by the Christian tradition.

- The intellectual aspect of formation is integrally related to the practical. The ability to see the whole of life through the lens of Christian faith requires a gradually deepening commitment to the practices through which Christianity is lived out in daily life, such as regular prayer and Bible study, the discipline of sabbath, stewardship of money and time, care for the poor, and commitment to sexual purity.
- In addition to the shared practices of the tradition, each Christian disciple receives a unique call from God to work with the Holy Spirit in the renewal of creation and the coming of God's kingdom.[15] Our fundamental call is to follow Jesus. But beyond this, God plants in each person a passion to play their part in the work of his kingdom, often in the sphere of their daily work or some other aspect of the wider community.
- In and through the redirection of affections, membership of Christ's Body, the adoption of the Christian tradition as a perspective on life, participation in Christian practices and response to God's individual call, Christians experience a transformation in attitudes. Their lives should increasingly be marked by qualities of life such as joy, compassion, kindness, patience, goodness, self-control and the willingness to forgive (Galatians 5.22–23; Colossians 3.12–14).
- Finally, formation involves the 'fellowship of Christ's suffering' (Philippians 3.10). The New Testament describes Christian believers as 'aliens and exiles' in relation to the wider community (1 Peter 2.11). Adopting the perspective and practices of Christian faith places the disciple at variance with the society in which she lives with the result that she is likely to be misunderstood and may even be hated and rejected by family and colleagues. But such hardship, when God allows it, also plays a role in building Christian character and dependence on God (Romans 5.3–5; James 1.2–4).

Implicit in this account of formation is the assumption that the Holy Spirit is present and active in all the processes of teaching and learning through which the disciple and minister is shaped.[16] Long ago, Dietrich Bonhoeffer wrote:

Formation comes only by being drawn into the form of Jesus Christ. It comes only as formation in his likeness, as *conformation* with the unique form of him who was made man, was crucified and rose again. This is not achieved by dint of efforts to 'become like Jesus', which is the way in which we usually interpret it. It is achieved only when the form of Jesus Christ works upon us in such a manner that it moulds our form in its own likeness.[17]

One of the greatest advantages of the term 'formation', then, lies in the intimate connection between formation for ministry and the transformation into the likeness of Christ that lies at the heart of discipleship.

This book is written from the perspective of my own Church, the Church of England, and with that Church specifically in mind. The starting point for other Churches, in Britain and overseas, may well be different. Theologies and practices of ministry emerge from different understandings of the church and its mission. Different cultures have differing expectations of both learning and leadership. On the other hand, most of the principles underlying the emerging paradigm I am presenting, both theological and pedagogical, are universal, and in constructing my argument I have drawn on the work of scholars in other countries and traditions. It will be the task of others more familiar with their own cultures of both church and society to discern how the proposals I make here might be applied elsewhere.

I have used the word 'Church' with a capital 'C' for institutions such as the Church of England or Methodist Church and 'church' with a small case 'c' to refer either to the whole church or the local church. I have also followed my normal practice in alternating between the use of 'he' and 'she' for the representative disciple or minister. I trust that this will be received as an acceptable way of avoiding the suggestion of gender bias.

No book can ever be the work of a single person and *Reimagining Ministerial Formation* would not have been possible without the help of many. I am immensely grateful to the following:

- My colleagues Beren Hartless, Tim Naish and Phillip Tovey met with me several times to explore the emerging new paradigm of ministerial formation; the table of grade descriptors for emotional intelligence in Appendix 3 is largely Phillip's work.
- During my work for the Diocese of Oxford between 2017 and 2020, my colleague Tina Molyneux introduced me to Personal Discipleship Plans; and area deans and deanery lay chairs from throughout the diocese helped me to think about the shape of locally based training.
- Nigel Rooms, ably assisted by Joel Denno, carried out the research that I describe in the Introduction.
- Dan Beesley, Anne Curtis, Nigel Featherstone, Susan Gill, Alexandra Hewitt, Michael Lloyd, Ross Meikle, Mark Philpott, Nadine Rose,

Cathy Ross, Rosemary Sandbach, Susanna Schneider, Sue Simpson, Bishop Humphrey Southern, Phillip Tovey, Rich White and Natalie Worsfold gave me permission to use the quotations from the report.

- Tina Hodgett from the Diocese of Bath and Wells, Luke Fogg and Rob Hay from the Diocese of Leicester, and Paul Bradbury of the South Central Regional Training Partnership's Pioneer Hub provided valuable insights into the training of pioneer ministers.
- Archdeacon Ambrose Mason commissioned the MA course for prospective ministry area leaders in the Diocese of Monmouth, on which I worked with my colleagues Rowena King and Janet Williams.
- Richard Hainsworth and Michael West shared with me their presentation at the 2019 conference of the British and Irish Association for Practical Theology on the educational philosophy of St Padarn's Institute, the training institution of the Church in Wales, and Manon James brought me up to date with the progress of ministerial formation in Wales.
- Jeremy Duff gave me permission to quote from his unpublished paper on the theological foundations for residential training in Wales.
- Ian McIntosh invited me to join the group working on the formation qualities for ordinands and clergy in the Church of England and worked with me on what became the detailed level description of those qualities in Appendix 4.
- Jane Leach allowed me to see an advance copy of her book, *A Charge to Keep*.
- Mandy Ford, Ian McIntosh, Nick Shepherd, Phillip Tovey, and John Valentine provided valuable comments on an earlier draft of the book.
- Jeff Astley, Keith Beech-Gruneberg, Quentin Chandler, Beren Hartless and Phillip Tovey provided valuable comments in the final stages of writing.

Needless to say, none of these people are responsible for the remaining shortcomings of the book.

Notes

1 David Heywood, *Reimagining Ministry*, London: SCM Press, 2011; *Kingdom Learning*, London: SCM Press, 2017.

2 For a fuller presentation of the argument for this position, see *Reimagining Ministry*, especially pp. 182–94.

3 David Heywood, *Divine Revelation and Human Learning*, Aldershot: Ashgate, 2004.

4 Archbishops' Council, General Synod Paper 2056, 'Setting God's People Free', www.churchofengland.org/sites/default/files/2017-11/gs-2056-setting-gods-people-free.pdf, p. 1.

5 Peter Senge, *The Fifth Discipline: The Art and Practice of the Learning Organization*, New York: Random House, 2006, p. 163.

6 Laurie Green, *Let's Do Theology*, 2nd edition, London: Mowbray, 2009, p. 135. Green writes: 'It is in the nature of oppression that the oppressed begin to think in the same categories as the oppressors', implying that clericalism shares in the 'nature of oppression'.

7 'Setting God's People Free', p. 2.

8 For an exploration of the language of 'powers and principalities', see *Reimagining Ministry*, pp. 91–108.

9 Archbishops' Council, *Formation for Ministry within a Learning Church: The Structure and Funding of Ordination Training*, 2003.

10 Although it is sometimes used to denote only the purely 'spiritual' aspects of ministerial training.

11 Jeff Astley, 'The naming of parts: faith, formation, development and education', in *Christian Faith, Formation and Education*, ed. Ros Stuart-Buttle and John Shortt, Cham, Switzerland: Palgrave Macmillan, 2018, p. 14.

12 Astley, 'Naming of parts', p. 23 (italics original).

13 Jeff Astley, 'In defence of "ordinary theology"', *British Journal of Theological Education* 13.1 (2002), p. 24; see also Astley, *Ordinary Theology*, Aldershot: Ashgate, 2002, pp. 47–52.

14 Elizabeth Jordan, 'Conversation as a tool of research in practical theology', *Practical Theology* 12.5 (2019), pp. 526–36.

15 Miroslav Volf, *Work in the Spirit*, Eugene, OR: Wipf and Stock, 1991, pp. 88–105; Volf, 'Work as cooperation with God' in *Work: Theological Foundations and Practical Implications*, ed. R. Keith Loftin and Trey Dimsdale, London: SCM Press, 2018, pp. 83–109.

16 I have explored the role of the Holy Spirit in Christian learning in depth in my book *Divine Revelation and Human Learning*, Aldershot: Ashgate, 2004.

17 Dietrich Bonhoeffer, *Ethics*, New York: Macmillan, 1986, pp. 80–1.

Introduction:
Ministerial Formation
for the Whole Church

Since the 1980s the Church of England's understanding and practice of ministry has been undergoing a process of transition. In the traditional model, 'ministry' was broadly understood as that of the ordained; it centred on the provision of worship and pastoral care in geographically based parishes. Over the past 30 years, that consensus has been breaking down under the impact of rapid changes in society and theological re-evaluation of our patterns of ministry. The Church is gradually coming to recognize that the primary meaning of 'ministry' must become the ministry of the whole church, clergy and lay together.[1] It is beginning to recognize and respond to its call to become a community of 'missionary disciples',[2] whose vocation is to cooperate with the Holy Spirit in the mission of God, the work of God's kingdom.

The church is thus experiencing a far-reaching change in its pattern of ministry: from a pattern centred almost entirely on the ministry of the clergy to one in which lay people play a full part, not simply as the supporters of the clergy but as fellow-workers, sharing in the responsibilities of leadership. Such a fundamental upheaval calls for changes in the pattern of ministerial formation. As long ago as 2006, Daniel Hardy had called for 'new conceptions of theological education and formation, not simply forms of the old adapted for wider use',[3] and in 2019 Bishop Jonathan Clark, Chair of the Church's Quality and Formation Panel, referring to the vision of a ministry involving all God's people, wrote:

> Putting this vision into practice requires a significant and concerted change in the learning and formational culture of the whole church. Bishops and their colleagues need to be committed to work collectively in their own contexts to enable the education and formation of the

whole people of God. This will need to be the first priority for all ministerial formation.[4]

In fact, as the Church's understanding of mission and ministry has developed, its patterns of ministerial formation have already begun to adapt to reflect some aspects of the transition. These developments have been far-reaching:

- It is now over two generations since all the Church's clergy have been full-time and paid a stipend. The past 50 years have seen the advent of self-supporting clergy and ordained local ministry, clergy whose calling begins with their local church and who are ordained to serve in that specific context.
- No longer are all clergy trained residentially. The majority now train on either part-time or context-based courses.
- Pioneer ministers are now recognized as a distinct specialism and receive dedicated specialist training.
- There has been a diversification in the range of lay ministry. Although the long-established office of 'Reader' (often referred to as 'licensed lay ministry') continues, many more lay people are now authorized for ministries in the field of pastoral care, schools work, youth work, children and families work, community engagement and chaplaincy. Many more churches employ administrators and dedicated worship leaders.
- There is now an official acknowledgement of the centrality of reflective practice in training for ministry, written into the requirements for all training institutions.
- There has been a broadening of the range of options for assessment beyond the traditional essay.
- In a few places, there have been experiments in pedagogical practice, accelerated in 2020 by the use of online learning during the lockdown due to coronavirus.

The number and range of these developments suggest that the Church of England's inherited model or 'paradigm' of ministerial formation is nearing the end of its useful life. They express a growing sense that the Church's understanding of ministerial formation is no longer 'fit for purpose'. The paradigm has reached that stage in its 'life cycle' at which it can only be sustained by multiple adaptations and is ripe for replacement.

Whole-life discipleship

The urgency of such changes is further emphasized by the publication of 'Setting God's People Free', which calls for a 'seismic revolution in the culture of the Church' through a renewed emphasis on the equipping of lay people for discipleship and ministry. The report frames the challenge in this way:

> Will we determine to empower, liberate and disciple the 98% of the Church of England who are not ordained and therefore set them free for fruitful, faithful mission and ministry, influence, leadership and, most importantly, vibrant relationship with Jesus in all of life? And will we do so not only in church-based ministry on a Sunday but in work and school, in gym and shop, in field and factory, Monday to Saturday?[5]

'Setting God's People Free' is the latest in a series of reports calling for the recognition of the ministry of the laity.[6] But it goes further in declaring that the ministry of the laity and their ability to exercise leadership in a Christian way in both church and secular contexts is founded on and emerges from discipleship in everyday life. The full breadth of 'whole-life discipleship' or 'everyday faith' is explored in the description of 'formation' in the Preface. Briefly expressed, it has several dimensions:

- a growing ability to draw on Christian faith when making important decisions
- a growing ability to discern God's presence and action in places of work and everyday life
- a growing ability to sense God's call in the here and now as well as for the future
- a growing ability to explain Christian faith to others
- a growing recognition of our interdependence as members of Christ's Body, the church
- and, above all, the 'love which binds everything together in perfect harmony' (Colossians 3.14), a growing ability to show love towards family, friends, colleagues, and those we find it hard to like.

Moreover, whole-life discipleship is 'missionary discipleship'. The changed lives of Christians and the mutual love of Christian congregations are among the means through which the Holy Spirit commends the gospel to a sceptical society. Calling for two 'essential shifts in culture and practice',

'Setting God's People Free' declares that 'Until, together, we find a way to form and equip lay people to follow Jesus confidently in *every* sphere of life in ways that demonstrate the gospel we will never set God's people free to evangelise the nation.'[7] However, the report acknowledges that the obstacles to such confidence are considerable and deeply rooted in the Church's existing culture. They include:

1 *The lack of a theology of lay discipleship*

For over 1,000 years, Christian theology and practice has been rooted in the system of assumptions generally known as Christendom. Since the late Roman Empire, in all the cultures and societies acknowledging some degree of continuity with Rome, the church occupied a privileged place in civil society. This allowed an appreciable proportion of the population to maintain a nominal allegiance to Christianity and a broadly Christian understanding of the nature and purpose of human life without requiring more than a superficial understanding and commitment to the practices of Christian discipleship. The consequence was a distinction between the realm of the 'sacred', the province of those seen as especially dedicated to religious practice, chiefly the clergy and members of religious orders, and the 'secular' world of everyday life. As a result, Christians, both clergy and lay, frequently fail to recognize their everyday lives as a sphere in which God is active and in which he calls them to participate in his mission.

In *Reimagining Ministry*, I suggested that the theological foundation that we require is to be found in the work of Miroslav Volf, who defines 'work in the Spirit' as cooperation with God in the transformation of creation.[8] Moving beyond the theology of Luther and Calvin, in which vocation is seen as God's call to serve him in a particular sphere of life, Volf suggests that each person (Christian or otherwise) has a distinctive call from God to work with the Holy Spirit to realize God's new creation in a specific way. Daily work thus becomes participation in the mission of God, a means for the realization of God's kingdom in the midst of the old creation.

This raises key questions about the formation of lay Christians. It challenges local churches to become learning communities with the ability to discern together the action of God in the world. It implies an aspiration for the 'theological education' of all God's people, although not in the traditional sense. According to Rowan Williams:

4

A theologically educated person is someone who has acquired the skill of reading and interpreting the world in the context and framework of Christian belief and Christian worship ... not someone who simply knows a great deal about the Bible or history of doctrine but somebody who is able to engage in some quite risky and innovative interpretation and ... to recognize holy lives.[9]

The goal of ministerial formation for the whole people of God will not be to make everyone an expert in biblical studies and 'formal' or 'academic' theology. It will be to enable them to use the Bible and the resources of the Christian tradition to interpret their everyday situations and the communities in which they live and work as places where God is alive and active, and to equip them with the skills to recognize his activity and the ways in which he is calling them to join in, sometimes as individuals but more often and more effectively together as members of his Body, the church.

2 The weakness of the lay voice in the life of the Church

'One of the most significant challenges lay leaders say they struggle with is a perceived lack of understanding within the Church about their vocation and calling as people of influence in their wider communities and workplaces.'[10] Robert Warren records how at a church function the head of planning for one of the largest cities in the UK was introduced to the bishop as 'one of our senior servers'.[11] 'Setting God's People Free' includes the lament of a senior civil servant who records that, 'At no time did my clergy colleagues ever take any interest in my working life ... despite the fact they were aware of the pressure I was under.'[12] Describing the second of the essential shifts in culture and practice it calls for, 'Setting God's People Free' declares: 'Until the laity are convinced, based on their baptismal mutuality, that they are equal in worth and status, complementary in gifting and vocation, mutually accountable in discipleship, and equal partners in mission, we will never form Christian communities that can evangelise the nation.'[13]

However, as I pointed out in *Reimagining Ministry*, the principal reference group for members of the clergy tends to be other clergy.[14] Their formation and training distances them from their own and others' experience of working life and runs the risk of creating a ministerial caste, separate from and with a weak understanding of the everyday life of lay Christian disciples.[15]

3 The 'damaged' relationship between clergy and laity, which is a feature of the Church's culture

In some places, this takes the form of insecure or overbearing clergy, unwilling or unable to allow the laity their proper role in the life of the church; in others, of a passive or demanding laity, unwilling or unable to play their part and throwing the responsibility back on to the clergy.

As I recorded in *Kingdom Learning*, a survey of lay church members in the Diocese of St Albans in 2014 demonstrated that the 1,385 lay Christians who completed it had a sound grasp of the theological basis for lay ministry. Almost 90% saw lay ministry as important in the life of the church and a significant proportion disagreed with the idea that lay ministry consists of 'helping the vicar'. The survey also revealed considerable frustration, in some cases amounting to impatience, with the failure of clergy in many places to recognize the place of lay ministry, especially of ministry in the wider world, or to enable or equip lay people for ministry.[16]

A recent piece of research as part of the Church's Living Ministry research programme explored the difficulties experienced by two recently appointed vicars, each of whom had come to their new parishes with the desire to encourage collaborative ministry. In each case, the obstacles they encountered included embedded cultures of deference and expectations that clergy would operate as 'solo practitioners'; linked to a shared self-perception on the part of the laity that it was not their role to exercise leadership or to share responsibility for the church's mission. Neither vicar had been equipped by their training for such a situation. Both had experienced collaborative ministry during their curacies in well-resourced churches where shared ministry was the norm but neither of their training incumbents had intentionally equipped them with the skills for collaborative leadership. Moreover, neither had been equipped with the relational skills required to manage the expectations of themselves and others or to enable such profound culture change.[17]

4 Inadequate resources for lay training and support

By the time of the publication of 'Setting God's People Free', a Church of England report on 'Education for Discipleship' published in 2006 appeared to have sunk without trace.[18] That report had aspired to lay the foundations for nationwide provision of further learning for lay Christians with the aim of resourcing discipleship and ministry in everyday life. Despite this, a report of 2015 entitled 'Developing Discipleship' could state that 'There is no well-developed authoritative source to which the Church of England can readily look to inform its teaching.' That report concluded that the Church's understanding of ministry was 'lop-sided', neglecting the call to lay Christians to live out their Christian faith in the world.[19]

Consequently, 'Setting God's People Free' included yet another call for the Church to become far more intentional and to devote a greater proportion of its resources to the equipping of lay Christians. 'Few churches,' the report observes, 'have developed the kind of learning culture that would illuminate the resource and support that is required to develop lay people. Few churches are equipped with the kind of "action learning" approaches that we see in Jesus' disciple-making and in best practice adult learning models in wider society.'

On the other hand, a survey of lay people 'at the front line' had clearly identified what would most help them to become confident, effective and fruitful in the area of their calling and vocation, whether in the gathered church or dispersed church setting:

- support for discovering lay vocation and gifting
- opportunities and the encouragement to step into these areas
- fit for purpose, easy to access, contextual training
- connections to others to learn from and share with
- a framework for local accountability and learning
- and appropriate affirmation.[20]

What equips ministers to enable disciples?

If there is to be ministerial formation for the whole church, then any reimagining of ministerial formation must include not only formally recognized lay ministry but the equipping of the whole people of God for mission and ministry in their places of daily life and work. In 2019, I commissioned on behalf of the Diocese of Oxford a small piece of research about ministerial formation as part of our response to 'Setting God's People Free'. Our research question was, 'What equips ministerial trainees to enable whole-life disciples?'

We invited our curates and licensed lay ministers to complete a questionnaire about their experience of ministerial training and received replies from 43 lay ministers and 33 curates. Of these, 24 volunteered to attend focus groups where the issues raised by the questionnaire were explored in greater depth. We also conducted semi-structured interviews with representatives of the five Theological Education Institutions (TEIs) located in the diocese.

The outcome of the research appears to be strikingly relevant not simply in relation to the specific question of equipping lay people for discipleship and ministry but for the light it throws on the whole process of ministerial training. The question about equipping ministers to enable whole-life discipleship turned out to be a 'threshold question', in that the answers to it posed many more deep and searching questions around the place of the church in the world and the whole process of ministerial formation. Here, in summary, are the key findings along with some quotations from the ministers' responses, the focus groups and TEI interviews, used in all cases with permission:

1 The TEI representatives and our self-selecting group of ministers shared a strongly held 'espoused theology'[21] of the importance of lay discipleship as a key element in God's mission along with a recognition that the Church does not do well in supporting whole-life discipleship. These are some comments from the focus groups:

> [The task of ministers] is to help people realise that what they do in their everyday life is shaped by their faith; it's not secular life and Christian life; it's life, all in one ... we've been very good as churches at encouraging teachers and nurses. What church doesn't pray for teachers and nurses? How many churches pray for accountants and hedge fund managers, shop-floor workers, packers in a factory ...

> It's priesthood isn't it ... I think one of the challenges for the Anglican Church is that we've possibly elevated and put priests on a pedestal, such that it's disempowered the laity, whereas actually, the reality is that we're all called to be priests, a royal priesthood who offer glory to God and be a blessing to the world.

2 Spiritual practices are clearly seen as the most helpful factor in equipping ministers to enable whole-life discipleship. Given a list of possible factors, the top three were 'personal reading and reflection' (96%), prayer (78%) and Bible study (69%). Likewise, the TEI representatives all saw the context of prayer as vital for the work of ministerial formation:

The practice of what we might loosely call theological thinking is ... that these three strands [of the Benedictine rule], study, prayer and work, were stronger when woven together.

We break down any kind of sacred/secular assumptions there might be simply by bringing prayer into the lecture space, into the pastoral space ... into our meetings ...

3 The three most significant obstacles preventing ministers from enabling whole-life discipleship are a) the culture of busyness in ministry including the requirements of administration; b) reluctance, fear or shyness about intervening in people's personal lives; c) the culture of pluralism in the wider society that actively discourages the mention of faith in connection with everyday life.

4 When asked about how the connection is made between theology and everyday life, all the TEI representatives and most of the ministers saw the practice of theological reflection (TR) as central.

However, the problem for TEIs is that, having taught their students how to reflect, few have any way of observing how this teaching 'lands' once they begin ministry. Discussion in the focus groups provided some insights that begin to answer this question. The response to theological reflection ranged from those who adopted it enthusiastically, to those who saw it as natural and something they did all the time, to others who were left cold by it and several who had been put off by having it taught as an academic exercise.

The teaching of theological reflection is an issue that I will examine more closely in Chapter 2. However, two points emerged from the report that are worth remarking on at this stage. One is the connection between theological reflection and prayer. In a recent article, Quentin Chandler reports how, in the course of his own research into the way students learn TR, he was led to recognize that for many of them learning to listen to God in prayer played the role of TR.[22] The same point was made by one of the TEI representatives:

... not just in terms of models of theological reflection, but also looking at prayer as a model of theological reflection ... there are spiritual exercises like the Examen, which actually are a way of theologically reflecting and joining up the dots.

Second, there was criticism that TR was frequently taught as an individual activity, whereas it is potentially far more powerful as a corporate practice. The Church's tradition of faith, on which we draw in TR, is the product of the faithful community and it is as part of that community that we reflect. Moreover, when using TR to discern the presence of God in a situation, it is far more effective when undertaken corporately, rooted in the loving relationships of a group or ministry team. This observation highlights the individualized culture of ministerial formation, which, as we shall explore in greater detail in Chapter 1, disables a collaborative approach to ministry.

5 Ministerial formation concentrates on training for leadership in the gathered church at the expense of leadership for the dispersed church, and for leadership of an institution rather than of a disciple-making community. This was a frequent theme in the focus groups:

> What we do on Sundays is we give a lot of information and then we expect innovation. So, we kind of communicate a message and we say, right now, go out and live your lives differently ... but we miss out the imitation aspect ...

> I look at and research a lot of questions people are asking ... and I make videos about them. And yet all of those questions you can easily find in a Google search we don't address at church. And that's why I say there's a disconnect: we're teaching from the Bible ... but they're going, my friend's asking this question. You haven't equipped me.

The frustration was summed up by one curate in the questionnaire:

> Rather than equipping us to know how to enable a culture of disciples who make disciples, we are equipped to be experts in theology, lead worship within a rigid framework, to be 'the minister' for the occasional offices, and warned about the legal ramifications of getting it wrong. We then minister in a culture of bureaucracy, budgets and parish shares, with congregations who expect high standards and things to be done the way they like it.

The same frustration was shared by at least some of the TEI representatives:

I think the way training is set up is very focussed on church-as-institution ... and we forget that church exists only for the sake of the world and for the sake of daily lives.

I think what we're doing is preparing people to be priests in the Church of England, which, as far as I can see from the hidden and overt curriculum, means how to do it in church ... but if that's all you think that faith is about, then to me that's about one tenth of the story.

Despite these reservations, in almost every case curates and lay ministers reported that ministerial training had increased their confidence in enabling whole-life discipleship. However, it was noteworthy that, when asked whether their training had increased their confidence to engage in eight skills or activities related to the ability to enable whole-life discipleship, confidence in skills to do with Sunday church, such as preaching a sermon related to everyday life, had increased by far more than skills exercised outside the Sunday context, such as 'enabling a Christian to make informed decisions about how they use their time outside of work'.

6 Of the five TEIs, only one was intentional about equipping ministers to enable whole-life discipleship. This is expressed in several specific ways:

- Ordinands and candidates for lay ministry train not only alongside each other but alongside 'interested learners', who enrol on a term by term basis.
- Individual learning programmes are carefully planned to take previous experience into account.
- Annual reporting is linked to experience in work and everyday life as well as progress in training.
- Teaching on ministry specifically emphasizes its corporate and collaborative nature.
- TR is practised as a corporate activity and linked to issues that arise from everyday experience in the students' training contexts.
- Students are offered opportunities to share and even teach what they have learned from their previous experience of work.

Above all, however, the representatives of this TEI pointed to the overall ethos of the course:

> We've been very influenced by the Local Ministry movement, the theory that ministers, whether lay or ordained, arise up from the local church rather than being selected and plucked down, and therefore we've tailored our training such that they are not taken out of context …

> I believe that I'm training people to equip others as a basic philosophy of what I'm doing … The whole point of having such courses is to teach them that they're there to teach others … We're trying right across the board to say, it's in order that you might serve the Body of Christ and equip it.

In contrast, the other TEIs worked on the assumption that students would be equipped to enable whole-life discipleship without the need to give this aspect of their training special attention:

> I think quite a lot happens through the practice and the discipline of their relationships with each other – so it might happen at a slightly unconscious level.

> If they're people who are formed by this habit of frequent and regular public prayer – and also within that the spaces they have for their own prayer life.

Sadly, however, the research quoted in 'Setting God's People Free' demonstrates clearly that lay people are not being enabled for whole-life discipleship in large numbers and therefore strongly suggests that clergy and lay ministers are not being equipped to enable them.[23]

7 The teaching of theology has an adverse effect on ministers' ability to enable whole-life discipleship because it is taught in a way that fails to connect with everyday life or ministerial practice. Here are some expressions of this disconnect from the focus groups:

> I was coming at it from the point of view of someone who's late to her first degree and is now serving in a parish where 25% of the working age population have no academic formal qualifications. I'm

aware that when I use complicated vocabulary – because that's what I've been trained to do in essays – that I'm speaking in a language that they just don't understand. So I've been mentored through three years of: use more complicated language, get your sentence structure right ... and I'm speaking to a bunch of people who don't know what I'm saying any more. I've been over-educated to connect with my population.

The people that taught us are probably ministering in parishes but they seem to be more in their books and in what the Greek or Hebrew said, or what some guy with a German name said ... You know, it was books, books, books and dons and ivory towers ... I would have said that I was more academic than not before I started and discovered I'm not really compared to some Anglican circles.

The TEI representatives were passionate about making theology accessible and relevant:

I think my particular ministry as I see it has always been to try to bridge the academic world and the church and to keep the two in conversation rather than see them drifting off further and further apart to their mutual impoverishment. One of the things one hears a lot about the academic world is the talk about academic ivory towers. You get it in a particular form in the Church ... I want to say passionately that there is no such thing as an ivory tower. Human beings have problems wherever you put them and you do not get away from those issues in the academic world any more than anywhere else.

I think we are made in the image of God; we are there to reflect God. And that's why, I think, if we are not exciting people about God, they won't know how to do that: it won't have shape, it won't have content, it won't have passion, it won't have coherence.

These tutors tended to locate the cause of the resistance to theology they encountered in their students in a prevailing anti-intellectualism:

There's always been anti-intellectualism in the Church, but this is a new kind and it's a sort of mission-shaped anti-intellectualism which says, we don't need all this hifalutin theology; we need people who will go out there and do the job. What is the job? It is offering God; that is theology.

The ministers, however, refute this. They discern a clear distinction between the study they were asked to do in training and the study that equips them for ministry:

> I mean there were academic books and there were other books, and I've got a whole pile of books that looked interesting but weren't relevant to the essays, which I really need to get stuck into.

> Maybe when I get out the other side of this then I will find some useful books that I can read that will connect with me and my situation but through this last three and a half years it's been so many books to read that are useful for writing the essays but maybe not for anything else.

In summary, the TEIs are offering a training that they passionately believe is appropriate but is failing to excite their students, connect with their situations or empower their ministry. There is little sense from the discussions in focus groups of the ministers having had their theology shaped in dialogue with their experience. In Chapter 2, I will suggest that the reason for this is a failure to distinguish between two different though related practices: ministry and theological scholarship. Despite their avowed purpose of equipping people for ministry, institutions continue to offer a theology shaped by and geared to the world of theological scholarship, whose effect is to disable their students for ministry.

The emerging paradigm of ministerial formation

What, then, is the shape of the emerging paradigm of ministerial formation, adequate to the demands of ministry and mission in the post-Christendom age and capable of equipping ministers to enable everyday faith? Chapter 1 explores the basic features of the new paradigm. I argue that, notwithstanding the multiple adaptations of the last two or three decades, the inherited model of ministerial formation rests on four basic assumptions:

- Ministry conceived as that of an isolated and usually ordained individual.

- One-size-fits-all. The ministry of the traditional vicar as the standard pattern.
- Front-end-loading. Ministerial formation takes place during a defined period prior to ordination or licensing.
- An 'academic' or theory-to-practice model of learning.

Correspondingly, the elements of the emerging paradigm are these:

- Ministry is by its very nature collaborative.
- Ministry is varied and diverse.
- Formation for ministry is a life-long process.
- The appropriate model of learning for ministry is experiential learning or reflective practice.

At its heart, the new paradigm is a response to the need to develop and inhabit with confidence a new relationship between church and society in the post-Christendom age. In the Christendom age, the Church functioned as a religious institution; in the post-Christendom age, the primary character of Christianity will need to become a way of life based on relationship with God through Jesus Christ. Everyday discipleship moves to the heart of what it means to practise Christian faith and forms the core around which other aspects of participation in the life of the church revolve.

The fourth element of the new paradigm, a shift away from an 'academic' approach to teaching and learning towards reflective practice, requires an argument in greater depth and is the subject of Chapter 2. The 'academic' model of learning developed within the Enlightenment university. In this model, 'real' knowledge is understood to consist of a complex, multi-faceted and inter-related theory. The task of the university is to refine that theory through the work of research, to initiate people into the world of theory-making through a university education and to influence the life of the wider world through dissemination of the knowledge gained through research.

The university model of education is currently facing increasing criticism. I argue that the most fundamental reason for this is that the idea that 'real' knowledge is abstract and theoretical is in error. Rather, knowledge is specific to and embedded in practices, which is why experiential learning or reflective practice is the most effective approach to learning.

The adoption of a new paradigm requires intentional action in a number of different areas. In Chapter 3, I make some specific recommendations:

- Reimagine ministerial formation as a life-long process.
- Enable 'whole-life discipleship' or 'everyday faith'.
- Resource locally based training.
- Develop more flexible patterns of commissioning and authorization.
- Balance the need for dedicated learning communities with the need for cross-fertilization.
- Bring ministry and training together.
- Think strategically about residential training.
- Ensure that the contexts in which formation takes place model diverse and collaborative patterns of ministry.
- Incorporate intentional training in the competencies of emotional intelligence (EI) into strategies for teaching and learning.
- Assess 'wisdom and godly habit of life'.
- Assess practice rather than theory.
- Broaden learning objectives to include EI competencies and dispositions.
- Train theological educators in experiential learning.
- Review the aims, content and learning outcomes of existing modules of the Common Awards curriculum and/or encourage the development of new modules.
- Provide reflective supervision for clergy.
- Share good practice.

The final chapter takes the form of a retrospect in which I imagine how the new paradigm might take shape in practice and how it might bring new life to the Church. It looks forward to a Church growing in numbers and influence in society, with articulate Christians equipped to see their work as cooperation with God for the coming of his kingdom everywhere from the cabinet table to the outer urban estates; a Church increasingly seen as a force for good in the community as more of its members are empowered for ministry. However, it is important to acknowledge that the picture it provides can only be tentative and provisional. The transformation the church requires takes the form of a process of adaptive change, the kind of change on which we embark not yet knowing where it will lead. Having said this, past experience suggests that change is more likely to arise from the 'bottom up' and that the renewing work of the Holy Spirit is likely to be found on the 'edges' of church life. While I considered it important to provide a description of the shape a reimagined approach to ministerial formation might take, it is equally important to acknowledge that the picture can only ever be a provisional one.

Notes

1 In the words of the ecumenical Lima Document, 'The word *ministry* in its broadest sense denotes the service to which the whole people of God is called.' World Council of Churches, *Baptism, Eucharist and Ministry*, Geneva: World Council of Churches, 1982, §7.

2 A phrase used several times by Pope Francis in his *Evangelii Gaudium*, London: Catholic Truth Society, 2013.

3 Daniel W. Hardy, 'Afterword' in *Local Ministry: Story, Process and Meaning*, ed. Robin Greenwood and Caroline Pascoe, London: SPCK, 2006, p. 147.

4 Church of England Ministry Council, 'Ministerial Formation for the Church of England', October 2019, p. 4.

5 Archbishops' Council General Synod Paper 2056, 'Setting God's People Free', 2017, pp. 1 and 2, available from www.churchofengland.org/sites/default/files/2017-11/GS%20Misc%202056%20Setting%20God%27s%20People%20Free.pdf accessed 10 December 2020.

6 Previous reports include 'All Are Called: Towards a Theology of the Laity', London: Church House Publishing, 1985; and 'Called to New Life: The World of Lay Discipleship', London: Archbishops' Council, 1999. Each of these reports, as well as 'Setting God's People Free', looks back to 'Towards the Conversion of England', Church of England Commission on Evangelism, 1946. However, 'Setting God's People Free' comments: 'This material often fails to make inroads beyond specific constituencies, or has difficulty achieving long-term currency, let alone significantly informing policy and practice across the Church of England' (p. 14).

7 'Setting God's People Free', p. 3.

8 See further David Heywood, *Reimagining Ministry*, London: SCM Press, pp. 62–3; Miroslav Volf, *Work in the Spirit*, Eugene, OR: Wipf and Stock, 1991.

9 Rowan Williams, CEFACS Lecture, Birmingham – Centre for Anglican Communion Studies, 3 November 2004, available at http://rowanwilliams.archbishopofcanterbury.org/articles.php/1847/cefacs-lecture-birmingham-centre-for-anglican-communion-studies.html accessed 20 February 2021.

10 'Setting God's People Free', p. 15.

11 Robert Warren, *Being Human, Being Church*, London: Marshall Pickering, 1995, p. 33.

12 'Setting God's People Free', p. 16.

13 'Setting God's People Free', p. 4.

14 *Reimagining Ministry*, pp. 6–7.

15 'Setting God's People Free', p. 16; 'Ministerial Formation for the Church of England', p. 6.

16 Presented to St Albans Diocesan Synod on 14 March 2014 by the Revd Canon Tim Bull, Director of Ministry for the Diocese.

17 Hilary Ison and Liz Graveling, 'Collaborative Ministry and the Transition to First Incumbency', Church of England Ministry Division, 2019.

18 The report appeared in Archbishops' Council, *Shaping the Future: New Patterns of Training for Lay and Ordained*, London: Church House Publishing, 2006.

19 General Synod Paper 1977, 'Developing Discipleship', §§33, 37, 38.

20 'Setting God's People Free', p. 18.

21 Helen Cameron and her colleagues distinguish between 'four voices' in theology: 'espoused theology', the theology embedded within a group's articulation of its beliefs; 'operant theology', the theology embedded within the group's actual practices; 'normative theology', the scriptures, creeds, liturgies and official Church teaching; and 'formal theology', the academic study of theology. Helen Cameron et al., *Talking about God in Practice*, London: SCM Press, 2010, pp. 53–6.

22 Quentin Chandler, 'Cognition or spiritual disposition? Threshold concepts in theological reflection', *Journal of Adult Theological Education* 13.2 (2016), pp. 90–102.

23 'Setting God's People Free', pp. 3–4.

I

An Emerging New Paradigm

The existing paradigm of ministerial formation is no longer 'fit for purpose'. It is kept alive only by an increasing number of adaptations and is ripe for replacement. Moreover, some aspects of the existing paradigm not only fail to equip ministers for some of their most essential tasks but actively disable them.

Over the past few years, a new paradigm for ministerial formation has been gradually emerging. The purpose of this book is to explore that new paradigm and to argue for its adoption as the guiding principle in the Church's pattern of ministerial formation.

The paradigm of ministry and formation we have inherited from the nineteenth century, when intentional ministerial formation first began, may be characterized by the following four basic assumptions:

- Ministry conceived as that of an isolated and usually ordained individual. In a paper of 1992, Craig Dykstra pointed out that we usually imagine ministerial practice in terms of activities carried out by an individual clergyperson: preaching to a congregation, leading a meeting, or visiting a person in need. 'Theology and theological education,' he wrote, 'are burdened by a picture of practice that is harmfully individualistic.'[1]
- One-size-fits-all. The ordained parish minister is thought of as the standard pattern of ministry consisting of a broadly similar ministry of word, sacrament and pastoral care. The ministry for which nearly all ordinands are formed is conceived in terms of the traditional activities of the parish clergy. Moreover, 'lay ministry' is thought of in the same terms as the ministry of the ordained, so that formation for licensed lay ministry echoes the pattern of training for ordination. Locally based training also tends to focus on training for pastoral care teams, leading intercessions and other church-based activities.
- Front-end-loaded. The Church operates what has become known as a 'just-in-case' rather than a 'just-in-time' model of training. Ministerial formation is conceived as taking place in a defined period preliminary to

ministry. University accreditation has reinforced the standard pattern for both clergy and lay ministry as a two- or three-year period of training for an initial qualification. This pattern inevitably leads to anxiety about the Church's capacity to offer all the requisite training in the time available, and regular reviews of the content of the curriculum.

- An 'academic' or theory-to-practice model of learning, and in the last 30 years or so an acceptance of university validation.

The adoption of a new paradigm requires a comprehensive 'reimagining' of what we mean by 'mission', 'ministry' and 'church' in addition to a new model of ministerial formation.

A new model of ministerial formation

This new model has four elements:

Christian ministry is by its very nature collaborative

The most important and distinctive characteristic of genuine Christian ministry is love. Of all the commandments in the Law, Jesus picked out two as most important: to love God with all our heart, soul, mind and strength and to love our neighbour as ourselves (Mark 12.30–31). The love of Christians for one another is to mark us out as followers of Jesus (John 13.14).

Christian love does not come naturally. It is a fruit of the Holy Spirit. It emerges in our lives only to the extent that we 'live by the Spirit' and not according to what Paul refers to as 'the flesh' (Romans 8.5–8). It is perfectly possible to engage in ministry to fulfil our own needs, such as to be noticed, to be significant, to be needed, or to gain power in the church. The presentation of the disciples in the Synoptic Gospels often reads like a series of object lessons in the kind of attitudes the Christian minister should be careful to avoid. The pride that led James and John to believe they had a right to the principal seats in heaven (Mark 10.35–37) was quite invisible to themselves but only too visible to their colleagues and, moreover, led to indignation and potential division.

Thankfully, we discover later in the Gospel story that Jesus did not expect the disciples to have become perfect before he entrusted them with the responsibility for preaching the gospel and working for the coming of his kingdom. Rather, he used the call to ministry as a means of perfecting them. In response to James and John, Jesus pointed out that his call was to be a servant. It was in taking the role of a servant that Jesus demonstrated the kind of love his disciples were to display towards one another (John 13.1–17). The servant does not have an agenda of his or her own. He does not expect recognition other than that of a job well done, or reward other than having satisfied his master. The call to ministry thus 'crucifies' the 'fleshly' part of us by demanding a self-forgetful and self-giving love, the attitude that Jesus himself displayed (Philippians 2.5–8).

But why love? Why is the church called to be a community whose members are learning to love one another and the wider world? Few secular charitable organizations make this their explicit aim, although many recognize the need for alignment between the character of the organization and its goal of serving those in need. The answer lies in the nature of the Trinity. God is three persons in loving relationship. The loving relationship of Father, Son and Holy Spirit is revealed in the ministry of Jesus and the life of the church. Jesus modelled perfect loving obedience towards God his Father. His whole aim was to glorify the Father, while at the same time God the Father glorified him and drew people to follow him. And the Holy Spirit points towards the Father and the Son. The Spirit is given, in the words of Tom Smail, to enable us to make two confessions: 'Abba, Father' and 'Jesus is Lord'.[2]

The Creator of the universe is a relationship of love. Because God is a relationship, the created world is a social world. We are made in the image of God and share the mystery of personhood, symbolized by the fact that we have names, which point to our uniqueness and mystery. To be made in the image of God means existing in relationship. Our fundamental relationship is to God, origin of our being, and the fact this relationship is broken is the source of all the world's troubles.

But secondarily we are in relationship with one another. The individual does not precede society; to be human is to be in relationship. Our identity, our sense of who we are, our personal significance, our place in the world, our purpose and destiny, are formed in relationships. Some relationships are healthy and nurturing and help us to grow well. Others are toxic, stifling, damaging and leave us less well able to face the world. The essential characteristic of the first kind is, of course, love.

God's desire for each of us is to grow to our full potential and this is something that can only take place in loving community. The church is called to be that community, in which, through the loving power of the Holy Spirit, each person experiences healing from the toxic relationships of the past, is challenged to renounce sinful patterns of life, and learns to love and be loved. In this way, the church is called to a 'foretaste, sign and agent' of God's kingdom,[3] a sign to the world of God's being and purpose.

The church's ministry must partake of and display the nature of the church. Ministry is rooted in the call to love one another. In a collaborative pattern of ministry, each of the partners is committed not just to the purposes of God but to the fullest possible flourishing of each of the other ministers. By working together in relationships of love and service to one another, we embody the nature of God at the heart of the church. For Stephen Pickard, Paul's phrase 'members one of another' (Romans 12.5) sums up the relationship in which Christians stand and from which all ministry must emerge. 'Collaborative ministry is not an optional extra but the manner in which the ministry of the gospel is a gospel ministry.'[4]

There is, therefore, a world of difference between ministry conceived of in institutional terms and a collaborative pattern of ministry rooted in the priesthood of all the baptized, Christian *koinonia* or fellowship and the call to whole-life discipleship. Accordingly, I differ from the accepted position of the Church of England, in which the term 'ministry' is reserved for 'licensed ministry', lay or ordained: that is, for ministry officially recognized by the Church.[5] Ministry cannot be severed from its roots in discipleship. The participation of all is rooted in lives open to transformation and the confidence that arises from the experience of God at work in the warp and weft of everyday life. The paradigm change we require will only have taken place when the word 'ministry' ceases to be defined in institutional terms and when its primary meaning ceases to be the ministry of the ordained and becomes the ministry of the whole church arising from its shared life and rooted in everyday faith.

Ministry is by its nature varied and diverse

As Paul frequently reminded his churches, the Body of Christ consists of unity in diversity. No one person has all the gifts necessary for the mission of God. All display different facets of the call of Jesus and all are called to love the others into the full realization of that call until 'all of us come to the unity of the faith and of the knowledge of the Son of God, to maturity, to the measure of the full stature of Christ' (Ephesians 4.13).

Moreover, because the outworking of mission is shaped by the context in which it takes place, the shape of ministry also varies according to context. As the church in Britain seeks to adapt to ministry within a changed context, at least three types of ministry are currently emerging to complement the traditional focus on word, sacrament and pastoral care:

- A variety of specialist ministries. Some are of long standing, many only recently emerging and many in response to specific local circumstances. They might include children, youth and families workers; evangelists and evangelism enablers; specialists in training; prayer guides or spiritual directors; administrators; pioneer ministers and members of church planting teams; chaplains in both the traditional settings of the health service, prisons, armed forces and education, and in the many new informal chaplaincies, such as to retail centres, agriculture, sports venues etc.; coaching and mentoring; ministry to care homes; liaison with local authorities; community organizing; and this list is far from exhaustive.
- Focal ministry. Particularly in multi-parish benefices, when the ministry of stipendiary clergy is stretched over several locations, a focal minister provides the 'face of the church' to their community and the potential for embedded leadership of the congregation. As early as 1980, Anthony Russell foresaw the need for the leadership of the church to be entrusted to local groups, at the centre of which would be a 'focal person' occupying a role which 'involves responsibility for the life and leadership of the local church'; and in 1993 painted a picture of churches in a rural setting to be led by small leadership teams drawn from their congregations, resourced and led in their turn by the clergy.[6] Local leadership, moreover, expresses the theological truth that each local church represents the whole church in its context, rather than merely a branch of a particular denomination.

  Research by Bob Jackson suggests that experiments with focal ministry are leading in many places to an upturn in church attendance and mission capacity.[7] Focal ministry may be carried out by a single person or a small team, depending on circumstances. The single person may be a retired clergyperson, a lay minister, a churchwarden or simply the long-standing member of the church who is identified and accepted by the local community as the church's representative. As yet, there is no consensus between dioceses experimenting with focal ministry about the precise shape of such ministry. My suggestion is that, just as the days of the one-size-fits-all parish clergy are coming to an end and the ministry of lay ministers is increasingly varied, so the precise shape of focal ministry will depend largely on the context and the gifts of the minister.

- Oversight. As ministry becomes increasingly varied, specialist and collaborative, the episcopal dimension always present in the inherited model of ordained ministry becomes increasingly important. Many full-time clergy are experiencing the need to give more and more time to oversight of the ministry of others. In his book *Ministry in Three Dimensions*, Steven Croft examines this aspect of ministry in detail, suggesting that the characteristics of oversight ministry are 'watching over' oneself and others, enabling the ministry of others and building missionary communities.[8]

  For some years I was involved in a training course for 'ministry area leaders' in the Church in Wales Diocese of Monmouth. Even those in urban contexts faced the task of leading not less than four churches; in more rural situations it might be more than twice that number. These clergy, originally trained for the traditional role of the parish priest, did not find it easy to make the transition from one style of ministry to another, from regular involvement in the day-to-day life of a church to the need to form, lead and equip a ministry team. But where they were successful, the fruits of mission were striking.

These changes in the understanding and approach to ministry require a change of paradigm complementary to and in many ways even more far-reaching than the new paradigm for ministerial formation advanced here. Not only is 'ministry' the responsibility of the whole church, but the focus of both ministry and discipleship becomes cooperation with the Holy Spirit in the coming of God's kingdom in the whole of life. Clergy see themselves as overseers of the ministry of the whole church while church members cease to see themselves as 'clients of the clergy' but rather as 'missionary disciples'.

Formation for ministry is a life-long process

We live in an age of life-long learning, in which lay Christians, in common with colleagues in most jobs and professions, are expected to constantly update their skills and expertise. For most Christians, both lay and ordained, vocation to ministry is a step-by-step process of gradual discernment, in which the focus of ministry is likely to change over the course of their lives. The overwhelming majority of those embarking on training for ordained ministry have previous ministry experience: as youth workers, churchwardens, chaplains and so on. Ministerial development is a life-long process.

Much more fundamentally, formation in Christian discipleship is a life-long commitment. Christian character develops over many years as the fruit of the Holy Spirit. Ministry, which arises from discipleship, is itself an aspect of discipleship. It challenges us through the calling to serve, to put the needs of others before our own. It teaches us more about the nature of sin, both the structural sin of society and the sinful tendencies of our own hearts. It teaches us more of the goodness and mercy of God, his compassion for the poor and marginalized and his strength in our weakness. Ministry challenges us beyond our own strength, places us in situations where we need to depend more fully on God and acquaints us with suffering.

It is a fundamental principle of adult education that adults learn best when they recognize the need for new learning, have the opportunity to put the new learning into practice, and are able to reflect on their own performance, in company with others. An initial course of training incorporating all the learning likely to be relevant to the future role may be a convenient way of gaining a qualification, but it is not the most effective learning strategy. A life-long model of formation redistributes learning for ministry for all, including the clergy. Although this does not mean doing away with appropriate qualifications, it does require a stepping away from the inherited pattern of training and assessment including a rebalancing of the funding between training for lay and ordained ministry.

The early stages of formation for ordained ministry will take place in local church settings as candidates, already engaged in ministry as lay people, take their first steps in the company of others. The transition to ordained ministry may require some learning as initial orientation, and to ensure 'fitness to practise' for a role in which clergy are called to exercise a representative ministry, but much of their continuing formation will take place following ordination as part of continuing ministerial development.

The appropriate model of learning for ministerial formation is experiential learning or reflective practice

This element of the new paradigm is by far the most complex and will be the subject of the following chapter. In a nutshell, the 'academic' model of learning is that developed within the Enlightenment university, a model of university education generally held to have its origins in the founding of the University of Berlin in 1810. In this model, 'real' knowledge is understood to consist of a complex, multi-faceted and inter-related theory about the world and everything in it. The task of the university is to refine that theory through the work of research, to initiate people into the world of theory-making and refining through a university education and to influence the life of the wider world through dissemination of the knowledge gained through research.

While the Enlightenment university has had spectacular successes over the past 200 years, especially in the fields of science and technology, its model of education is currently facing increasing criticism and may even be approaching a crisis.[9] I contend that the most fundamental reason for this is that its model of knowledge is in error. Knowledge does not consist of a universal theory, but is specific to and embedded in practices, which is why experiential learning or reflective practice is the most effective approach to learning.

This critique of the Enlightenment university has important implications for the way the discipline of theology has been conducted. I will argue that the pursuit of 'academic' theology prepares people directly for the practice of theological scholarship but only indirectly for the practices of Christian discipleship and ministry, that what theology 'means' for the practice of theological scholarship is in crucial ways different from its meaning for the practices of discipleship and ministry. Moreover, because the pursuit of theology in the university has been constrained by the criteria for rational scholarship emerging from the Enlightenment, what has emerged is what might be called 'secular' theology, differing in fundamental ways from what the Bible and Christian tradition recognize as the 'knowledge of God'.

The analysis I shall present is, however, a source of hope, not only for ministerial formation but also for the university. The Christian should not be surprised to find that the approach to knowledge in what the Bible and Christian tradition recognize as the knowledge of God lies much closer to what knowing something really involves than does the Enlightenment concept of knowledge as universal theory. The 'Preface' to the Common Awards, the curriculum for ministerial formation shared by Church of England and several other denominations, raises the possibility of a 'wider and deeper epistemology' that 'shapes the emotions, hones virtue and fuels passion after the pattern of Christ' and that '(re-)asserts the necessary unity of faith and learning, of knowledge and divine revelation, of the pursuit of truth and the nurturing of virtue'.[10]

In 1987, the report *Education for the Church's Ministry*, commonly known as 'ACCM 22', proposed that the 'central thrust' of what was then known as 'theological education' should be seen as the 'wisdom and godly habit of life which are engendered by God's self-presentation in the world and by his grace in the Christian and how they are to be exercised in and through the corporate ministry of the Church of England for that world'.[11] In other words, formation for ministry is essentially formation in character and discernment. Specific knowledge and skills for ministry are to contribute and flow from this, in what might now be called a 'virtue ethic' for ministry.[12]

The end of Christendom

The context in which this new paradigm is presented is the loss of the privileged place in society previously occupied by the Church. Whereas allegiance to the Christian faith was once widely understood as one of the foundations of social cohesion, the Church is now increasingly marginal to society. Even in the 1990s, I was encountering couples requesting baptism for their children who did not know that Christians believe Jesus to have risen from the dead. We also discovered to our surprise that many from the local community who brought their children to a pre-school group or came to a badminton club in our dual-purpose building on a daily or weekly basis had no idea that it was a Christian church, despite the presence of the church notice-board and a large cross on the wall outside.

Since the European Enlightenment, the distinction between the sacred and secular spheres of life, so much a feature of Christendom, has become an article of faith. The Enlightenment world-view insists that public life be regulated solely by the dictates of human reason and views any appeal to religious tradition with profound suspicion. In place of the centrality of faith and the power of the church characteristic of the Middle Ages in Europe, in the modern age both religious practice and religious institutions have been pushed to the margins and the God-centred world-view of earlier ages replaced by what philosopher Charles Taylor has called the 'immanent frame', a world-view in which human reason is taken as the measure of all that is believable or even acceptable.[13]

Once religious allegiance no longer plays a role in maintaining social cohesion, it becomes necessary to find some other basis. Britain in the early twenty-first century is a pluralist society. Our form of pluralism rests on the widely shared belief that society consists of a variety of sub-cultures, that most people will continue to inhabit the culture into which they are born, but that everyone possesses the right to choose their culture (although in practice such a choice is only open to those with sufficient money, education and life skills). The maintenance of harmony in a pluralist society depends on a belief that 'truth' is contextual rather than absolute, a commitment to the equal status of the choices open to members of society, and tolerance of diversity. Religion therefore poses a potential threat to social cohesion since it proposes a reference point beyond the reach of social control and puts forward claims to absolute truth. Moreover, from a pluralist point of view such a claim to know the truth can only ever be an exercise of power with the aim of 'imposing' religious beliefs on the rest of society.

At the time of writing, this shaky consensus is threatened not only by its own internal contradictions but by increasing inequality between rich and poor, exacerbated by the policies of austerity; by the deep divisions in society caused by the failure of successive governments to find a realistic role for Britain in the world following the end of the empire, culminating in Brexit; and by the emergence of right-wing populism. It is hard to be sure at the present time what the response to these developments is likely to be. One possibility is the re-emergence of a focus on the importance of character and with it a search for shared values. It may be that the Christian churches have a contribution to make, albeit as one of a number of faith communities and on terms set by the assumptions of a pluralist society.[14]

It should not be assumed that the marginalization of faith in the public square means its disappearance. Although the age of Christendom is coming to an end, elements of Christendom persist. As Malcolm Brown, Director of Mission and Public Affairs for the Archbishops' Council, points out, Britain is an 'old country' and the churches are deeply embedded in society. The bishops in the House of Lords speak with the authority of a Church that is present in every parish.[15] In 2011, 20% agreed that the Church of England was 'very important' in defining Britishness.[16] The Church of England and the Roman Catholic Church maintain a significant presence in schools and some higher education institutions. In cities, towns and villages throughout the country, church buildings offer not only a visible reminder of the role of Christian faith in the country's history but visible places of sacred space in the present. And many secular charities, such as the Samaritans, draw on Christian roots.

Nor does the end of Christendom mean the demise of people's awareness of a spiritual dimension to life. A survey of 2005 revealed that 86% of the population had visited a church building at least once in the previous year. Of the reasons given, 50% were at a wedding, 50% at a memorial service, and 40% attended a Christmas service. Perhaps more significantly though, 20% gave as one of their reasons that they were 'walking past and felt the need to go in', while almost the same proportion attended specifically to 'find a quiet space'.[17] The persistence of this sense of connection to the life of the church was further demonstrated by the large number of people who were not regular churchgoers but sampled online worship during the lockdown of 2020.[18]

Further evidence for the persistence of interest in spirituality into the post-Christendom era comes from the Soul of Britain surveys of the late twentieth century, which found significant increases between 1987 and 2000 in such things as belief in providence, awareness of a prayer being answered and belief in a power of evil;[19] from the 'Beyond the Fringe' research carried out by the Diocese of Coventry in 2003, which reported the persistence of questions of identity, destiny, creation, the supernatural and moral values;[20] and a survey of 2017 for Tearfund by ComRes, which revealed that 51% of the population prays either regularly or occasionally, including 45% of people aged 18 to 34 who prayed at least once a month, of whom 20% prayed regularly.[21]

This openness to spirituality is usually expressed, however, as 'spiritual but not religious'.[22] In a pluralist culture, the moral authority of institutions, including that of the churches, is in decline. Religious institutions are also widely seen as committing the cardinal sin of telling people what to think. Moreover, it is not only among the non-religious that church membership fails to appeal. Statistics of church leaving suggest that Christians too are becoming disillusioned with the institution of the church. Among those who leave, many after a lifetime of regular attendance and roles in church leadership, are a significant proportion who consider themselves to have 'grown out' of church; who are frustrated by lack of opportunities to serve; or who sense God's call to leave their local church in order to engage in mission in one form or another. Concluding his survey of over 800 Scottish church leavers, Steve Aisthorpe wonders whether what is happening might be the 'rewilding' of the church, a return to simpler and more fluid forms of Christian affiliation.[23]

The importance of this for our present purpose is that each of the four features of the inherited paradigm of ministerial formation listed above – ministry as the province of the sole religious practitioner; the shape of ministry as that of the vicar in the parish; front-end-loaded training regarded as a necessary prior qualification for ministry; and the 'theory-to-practice' approach to learning – belongs to a world that is passing away. They belong to the world of Christendom in which a religious institution staffed by religious professionals played an essential role in society. In a pluralist society (and in whatever may be about to take its place) these assumptions are both outdated and irrelevant.

Christianity after Christendom

Over the past generation, one of the most important contributions of the missionary movement to the old-established churches currently emerging from the era of Christendom has been an emphasis on contextualization. The church has long been familiar with the need to proclaim the gospel in terms that are readily understandable in contemporary culture. However, contextualization goes further than this. The way in which Christian faith is expressed is inevitably shaped by the context in which it emerged. When that context changes, it is necessary to reimagine the outward expression of faith not simply to connect with the changing culture but to retain its essential meaning.[24]

Contextualization has been a feature of Christian faith from its earliest days, readily discernible in the New Testament as the infant church made the transition from a renewal movement within Judaism and accepted a mission to the entire Roman world. The choice of the word *ecclesia* rather than *synagogue* for the gathering and common life of believers is an example of contextualization, and the avoidance of the words *archon* (ruler) or *hiereus* (priest) to describe church leaders in favour of words like *proistamenos* (one who takes responsibility) indicates a distinctive, counter-cultural approach to leadership.[25]

One of the most fundamental tasks for the Church at the present time is to recontextualize the practice of Christian faith for a post-Christendom age. As always in the task of recontextualization, scripture and Christian tradition supply the necessary resources. In the age of Christendom, the form in which Christianity presented itself was primarily as a religious institution with the emphasis on the church gathered for worship, so that the popular understanding of a Christian in society is someone who 'goes to church'. While the gathered church in worship will continue to be important, the post-Christendom age requires a balancing emphasis on the church in mission and the life of the dispersed church in the world.

In the New Testament Church, Christian faith was known simply as 'the Way' (Acts 9.2, 22.4). Christianity was at its heart neither an institution nor a Sunday gathering but a shared way of life. This way of life emerges from and is empowered by Jesus' resurrection, through which he is proclaimed as Lord of the new creation that is coming into being. In a recontextualized Christian practice, the core definition of a Christian will be someone who 'follows Jesus'. Discipleship consists not in a set of religious practices but in the life of the new creation lived out in the midst of the old, affecting every sphere of life and relationship. I suggest that this renewed emphasis on the dispersed as well as the gathered church, on everyday faith as well as Sunday worship, will result in a reconfigured practice of faith encompassing:

- face-to-face community in a world where many experience loneliness and isolation
- an acknowledgement of the importance of spirituality that affirms the sense that there is more to life than the pursuit of material well-being
- worship that expresses the centrality of God in every sphere of life
- the invitation to explore questions of life, faith and spirituality without being directed to the 'right' answer
- an awareness of the call to make a difference in the community or the wider world in the service of God's coming kingdom
- a way of life that helps to provide a unified sense of identity in an experience that is often fragmented, a moral compass that provides the guidance needed for a satisfying way of life and addresses the pain that many carry as a result of past experience.

Such a definition, I would contend, provides a satisfying picture of what it means to practise Christian faith with the potential to attract those for whom the idea of regular churchgoing fails to connect.

The goal of the reimagined paradigm of ministerial formation I am presenting is the fruitfulness and flourishing of the Church as a 'foretaste, sign and agent' of God's kingdom. It is a model of training for ministry that accords with the new situation of the Church as a mission community in which every member is called to live out their discipleship in the world; in which 'ministry' is the vocation of all and emerges from the shared practice of discipleship; and in which the role of ordained leaders is to nurture and enable this shared ministry as well as to represent it to both the church and the wider world. This paradigm assumes that it is the call of all Christians to grow to maturity in Christ over the course of their lives, and that accordingly the appropriate model of ministerial formation is one of life-long learning. It assumes that the ministry of God's people is both diverse and exercised in collaboration. Before examining in greater detail the fourth element of the paradigm, the shift from theory-to-practice to experiential learning or reflective practice, it may be worthwhile to draw on two biblical passages to highlight the essential nature of discipleship and ministry.

The Beatitudes have long been recognized as a core text for the practice of discipleship, a summary of the transformed life that Jesus' disciples are empowered to live and of their inheritance in the new creation. Taking the observations of Kenneth Bailey[26] on the structure of Jewish rhetoric as a guide, it is apparent that the Beatitudes exhibit what Bailey calls 'ring composition'. Their theme is announced at the beginning and the end: the manner of life through which the disciple receives or comes to inhabit the kingdom of God. Between the introductory statement and the conclusion are two sets of three statements, in each of which the central line of the three conveys the core or foundation of the teaching. We can thus set out Matthew 5.3–10 as follows:

Blessed are the poor in spirit, for theirs is the kingdom of heaven.

Blessed are those who mourn, for they will be comforted.
  Blessed are the meek, for they will inherit the earth.
Blessed are those who hunger and thirst for righteousness, for they
  will be filled.

Blessed are the merciful, for they will receive mercy.
  Blessed are the pure in heart, for they will see God.
Blessed are the peacemakers, for they will be called children of God.

Blessed are those who are persecuted for righteousness' sake, for theirs
  is the kingdom of heaven.

In many respects the qualities listed here overlap with one another. All flow from the terms of entry to the kingdom of God, the recognition of our dependence on God's mercy. Thus, poverty of spirit is the essential quality of life in the kingdom. It means the acknowledgement of our need for grace and the impossibility of serving God or realizing our best hopes for ourselves without his life within us.

The seven promises (the introduction and conclusion repeat the same promise) are all present to some extent in our life on earth. Like any kingdom reality, we experience a foretaste or down-payment of them through the presence of God's Holy Spirit in our lives. Their full realization awaits the final coming of the kingdom.

At the centre of each group of three, forming the heart of the teaching, is a statement about the relationship with God that Jesus looks for. Meekness is the quality of radical obedience. It refers to human strength and aspiration offered to God and under his control. The meek are those who are subject to God's will and ready to do his bidding. The pure in heart are those for whom God is the sole object of desire and worship. They are those who have recognized the one thing that is needful (Luke 10.42), who, like the psalmist, ask one thing of the Lord, to dwell in his presence and thus to 'behold the beauty of the LORD' (Psalm 27.4), to 'see God'.

The first line of each group of three is a statement about relationships with others. They are marked by a quality of mercy, a willingness to be touched, to share the suffering of others, to mourn for the griefs of the world. They describe people who, like the Good Samaritan, instinctively show mercy and compassion where it is needed. The third line of each group is a statement about engagement with society. Disciples share a passion for righteousness and peace (*shalom*). They are those in whom steadfast love and mercy meet, and righteousness and peace kiss each other (Psalm 85.10), and who bring those qualities to their life in the world.

The conclusion is a statement about the likely outcome of living out these qualities in the world. To do so is to demonstrate that the world is wrong about sin, righteousness and judgement (John 16.8). It is to live in the opposite spirit to that of the powers and principalities that dominate the corporate life of society. It is thus to incur suspicion, hostility, ostracism and persecution. But although they may be excluded from enjoyment of the good things of this world, the inheritance of disciples is the kingdom of God, a reality of which they already experience the first fruits.

Ministry emerges from discipleship. In *Reimagining Ministry* I suggest that the biblical model for Christian ministry is found in the figure of the Servant of the Lord in Second Isaiah, a model completely fulfilled in the life, death and resurrection of Jesus.[27] By comparing the characteristics of the Servant with the qualities outlined in the Beatitudes the relationship between ministry and discipleship becomes even clearer.

In the first place, the Servant is poor in spirit. He acknowledges his utter dependence on God, who named him in the womb (Isaiah 49.1), upholds him (42.1) and sustains him when he comes to the end of his strength (49.4). He is rooted in his relationship with God, chosen by him and empowered by his Spirit (42.1), guided by obedient listening (50.4–5). He is compassionate, listening for the word that sustains the weary (50.4), unwilling to break a bruised reed or quench a dimly burning wick

(42.3). He engages not only with individuals but with the life of society, where his purpose is to bring the justice and righteousness of God to the nations, that God might be glorified through him (42.1, 4, 6). As a result, he experiences persecution (50.6; 53.3–9) but is sustained through discerning the eventual reward for his faithfulness (49.4; 50.7–9; 53.10–12). It is through ministry of this character that God declares he will make his glory evident to all nations, so that even those involved in the persecution will be surprised when they recognize the purpose and presence of God in and through the Servant (42.5–6; 49.6; 52.13–15).

In the words of Daniel Hardy quoted in the Introduction, formation for such a ministry 'will call for new conceptions of theological education and formation, not simply forms of the old adapted for wider use'.[28] The next chapter explores the reasons that the traditional 'theory-to-practice' approach of academic life is completely unsuited to ministerial formation and presents in its place a style of teaching and learning in which growth in knowledge and skills for ministry are but two aspects of an overarching growth in 'wisdom and godly habit of life'.

Notes

1 Craig Dykstra, 'Reconceiving practice' in *Shifting Boundaries*, ed. Barbara G. Wheeler and Edward Farley, Louisville, KY: Westminster John Knox Press, 1992, pp. 35–6. Dykstra added that our picture is also harmfully 'technical, ahistorical and abstract'. He meant that practitioners are usually thought of as doing something 'to' others which they have been trained to do by theory-to-practice methods.

2 Tom Smail, *The Giving Gift*, London: Hodder and Stoughton, 1988, p. 13.

3 Lesslie Newbigin, 'On being the Church for the world' in *The Parish Church*, ed. Giles Ecclestone, London: Mowbray, 1988, pp. 37–8, reprinted in *Lesslie Newbigin: Missionary Theologian*, ed. Paul Weston, London: SPCK, 2006, pp. 138–9. See also the masterly foreshadowing of the message of 'Setting God's People Free' in the chapter 'The congregation as the hermeneutic of the gospel' in Newbigin, *The Gospel in a Pluralist Society*, London: SPCK, 1989, pp. 222–33.

4 Stephen Pickard, *Theological Foundations for Collaborative Ministry*, Farnham: Ashgate, 2009, p. 7, and see further especially pp. 139–50.

5 See, for example, Archbishops' Council, *Shaping the Future: New Patterns of Training for Lay and Ordained*, London: Church House Publishing, 2006, pp. 4–5; Faith and Order Advisory Group of the Church of England, *The Mission and Ministry of the Whole Church*, London: Church House Publishing, pp. 62, 64; Martin Davie, *A Guide to the Church of England*, London: Continuum, 2008, p. 108.

6 Anthony Russell, *The Clerical Profession*, London: SPCK, 1980, pp. 303–4; *The Country Parson*, London: SPCK, 1993, pp. 161–87.

7 Bob Jackson, *Leading One Church at a Time*, Cambridge: Grove, 2019.

8 Steven Croft, *Ministry in Three Dimensions*, London: Darton, Longman and Todd, new edition 2008, pp. 141–92. In an earlier work Croft added the dimension of connecting the local church with the wider church; see 'Leadership and the emerging Church' in *Focus on Leadership*, Foundation for Church Leadership, 2005, pp. 7–41. See also Stephen Pickard, who picks up the position set out in the Church of England's 1987 report, *Education for the Church's Ministry*, which sees the clergy as 'animators' of the ministry of the whole church: *Theological Foundations for Collaborative Ministry*, Farnham: Ashgate, p. 102; see Advisory Council for the Church's Ministry, *Education for the Church's Ministry*, 1987, §29; Robin Greenwood, who offers the metaphor of 'navigator': *Parish Priests for the Sake of the Kingdom*, London: SPCK, 2009, pp. 90–120; and Nigel Rooms and Pat Keifert, who offer the pattern of the 'spiritual leader', a key element of the Partnership for Missional Church Process: *Spiritual Leadership in the Missional Church: A Systems Approach to Leadership as Cultivation*, Cambridge: Grove, 2019. For information about Partnership for Missional Church, see https://churchmission society.org/churches/partnership-missional-church/ accessed 10 December 2020.

9 See David Ford, 'An interdisciplinary wisdom: knowledge, formation and collegiality in the negotiable university' in *Christian Wisdom: Desiring God and Learning in Love*, Cambridge: Cambridge University Press, 2007.

10 'Preface to the Common Awards' 2012, p. 2, available at www.dur.ac.uk/ common.awards/programmes/. I will also be drawing on the work I did for my doctoral thesis on learning and revelation, published as *Divine Revelation and Human Learning*, Aldershot: Ashgate, 2004.

11 Advisory Council of the Church's Ministry, *Education for the Church's Ministry*, 1987, §46. In 2003 the 'Hind' report asked that the Church of England's training institutions seek to enable their students to appropriate theology as 'inhabited wisdom' and calls this a 'guiding principle' of ministerial education; Archbishops' Council, *Formation for Ministry within a Learning Church*, London: Church House Publishing, 2003, p. 45.

12 The idea of a 'virtue ethic' specific to particular 'people professions' is embraced by the editors of *Towards Professional Wisdom*, ed. Liz Bondi et al., Farnham: Ashgate, 2011; see especially the contribution of Joseph Dunne, '"Professional wisdom" in "Practice"', pp. 13–26.

13 Charles Taylor, *A Secular Age*, Cambridge, MA: Belknap Press, 2007, especially pp. 539–93.

14 For the renewed focus on character in recent years see, for example, the Oxford Character Project at https://oxfordcharacter.org/; the Jubilee Centre for Character and Virtues at the University of Birmingham, www.jubileecentre.ac.uk/; and Jonathan Birdwell, Ralph Scott and Louise Reynolds, 'Character Nation, a Demos Report with the Jubilee Centre for Character and Virtues', London: Demos, 2015, www.demos.co.uk/publications/character-nation accessed 10 December 2020. I refer to the importance of the renewed emphasis on character for ministerial formation in *Kingdom Learning*, London: SCM Press, 2017, pp. 61–71 and later in this book, pp. 39–40, 47–8 and 70–1.

15 Malcolm Brown, 'Church and state: living in an old country', *Church Times*, 14 February 2014.

16 The figure comes from a YouGov@Cambridge poll of 2011, reported at www.brin.ac.uk/yougovcambridge-launched/ accessed 10 December 2020.

17 Opinion Research Business, national poll for the Archbishops' Council, November 2005; reported in Lynda Barley, *Community Value*, London: Church House Publishing, 2007.

18 See further David Walker, *God's Belongers*, Abingdon: Bible Reading Fellowship, 2017, for some interesting research on the different ways in which people maintain a sense of 'belonging' to their local church without participating in regular worship.

19 David Hay and Kate Hunt, 'Understanding the Spirituality of People Who Don't Go to Church', University of Nottingham, 2000, p. 14; reported in Mark Ireland and Mike Booker, *Evangelism: Which Way Now?*, London: Church House Publishing, 2006. Hay concludes that the increased frequency of reported spiritual phenomena is due to the increased 'social permission' people have to talk about such experiences in a post-modern age.

20 Reported in Nick Spencer and Graham Tomlin, *The Responsive Church*, Leicester: IVP, 2005; and Steven Croft et al., *Evangelism in a Spiritual Age*, London: Church House Publishing, 2006.

21 See www.comresglobal.com/polls/tearfund-prayer-survey/ accessed 10 December 2020.

22 The importance of spirituality has become a major theme in the work of Linda Woodward, in part arising from the 'Kendal Project' reported in Woodward and Paul Heelas, *The Spiritual Revolution*, Oxford: Blackwell, 2005. In my opinion, however, this research is significantly flawed. It begins with an overt value statement as a description of what the researchers call the 'holistic milieu': 'The good life consists of living one's life in full awareness of one's state of being; in enriching one's experiences; in finding ways of handling negative emotions; in becoming sensitive enough to find out where and how the quality of one's life – alone or in relation – may be improved. The goal is not to defer to higher authority, but to have the courage to become one's own authority' (p. 4). The research then assumes that Kendal is typical of the rest of the country. It concentrates on counting and contrasting the number of people in the town attending Christian churches and centres devoted to the 'holistic milieu' but fails to investigate the prevalence of beliefs and attitudes associated with the 'holistic milieu' among the population of the town taken as a whole. Finally, there is no significant theological reflection.

23 Steve Aisthorpe, *The Invisible Church*, Edinburgh: St Andrew Press, 2016, pp. 201–2; and *Rewilding the Church*, Edinburgh: St Andrew Press, 2020; see also Alan Jamieson, *A Churchless Faith*, London: SPCK, 2002; Philip Richter and Leslie J. Francis, *Gone but not Forgotten*, London: Darton, Longman and Todd, 1998; and Francis and Richter, *Gone for Good*, London: Darton, Longman and Todd, 2007.

24 This claim is disputed by those who believe that the practice of Christian faith in its existing form expresses and conveys its essential message and that therefore no alternative form of Christian practice is legitimate. See, for example, Andrew Davison and Alison Milbank, *For the Parish*, London: SCM Press, 2010. The mistake of these authors is to forget that all the existing features of Christian practice that they defend emerged in a specific context. The parish was a creation of the

late Saxon period when parish churches took the place of minsters or mission communities. The change was driven by the desire of the aristocracy for control over the church, still expressed today by the juxtaposition of the church and the manor house in many rural communities. See John Blair, *The Church in Anglo-Saxon Society*, Oxford: Oxford University Press, 2005, pp. 426–98.

25 Ian Parkinson, *Understanding Christian Leadership*, London: SCM Press, 2020, pp. 81–92.

26 See Kenneth Bailey, *Jesus through Middle Eastern Eyes*, London: SPCK, 2008 and *Paul through Mediterranean Eyes*, London: SPCK, 2011.

27 *Reimagining Ministry*, pp. 177–82.

28 Daniel W. Hardy, 'Afterword' in *Local Ministry: Story, Process and Meaning*, ed. Robin Greenwood and Caroline Pascoe, London: SPCK, 2006, p. 147.

2

Moving on from the Academic Model

'Much of the dissatisfaction that currently exists comes from the belief that present patterns of training are either too academic or too influenced by university models.' This statement formed part of an address given in 1986 entitled 'Theological Education Today' by the then Archbishop of Canterbury, Robert Runcie, himself the former principal of a theological college. Significantly, it was included in the Preface to the influential report, *Education for the Church's Ministry*, popularly known as 'ACCM 22' and published in 1987. That report points to the conventions generated by the study of academic theology as lying at the root of 'the present difficulties of theological education'.[1]

If we are to move on from patterns that are too influenced by university models of learning, it will be important to pinpoint where those models fall short. What exactly is meant by the idea that ministerial training is 'too academic'? What are the shortcomings of the academic model? What are the characteristics of the alternative approach, and how do they reflect the new paradigm of ministerial formation?

Universities in crisis

In 2015, the global accountancy firm Ernst and Young announced that it would be removing the minimum requirement of an upper second class degree when considering recruits for their graduate programmes. Their decision has since been followed by other graduate recruiters. Academic achievement is now only one factor in a broader strength-based assessment process. The decision was made after an independent study rated its in-house assessment as a more robust and reliable indicator of a candidate's potential to succeed. Academic performance was too blunt an instrument: there was no evidence to suggest that academic success was correlated with future success in the workplace.[2]

One of the evident shortcomings of a university education is that it pays too little attention to emotional intelligence (EI). Studies of leadership in the business world have suggested that, among the factors leading to success, EI exercises greater influence than intellectual ability.[3] If EI has this degree of importance for the business world, it is likely that in the people professions its significance is even greater, and what applies to the people professions applies equally to Christian ministry.

Furthermore, the last 30 years have seen a significant movement in government thinking on the role of the universities in which their role in 'the transmission of that background of culture and habit on which a healthy society depends'[4] has been downgraded in favour of 'sustaining future economic growth and social mobility in an increasingly competitive global economy'.[5] In a stimulus paper for the Leadership Foundation for Higher Education, Kathleen Quinlan notes the lack of attention in higher education generally to the students' holistic development, by which she means 'Going beyond knowledge and skills to include other aspects of being a person in society (such as emotion, spirituality, moral judgement, embodiment)' and 'An integrative view of learning that emphasises the connections and relationships between thinking, feeling and action.' However, she goes on, 'Higher education is currently a contested and conflicted sector', where the pressures of the market are towards commodification in the service of economic outcomes. 'While these difficult times present us with the opportunity to re-examine our values', she continues, 'the values underlying this paper run counter to the current climate.'[6]

In the view of David Ford, 'current pressures', including globalization and the commodification of higher education, 'amount to a crisis' for the modern research university.[7] Tracing its origin to the foundation of the University of Berlin, Ford sees the Enlightenment research university as a distinct phase in the history of the university following the medieval university with its origin and exemplar in the University of Paris. However, Ford makes clear, the institution of the university requires for its stability and continuity a shared set of goals and values cohering with those of the wider society within which it is set along with the institutional means of embodying and continually refreshing those values and goals. He lists six current challenges that threaten the viability of the modern university, including the unity of research and teaching, the vocation of the university to produce well-educated people fitted for the professions and its commitment to holistic educational formation. The idea of forming wise people committed to the common good, he writes, is 'not on the agenda in most higher education institutions'.[8]

In *Kingdom Learning* I have argued that the heart of the problem facing the modern university is to be found in the shortcomings of its view of knowledge. According to the philosophy of the Enlightenment, 'real' knowledge consists of a general theory about the world. One of the tasks of the university is to extend and deepen that theory through the process of research. Moreover, the human capacity for critical reason was to be the means of investigating both the natural and the human worlds. The traditions of previous ages, including, of course, the Christian theological tradition, were discarded. The basic principles of human life were to be discovered by the exercise of rational thought, free from the dictates of religious or any other authority.

The Enlightenment's concept of knowledge not only separates theory from practice but also intellectual endeavour from values and disposition. It champions a public domain governed by verifiable theory and relegates the aesthetic, moral and spiritual realms to a separate world of private opinion. The university's failure to promote emotional maturity or growth in character is, therefore, simply a reflection of its governing philosophy.

The research university's conceptualization of knowledge is, however, seriously in error. As Michael Polanyi has pointed out, the foundation of our knowledge lies not in explicitly articulated theory but in 'tacit knowledge', the implicit assumptions we often find it difficult to articulate. Our knowledge is like an iceberg, in which 90% or more lies below the surface. 'While tacit knowledge can be possessed by itself,' Polanyi wrote, 'explicit knowledge must rely on being tacitly understood or applied. Hence all knowledge is either tacit or else rooted in tacit knowledge.'[9] In other words, all theoretical knowledge rests on and emerges from tacit knowledge, which is practical. His work is full of examples, from following a recipe to riding a bicycle to conducting a scientific experiment, to illustrate that the foundational level of knowledge is not abstract theory but rather 'practical know-how'.

Not only is the foundation of our knowledge practical and tacit rather than explicit and theoretical, but tacit knowledge is differently organized from explicit. Tacit knowledge is concrete and specific rather than general and theoretical, taking the form of active expectations for a given situation. This 'readiness to respond' unites cognition, affect and, crucially, values in a single representation of a situation. Moreover, this actively organized situational understanding comprises our 'operative' knowledge, the knowledge we use in everyday life. It grows and develops not simply through rational enquiry but through a much more complex process of experiential learning or reflection on practice. Writing from the point of view of his research on reflective practice, Donald Schön declares, 'I have become convinced that universities are not devoted to the production and distribution of fundamental knowledge in general. They are institutions committed, for the most part, to a *particular* epistemology, a view of knowledge that fosters selective inattention to practical competence and professional artistry.'[10]

The conventions underlying a university education are, therefore, unsuited to ministerial formation, requiring as it does the integration of the cognitive and affective, practical, dispositional and spiritual. However, this does not necessarily mean that the Churches should abandon their partnership with the university sector, nor the aspiration for university accreditation of their training programmes. The Preface to the Common Awards welcomes 'the exchange of ideas that being part of a vibrant, interdisciplinary community of scholars offers, and the breadth and depth of experience in the development and administration of higher education' that a partnership with the university brings, but it continues:

A wider and deeper epistemology that also embraces affective knowledge underpins the Common Awards. Such knowledge shapes the emotions, hones virtue and fuels passion after the pattern of Christ ... The Common Awards offer education that (re-)asserts the necessary unity of faith and learning, of knowledge and divine revelation, of the pursuit of truth and the nurturing of virtue, and so must reach beyond the aims of prevailing models of higher education and, in some sense, return to its Christian roots ...

The Common Awards adhere to an understanding of Christian education that is holistic, shaping intellect, spirit, affections, relationships and bodily life. It is more akin to the classical Greek conception of education – *paideia* – that was adopted and adapted by the early church, and within which attention is given to the formational dimensions of the pursuit of knowledge and the acquisition of skills. Formation relates to the transformation of learners into the likeness of Christ and into ways of being, knowing and doing that inhabit the kingdom of God and reflect the God-given callings for which learners are being prepared. It involves the cultivation of virtues, spiritual disciplines, self-mastery and self-awareness, but, above all, seeing the knowledge, love and worship of God as the only and ultimate goal of learning from which all other learning flows.[11]

As the Preface makes clear, the Church is expecting its validating university to make room in its processes for a 'wider and deeper epistemology'. Moreover, as long as the university is open to it, the location of such a programme at the heart of one of our universities has the potential to contribute to the renewal of academic life as a whole. Among the requirements for renewal, writes David Ford, are convincing ideas about the future of the university. These are likely to be found 'in traditions and communities that seek wisdom and have developed overall frameworks and core convictions'. It is, moreover, 'crucially important that these traditions be academically mediated'. Ford envisages intensive discussions between small numbers of stakeholders, each with a tradition of wisdom to contribute.[12] My suggestion is that the Church of England, through its adoption of a new paradigm of ministerial formation, would be well placed to be one of those communities.

Learning ministry as a practice

In *Kingdom Learning* I develop the idea of ministry as a practice or, rather, a cluster of related practices, and examine the way practices are learned. It will be as well to summarize here the main lines of that argument.

The definition of a 'practice' is taken from the work of Alasdair MacIntyre. A practice is:

- a coherent, complex and cooperative human activity
- which has both a social context and a history
- and a goal, recognized both by those engaged in the practice and those outside
- whose standards of excellence are 'internal' to the practice itself, that is, they are defined in relation to the goal, history and context of the practice
- and these standards of excellence can be, and frequently are, systematically extended.[13]

Christian ministry can readily be seen to conform to MacIntyre's definition of a practice or, to be more precise, a family of related practices. To take preaching as an example, it is a coherent and complex activity, its many facets the subject of numerous works of scholarship produced by a community dedicated to the pursuit of excellence. These works make frequent reference both to the history of preaching and the demands

placed on the preacher by the contemporary context. Like many practices, the precise goal of preaching is the subject of constant negotiation,
both within the church and between the church and wider society. As
the practice evolves in response to the demands of the context, so too do
recognized standards of excellence for the preacher.

I also referred in *Kingdom Learning* to the five stages suggested by the
brothers Hubert and Stuart Dreyfus through which a learner develops in
their mastery of a practice. It is worth repeating these, using the practice
of taking a funeral as an example:

- At the very start of the process, the 'novice' is taught a limited number
  of context-free variables and simple rules. In the case of funeral ministry
  these might include theories of bereavement, a general understanding
  of the Christian theology of death and resurrection, and an acquaint-
  ance with the liturgical resources available. Notice that in relation to
  the practice of conducting funerals, even with a considerable degree
  of understanding in these areas of theology and psychology the
  practitioner only advances to the first stage.
- The advanced beginner builds on these simple rules the ability to recognize situational variables. The funeral minister will learn to apply her
  general understanding of bereavement to recognize the responses of
  the people she encounters. She will learn to select from the liturgical
  resources at her disposal the most appropriate for the situation.
- Up to this stage, the minister is learning by following rules and
  recognizing their application in an increasing variety of situations.
  'Competence' arrives only when these rules are integrated and sub-
  sumed in a plan or goal. She plans and prepares the funeral with
  specific goals in mind, such as to bring comfort and reassurance, to
  enable the bereaved to make connections between their experience and
  a particular gospel theme, or to challenge a complacent congregation
  with the reality of death. She adopts these goals from the standpoint
  of a consistent set of values: openness to and love for the family and
  the decision to serve them; commitment to the Christian faith and the
  hope of resurrection in Christ. She also begins to draw on a repertoire
  of actions and responses embedded in habitual practice, sometimes
  using the same words as on previous occasions, sometimes varying the
  words to meet the demands of the situation. In her thinking, rules and
  variables have become part of an overall situation, with features that
  stand out as more or less important.

- Further progress is made as the minister gains experience in a variety of situations, learning to recognize the similarities and differences between them. At the same time, she is building up a repertoire of possible plans and responses and learning to deploy these intelligently and critically. She comes to recognize certain patterns: the difficulty people have expressing their feelings; their reluctance to share unhappy memories; the possibility of anger, expressed or unexpressed; anxiety about the content of the service; and develops a repertoire of ways of responding to these. She learns to recognize when the response she encounters is familiar and predictable and when it is not, and when there are factors in the situation that call for further exploration. At the stage of 'proficiency' she devises plans for an increasing number of situations with an increasingly developed ability to judge the likelihood of a fruitful outcome. Notice not only that proficiency requires the integration of knowledge, skill and disposition. It requires a specific set of dispositions, including empathy, vulnerability, courage and love.
- With further experience her deployment of this repertoire of responses becomes unconscious and intuitive: she is picking up familiar patterns and responding to them without the need of conscious thought. The patterns of events surrounding ministry at funerals and the variations on these stored in her memory gradually grow and she becomes adept at recognizing and responding to these in flexible ways. At the stage of 'expertise' the best response in each situation becomes as much a part of her store of experience as the ability to recognize those situations. 'The expert performer ... understands, acts, and learns from results without any conscious awareness of the process. What transparently *must* be done *is* done.'[14]

Funerals are the territory of the licensed or ordained ministers. For a second example, applicable to either lay or ordained ministry, take leading a project group. In fact, I am not aware of any programme of training for ministry that addresses this task and suspect that most of those who undertake it are drawing on experience gained from their work context and have learned almost entirely through participation in such groups and reflection on their experience.

- The 'beginner' may be familiar with some basic rules and variables, such as John Adair's 'three interlocking needs' in group life, achieving the task, caring for and developing the individual members of the group, and building and maintaining the team;[15] or the nine Belbin team roles.[16]

- The advanced beginner may build on these by identifying the gifts and preferred roles of each member of the group and planning the timescale and stages of the project.
- Competence arrives when the leader is able to set a clear goal for the group by which to relate process to outcome. He begins to learn to balance Adair's three variables, working out when to give attention to individual needs, when to work on the group dynamic and when to move the group on in its task. He is able to draw on the gifts of each group member and possibly identify others from outside the group who might contribute.
- Proficiency will require experience with several different groups. Balancing the needs of the group begins to become second nature. In addition, he becomes familiar with the various elements of what Jenny Rogers calls 'the secret life of groups', such as triangulation, transference and groupthink and learns how to counter them. He becomes comfortable with the life history by which a group progresses through 'forming' and 'storming' to 'norming' and 'performing'.[17] Most of this will be learned by using texts such as Rogers's for reflection on experience when puzzling about how best to steer the group and respond to challenges.
- The 'expert' will be able to master most of the complex dynamics of group leadership without conscious thought, though there will always be individuals and situations that challenge him to go back to basics and think about his best course of action.

The Dreyfus brothers' description makes clear that the style of learning involved in developing as a practitioner differs from that involved in academic study. Moreover, the form in which knowledge is held is also significantly different. The Christian minister growing in her ability to conduct a funeral and the lay church member leading a project group are not refining a theory for how to do it. They are accumulating instances and examples and learning to draw on these in a flexible way to meet the needs of concrete situations. Elements of theory, such as theories of bereavement or theology of death and resurrection, the interlocking needs or life cycle of a group play their part in a much more complex and multi-faceted process of reflective learning.

One of the colleagues with whom I have been discussing these ideas pointed out that there is another 'stage' that follows 'proficiency', complementary to the stage of 'expertise': the ability to stand back and analyse the practice. This capacity is the stance of the teacher. It consists in the ability to spot certain constants, such as the way the variety of possible goals for a funeral service interact with the expectations of the mourners, and become adept at helping others to reflect on their own practice. Thus, in preparing an introductory text for preachers, I set out to analyse the 'ingredients' of a competent sermon, such as a specific message, a structure best suited to the message or to the Bible text, the use of images, introductions, transitions, and conclusions.[18]

It is noteworthy that instruction in theory takes the practitioner no further than the first or possibly the second of the five stages. It is not surprising, therefore, that ministers trained by means of theory-to-practice methods frequently remark that their training has failed to equip them for the reality of ministry. The presupposition of those teachers who espouse the theory-to-practice approach characteristic of academic life is that their students have been equipped with 'real' knowledge, which has only to be applied to be recognized as all they need. In fact, they have been left woefully unprepared for the realities of ministerial practice, in which competence is gained only through the opportunity to reflect on experience.

Thus, when it came to preparing my students for the practice of preaching, I spent little time on the teaching of theory. I knew from the reports of their placements that they already possessed a great deal of tacit knowledge about preaching. Their positive sermon evaluations told me that they already knew tacitly several of the elements of a good piece of communication, already appreciated the need to adapt their presentation to the context and were beginning to recognize the importance of their relationship with their congregations. The preaching classes therefore consisted entirely of reflection on practice, in which they prepared an exercise on each of the 'ingredients' in turn and the class then reflected together on their efforts.

What I had done was to create in the preaching workshops a community of practice through which each student could learn from each other through shared reflection on practice. Reflection is a type of 'experiential learning', which begins with the learner's own experience and enables her to examine and explore it, draw her own conclusions about how to improve and formulate plans for the future. It creates a situation in which, as far as possible, learning and ministry are held together, each feeding the other, rather than being separated into distinct compartments.

A recognition that the activities of ministry, such as church leadership, leading worship, teaching, preaching, pastoral care, evangelism and church planting, leading groups, even administration, are practices, and that the knowledge required to grow in the practice takes the form of 'practical know-how', leads to a radically different assessment of how ministry is learned. As Etienne Wenger writes:

> If we believe that knowledge consists of pieces of information explicitly stored in the brain, then it makes sense to package this information in well-designed units, to assemble prospective recipients in a classroom where they are perfectly still and isolated from any distraction, and to deliver this information to them as succinctly and articulately as possible ... But if we believe that knowledge stored in explicit ways is only a small part of knowing ... then the traditional format does not look so productive. What does look promising are inventive ways of involving students in meaningful practices, of providing access to resources that enhance that participation ... and of involving them in actions, discussion, and reflections that make a difference to the communities they value.[19]

Like MacIntyre, Wenger believes that the baseline for understanding human action and interaction is the individual in community and that life in community consists of shared practices. From this perspective, learning is less the refinement of a theory of the world than the developing ability to participate in practices. 'Learning,' he writes, 'is a matter of competence with respect to valued enterprises.'[20]

This approach to knowledge as shared practical know-how also accords far more closely with the biblical understanding of knowledge than does the Enlightenment ideal of disinterested objective theory-making. For the people of God in both Old and New Testaments, the knowledge of God is always practical. For the prophets like Hosea, to know God was to share his characteristics of righteousness, justice, covenant love, mercy and faithfulness (Hosea 2.19–20). For Jeremiah it meant sharing God's concern for the poor (Jeremiah 22.16). For Paul, the knowledge of God is to lead to a life fully pleasing to him, bearing fruit in good works (Colossians 1.9–10). In my first book, *Divine Revelation and Human Learning*, I show that the process of revelation, through which we come to the knowledge of God, is, in fact, a process of formation through which, by the working of the Holy Spirit, our lives are gradually conformed to the character of Christ.[21]

Miroslav Volf points out that the phrase in Ephesians 4.15 traditionally rendered 'speaking the truth in love' translates the Greek *aletheuein en agape*: 'doing' or 'living' the truth in love. Truth, he concludes, is situated in community and is known only through the will to love.[22] Learning to love lies at the heart of the practice of Christian discipleship and sharing the love of God with the world at the heart of Christian ministry. Learning the knowledge and skills required for ministry is inseparable from the formation of character, not simply because the appropriate dispositions for fruitful ministry are as much a part of formation as the learning of knowledge and skills but because it is impossible to grow in the knowledge and skills required without the disposition to love God and neighbour.

Beyond Athens and Berlin

The publication of Edward Farley's *Theologia* in 1983 sparked a period of intense discussion in the United States about the nature of ministerial formation. Farley had suggested that developments leading up to the establishment of the Enlightenment research university had resulted in a changed concept not only of ministerial formation but of theology itself.[23] After a decade of uncertainty the publication of two works by David Kelsey, *To Understand God Truly: What's Theological about a Theological School* and *Between Athens and Berlin: The Theological Education Debate*, set the agenda for the next stage of the discussion.[24]

Kelsey identified two powerful models of ministerial formation, which he christened 'Athens' and 'Berlin'. The Athens model followed a Christian version of ancient Greek methods of education, known as *paideia*. The aim of *paideia* was to inculcate the virtues required for good citizenship. In the hands of Christian teachers such as Clement of Alexandria and Origen, *paideia* became a conscious ideal focussed on the inner and spiritual life. In *paideia* the teacher acts as a midwife to facilitate the growth of virtue, which can come about only through the student's contemplation of God. Christian texts are used as a source of wisdom in themselves and a stimulus to the pursuit of that wisdom in the student.[25]

The 'Berlin' model adopts the methods of the Enlightenment university. The agenda for the study of theology in the university was first set out by Friedrich Schleiermacher, who was himself instrumental in the founding of the University of Berlin. It was Schleiermacher's achievement to outline the terms on which theology was to play its part in the intellectual life of the reformed Prussian state.[26] Theology, he argued, had a place in the university as one of the professional faculties, along with law and medicine. As the university provides the required training for lawyers and doctors, so it is the place where clergy are trained to play their role in the life of the state. Theology, then, cannot be understood as the pursuit of 'pure' theoretical knowledge but is an example of a 'positive' discipline – that is, a discipline that arises to serve the needs of a professional endeavour. In the words of Edward Farley, it exists to 'give cognitive and theoretical foundations to an *indispensable practice*'.[27]

Second, Schleiermacher insisted, theology must adapt itself to the Enlightenment's approach to knowledge. It cannot proceed by allowing authority to Scripture and Christian tradition and using these as the bases for an enquiry into the nature of God. The nature of knowledge requires that Christianity can only be studied historically, as a concrete example of a religious community.[28] The church's history and its notions of God thus become the focus of critical study, and the study of systematic theology is not to be taken as an account of God's ways with the world directly informed by divine revelation, but as a theoretical, and above all critical, account of Christian belief and practice.

Kelsey concluded that contemporary theological training was uneasily poised *between* these two models of educational excellence. Most training institutions, he observed, attempt to honour both. Students are introduced to the critical study of theology on the one hand; on the other, through the corporate discipline of shared worship, reflection on practice and the 'hidden curriculum' of the training institution, they are to develop qualities of personality and character and learn to nurture healthy relationships. But these two approaches, Kelsey realized, are fundamentally incompatible. 'Between Athens and Berlin', he wrote, 'theological schools are caught between a rock and a hard place. The most that any school can do is negotiate some sort of truce, strike some sort of balance between them.'[29] This negotiation takes place not simply between two different approaches to *learning* theology, but between two fundamentally incompatible conceptions about *what theology actually is*: on the one hand the quest for a transforming knowledge of God, on the other the critical study of historical Christian practice. There is, he wrote, 'a deep *theological* incoherence' underlying the practice of theological training.

In the light of the discussion above, it is evident that the incoherence to which Kelsey draws attention stems from the incompatible requirements of two separate though related practices: the practices of theological scholarship and ministerial formation. The one values critical distance, the other obedience. The one works by analysis, the other requires integration. The one aims to train intellectual capacity, the other to integrate intellect, emotion and character. The one views theology as a theory to be refined through careful analytical enquiry, the other draws on theology as a resource for discerning the presence and activity of God.

Kelsey's distinction has set the terms for the ongoing discussion of ministerial formation in Britain and Australia as well as in the United States.[30] However, the assumption that, despite their uneasy relationship, both models of excellence have their place in ministerial formation has rarely, if ever, been challenged. Nor has attention been paid to the considerable flaws in Kelsey's work. His comparison of the two models centred on one issue: the quest for unity in diversity. What he conspicuously failed to do was to analyse either 'Athens' or 'Berlin' from the point of view of the relationship between Christ and culture, asking which of the models conforms most closely to a theological understanding of the requirements of discipleship and ministry. Furthermore, he fails to probe their claims to 'excellence' from an educational point of view, conceding that the debate had not until then focussed on pedagogical issues but had remained enclosed within the discipline of theology.[31] Thus he fails to consider which of the models best accords with recognized standards of good practice in education. Moreover, he fails to explore the approaches to teaching and learning that might play a part in a contemporary form of *paideia*. Instead, he contrasts an *ancient* approach to *paideia* with the *contemporary* practice of university education.

In hindsight, then, it is to be regretted that it was Kelsey, himself a practitioner within the 'Berlin' tradition, whose attempted resolution of the questions surrounding ministerial formation proved so influential, overshadowing the far more promising proposals of Craig Dykstra, mentioned above, and also those of Edward Farley and Charles Wood, each of whom advocated a version of reflective practice at the heart of formation.[32]

'Secular' theology

Kelsey explicitly treats his two models of excellence in education as 'non-theological' factors.[33] He describes the two approaches as culturally derived models of educational excellence, but without attempting to analyse either model from a theological point of view for its adequacy to a Christian understanding of human life and learning. When we make the attempt, however, it very quickly emerges that the terms on which theology was to be granted a place in the Enlightenment research university represent a surrender to the dominating principalities and powers of contemporary culture.[34]

The existence of the Church, the role of the clergy and the method of their training are all to be defined from the point of view of their role in the state. The role of the Church is the conduct of the religious dimension of social life and the clergy are to function as professional religious practitioners. That Schleiermacher should propose this as the basis of theology's role in the university is not surprising in the context of his time. Since the Reformation, the decision as to the form of religion to be followed in the German States – Catholic, Lutheran or Calvinist – had been in the hands of the governing authorities. Church and state were thereby integrally related.

However, a view in which the role of the church is to serve society in this way is very different from one in which the church's role is to serve the coming of the kingdom of God, which will supplant all human authority. Although the church does aspire to meet human need in a variety of forms as part of its God-given mission, it does so not as an agent of the state or even to fulfil an acknowledged role in society, but from commitment to God's kingdom. While churches may work in partnership with community and secular agencies, there must always be an element of reflection on the church's engagement with society to ensure that it is the values and purposes of the kingdom that are taking priority.[35]

Second, in the Berlin model, fidelity to standards of critical reasoning has been allowed to replace fidelity to Christ as the ultimate standard of truth. Rather than taking Christ as the one 'in whom are hidden all the treasures of wisdom and knowledge' (Colossians 2.3), the ultimate truths of the human condition are to be found through the process of scientifically conducted research. And rather than taking Jesus the *logos* as the world's inherent principle of rationality and revelation of the truth in person, theological study itself is to be subordinated and redefined according to the principles of Enlightenment critical reason. The authority of scripture and tradition has been replaced by the authority of 'critical thinking'.

Constrained by the epistemology of the Enlightenment, for which human reason was the incontestable and indispensable foundation for critical study, much academic theological study became imprisoned within what Charles Taylor calls the 'immanent frame'.[36] To adopt the standpoint of the Enlightenment required assent to the beliefs that God cannot be personally involved in the world of humanity, that Jesus could not have been both human and divine, have worked miracles or have risen bodily from the dead. If the study of theology were to fit the immanent frame, a radical reinterpretation of some of the fundamental tenets of Christian faith became necessary.

Moreover, the terms on which theology maintains its place in the university continue to be set by the state rather than the Church. In the secular university, the theologian is constrained by the insistence of the wider society on a 'value-free' approach to the study of religion, undergirded still by the Enlightenment ideal of rationality. In practice, that 'value-free' approach means that while the teacher of theology may be known as an adherent of a particular religious tradition, this may not be seen to affect their teaching, either in content or manner. Gavin d'Costa retells the anecdote of a theology lecturer who used to begin his lectures in patristics with a prayer until students complained and he discontinued the practice.[37] What is significant here is that in beginning with prayer the lecturer was remaining true to the essential insights of Christian faith and demonstrating these to the class. The Bible and Christian tradition are clear that knowledge and understanding of God only come about with the help of the Holy Spirit. God's thoughts are not our thoughts and his ways are not our ways (Isaiah 55.8). Prayer for the help of the Spirit is therefore an indispensable starting point.

In addition to the *a priori* beliefs I have listed above, theologians of the Enlightenment period and since have also been subject to some grave epistemological errors deriving from the Enlightenment's erroneous understanding of knowledge. One example is the claim of Gottholf Lessing that an 'ugly ditch' lies between contingent historical facts and the 'necessary truths of reason'. The truths of Christian faith, which in his view could only be of the latter kind, could therefore not be established by the historical facts of Jesus' life, death and resurrection, nor yet by the whole sweep of biblical revelation. Another is the positivist approach to history, the belief that it is possible for history, in the words of Leopold von Ranke, 'merely to show how things were'.[38] The immanent frame gives rise to the assumption that the 'Jesus of history' could not possibly be the same as the 'Christ' who was the centre of the faith of the early church; and the positivist idea of history led to the search for a 'historical Jesus', whose outcome reflected almost entirely the motivation and world-view of the individual searcher.[39]

A third aspect of the legacy of the Enlightenment is the fracturing of academic study into increasingly narrow and specialized fields. The factors contributing to this tendency include the pursuit of knowledge 'for its own sake' and the approach to knowledge as abstract theoretical generalization. These two tendencies combine to push research in the direction of analysing the conceptual implications of aspects of the overarching theoretical framework of the discipline. With the explosion of knowledge in the contemporary world it becomes impossible for any but the most practised expert to hold a detailed overview of the whole field of the discipline. This means that research degrees, the criteria for which include mastery of the relevant subject area, tend to focus on specialized areas within it. This yardstick for progress in the academic community is reinforced by the expectation of regular publication, pushing academics in the direction of increasingly specialized areas of experience.

The discipline of theology is no exception to this rule, divided as it is between biblical scholars, further sub-divided into Old and New Testament specialists; systematic theologians; ethicists; philosophers of religion; church historians and, in some places at least, practical theologians; with little in the way of cross-fertilization taking place between them. This feature of academic theology as a community of practice is completely antithetical to the requirements of Christian ministry. There the aspiring minister is required to integrate his understanding of the Bible, history, ethics and systematic theology, so as to bring the resources of his study to bear on the practical everyday problems of ministry.

Finally, the way in which academic theology is taught reflects the history and trajectory of the sub-discipline under study. The community's aim is to initiate the novice into the practices of academic study. For this to be successful, he must learn the issues at stake and the big names involved in the most significant controversies within the discipline; build a picture of how the discipline has been shaped by these, and what are its present interests and most important issues. All this is very different from the requirement of the Christian minister to be resourced by the key methods and insights of the discipline for the practice of ministry or of the disciple to draw on its resources for the practice of faith in everyday life.

Lest it appear that I am seeking to convey a wholly negative picture of academic theology, I should confess that I found the study of theology in the University of Durham as part of my own training for ordination one of the most stimulating and satisfying experiences of my life. It should also be acknowledged that the epistemological errors of the Enlightenment are in the process of breaking down, creating room for approaches in which faith and critical reasoning are avowedly interconnected. Moreover, most professional theologians and biblical scholars are also Christians for whom the practice of discipleship exercises a considerable influence on their work. Recent biblical study has begun to re-balance the dogmatic scepticism surrounding the historical nature of the Gospels. Scholars such as Richard Bauckham and Tom Wright have ably summarized the evidence that suggests that the Gospel accounts, including the resurrection stories, bear all the marks of eye-witness testimony.[40] Mark McIntosh is one of several scholars who set out to introduce the study of theology as a search for 'theological virtue'. 'Theology,' he writes, with a degree of irony, 'is in constant danger of getting carried away – from a respectable discipline managed by theologians to a mysterious sharing in God's way of life.'[41]

The point I wish to make is that, while it is undoubtedly necessary to draw on the resources of theological scholarship in the course of ministerial formation, there are dangers in so doing. There is always the risk of forgetting the distinction between formation for ministry and training in theological scholarship: of constructing courses of teaching that focus on the history and methods of a particular theological sub-discipline rather than the application of theology to ministry. Within that, there is the danger of initiating students into the mistakes of the past simply because they are an integral part of the history of the discipline.

As an example, I was once asked to review a course of teaching in Christology for the Common Awards level 5 module, Topics in Christian Doctrine. The course was wholly structured around the relationship between the 'Jesus of history' and the 'Christ of faith', tracing the question through the work of a series of theologians. It was the study of the way in which theologians had tried, with limited success, to reconcile an epistemological error originating in the Enlightenment with the traditional content of Christian faith. As an initiation into the practice of theological scholarship it could not be faulted, but one wonders what value the exclusive focus on an epistemological and theological mistake could have as an element in ministerial formation, especially when compared with the wide field of alternative possibilities with a greater potential for resourcing ministry: the role of Christ in creation as the origin of all things; in revelation as the image of God; in reconciliation through the atonement; in the new creation as the second Adam; in mission through his Body in the world; in ministry as the Servant of God; as King, victorious over powers and principalities.

Academic learning or ministerial formation?

Over the past 50 years the Church of England has attempted in a variety of different contexts to implement patterns of training more closely related to the demands of ministry than to the structure of theology as an academic discipline. One of these is the Diocese of Southwark, which saw the establishment of the Southwark Ordination Course in 1962, an attempt to extend ministerial formation to working-class candidates, who might otherwise be prevented by their cultural and educational background from training for ordained ministry. Later, in the 1990s, the Southwark Ordained Local Ministry Scheme set out to provide a pattern of training which would be:

- contextual: one in which supervised placements and involvement by candidates in their own local churches would play a core part in the training
- collaborative: in which candidates in training would be divided into small groups to work together, producing many of their assessed pieces of work as a group project
- integrative: in which the theological knowledge incorporated in the training would be organized around five central themes related to discipleship and ministry.[42]

At a later stage, the training course explicitly espoused a reflective pattern of training, based on David Kolb's cycle of experiential learning. One module required the student peer group to choose a passage from the eighth-century BC Hebrew prophets and work on an exegesis of the passage together. As individuals, they then applied this text to the worshipping life of their own congregations; and as a group they visited each other's congregations; they reflected on these visits as individuals and then brought together their observations to suggest the implications of the passage for each other's congregations.[43]

A module like this has the potential for a rich pattern of assessment. Whatever the method of final assessment, it may include:

- a grasp of the knowledge base required by the unit
- ability to apply this knowledge in concrete situations
- ability to reformulate the knowledge in order to teach it to others
- the ability to recognize the knowledge and skills of others and relate these to one's own.

The fact that the work is based in specific contexts offers the potential to assess:

- the student's ability to recognize and articulate the features of the context, such as the worshipping life of a congregation, the patterns of care and engagement in a community project, or the cultural make-up of a community

- the student's ability to interpret that context theologically
- the student's ability to learn by reflection on that context.

In addition, in a training pattern that is collaborative, the potential is there to assess:

- the student's ability to recognize and articulate the features of the learning group's group dynamic
- her ability to cooperate in a common task: to negotiate appropriate goals, to recognize the gifts she brings to the group, as well as the strengths and weaknesses offered by the other members
- the student's reflexivity: her ability to reflect on her own and others' shared assumptions and attitudes.

This process of learning and assessment takes the student into the territory of shared tacit knowledge: the shared knowledge of the learning group, of the context or community, as well as the knowledge embedded in the Christian tradition. It encourages and teaches her how to work with that shared knowledge base and how to assess her own contribution to the shared enterprise of Christian ministry.

At regular intervals, the Ordained Local Ministry (OLM) scheme was subject, as are all other training schemes in the Church of England, to inspection and revalidation. And on each occasion, along with some helpful observations on the pattern of training, the Southwark scheme had to face the demand from the inspectors for a greater degree of explicit theological knowledge. Stephen Lyon, the first principal of the scheme, records the wrestling of the scheme's Council with the request 'to define a core body of theological knowledge and understanding for its ordinands and indicate how and where within the context of training such knowledge and understanding are to be acquired'. Responding to such a request would, the Council responded, be relatively easy but:

> the request ... flies in the face of our basic approach. The Scheme, by its very design, has deliberately sought to integrate the acquisition of theological understanding and knowledge with ministerial and personal development. To extract from such a programme a 'core body of theological knowledge and understanding' appears at odds with such an approach.[44]

Five years later, the same request that 'some of these core curriculum areas were made more discrete and explicit' occurred again.[45] These requests and responses are a classic illustration of the difference in the meaning of 'theology' for two separate though related communities of practice. For the one, 'theology' is divided into discrete subject areas, the 'valued enterprise' is the accumulation of knowledge and expertise in each of these discrete areas and the ability to articulate it to a specialist audience. For the other, 'theology' is the ability to interpret and respond to a given context or situation in ways that reflect the Christian community's tradition of reflection on its life and practice. From the one point of view, the assessment process in the OLM scheme lacks sufficient academic rigour: it does not require the students to articulate the explicit definitions and generalizations or manipulate the abstract concepts that are the stock-in-trade of the academic community. From the other, the academic community's criteria of assessment simply fail to recognize, much less to engage with, the rich and multi-faceted corporate and reflective learning process the scheme had set out to create.

Within the context of their own communities of practice, *both* of these viewpoints may be said to be correct. There really is room for doubt as to whether the OLM trainees, who might be able to deliver an effective Christmas sermon to a mixed audience drawn from their local community, would be capable of writing an essay explaining the doctrine of the incarnation to the standard required by the academic community.

On the other hand, the practice for which the students are being trained is *ministry*, and the qualities required for effective and fruitful ministry are different from those required for academic success: in some ways less rigorous and in others far more demanding. The Christmas sermon requires far more than a competent understanding of the incarnation. It requires some of the competencies of emotional intelligence, the ability to read a context, and skill in communication. It is a far more complex performance than the writing of an academic essay.

Moreover, as will become clear later in this chapter, while the cycle of experiential learning that underlies reflective practice easily incorporates and applies the insights that arise from the theology of the academy, the academic approach to theology completely fails to comprehend the demands of reflective practice. For all its analytical rigour, academic theology represents only a small slice of the complete learning process. In demanding the definition of a core body of theological knowledge, the inspectors were asking for something simple enough for comprehension in terms of the methodology of academic scholarship. They failed to ascribe sufficient value to the rich and multi-faceted nature of the learning process they were supposed to be assessing.

Jerusalem and beyond

The story of the Southwark OLM scheme illustrates the way the relationship between theological scholarship and ministerial formation may go wrong as a result of the failure of professional scholars to recognize the demands of a different though related practice. Before attempting an alternative picture of a mutually fruitful partnership, it is worth taking time to review the developments that have taken place since David Kelsey summarized and provided a focus for the discussion of theological education in the United States. In this section, I examine some of the major contributions to the debate, some responding to Kelsey and others aiming to move beyond him.

1 Robert Banks: The 'Jerusalem' model

Kelsey himself pointed out that the Athens and Berlin models do not cohere and that the incoherence is theological as much as it is educational. Recognizing this incoherence, Kelsey wondered whether there might not be a third model of education. 'Indeed', he wrote, 'Tertullian's question, "What has Jerusalem to do with Athens?" might suggest that, with its roots in "Jerusalem", Christianity in fact theologically mandates a third type of excellent schooling altogether.'[46] This statement provided the opening for Robert Banks to propose a third, theologically grounded, model, which he suggested might be the 'Jerusalem' model Kelsey had hinted at.[47]

As a scholar in the evangelical tradition, Banks argues strongly that the Bible provides the models of Christian formation we require on which to base our approach to ministerial training today. He asks why more had not been made of the biblical meaning of the Hebrew word *yada*, meaning 'to know'. In both Old and New Testaments, to 'know' God is to be drawn into a relationship with him. In the New Testament:

> This involves a considered and heartfelt acceptance of the message about [Christ], leading to a lifelong commitment to his way of life and purposes ... At the heart of this view of personal and corporate knowing – affecting mind, heart, and will – is the work of the Spirit initiating, directing and completing our knowing ... Implicit in all this is a Trinitarian basis for knowing, relating and doing.[48]

At the heart of the Jerusalem model as Banks presents it is mission. Mission, he points out, is both the goal of the church and the context of discipleship. He points to the practice of Jesus with his disciples and of Paul with his missionary teams, finding in these a model of learning in community in the context of mission, forsaking family and other ties in order to learn from and serve alongside a leader. In both cases, missionary disciples model themselves on the example of Jesus, in the case of Paul's teams and churches because he presents his own example, modelled on that of Christ.

Although Banks makes these important points about the recruitment of the disciples and the context of their training, he does not make as much of the example of Jesus as a teacher as does Sylvia Wilkie Collinson. In her study of the Gospels, Collinson perceptively shows how Jesus employed not only formal teaching methods but action-reflection in community, finding in this the key that enables the whole community to grow in discipleship together. 'The action-reflection method,' she writes, 'provides a solution to every caring teacher's problem, that of encouraging those not gifted academically to learn and operate successfully at their own level of giftedness.'[49]

Although Banks recognizes that ministerial formation takes place in the context of discipleship, his focus is on the training of church leaders rather than the formation of the whole church, citing the fact that the disciples broke with old ties and left their homes to join Jesus' mission as a justification for the institution of the seminary and drawing on his own experience of theological education in both Australia and the United States. Without a specialist understanding of educational method, he nevertheless places theological reflection at the heart of learning in context, quoting the work of Donald Schön and taking as his model Thomas Groome's version of the pastoral cycle supplemented by the work of Don Browning.[50] His conclusions for the practice of theological education can be summarized as follows:

- The vision and culture of the educational establishment, including both its overt and 'hidden' curriculum, must be aligned with a missional goal.[51]
- It is important to integrate learning with ministry, prioritizing 'in-ministry formation'. The seminary may be a 'model' of a life-context, but that is all it can be.[52]
- His aspiration is that the local church should become a genuine learning community and, as such, a viable context for ministerial formation.

This involves 'reinventing' the congregation as a relational and missional community, quoting with approval the 'dream' of Bishop Wesley Frensdorff: 'Instead of a community gathered around a minister, a ministering community; instead of a community gathered around a learning person, a learned and reflecting community, a theologically reflective community, knowledgeable in its basic traditions.'[53]
- He recognizes ministry as a cluster of practices, preparation for which involves the formation of attitudes and the areas of understanding that undergird these, and that 'formation-in-ministry' is the best way to achieve this.[54]
- He recognizes the value of 'learning how to learn' and the importance of 'doing' as well as learning theology.[55]
- Teachers serve as role models and should be able to draw on practical ministerial experience.[56]
- Fieldwork should be integrated into the academic curriculum and the role of the fieldwork supervisor strengthened to enable good-quality theological reflection to take place in context.[57]
- There needs to be a break with the 'professional guild mentality' in order to free the ethos, curriculum and teaching methods from those of the academy.[58]

All this represents a considerable step forward. Without deploying very much in the way of educational theory, Banks' theological starting point leads him to see clearly the need for a missional focus and the importance of bringing ministry and learning together. Although his model remains firmly rooted in the seminary, he nevertheless recognizes the importance of the local church as a learning community, and although his focus is on the professional training of church leaders, he anchors this in discipleship and recognizes ministry as a practice in the formation for which attitudes play a crucial point. In the course of the book, he also provides a wealth of examples of good educational practice. Banks' work therefore provides a firm basis for a move beyond the incoherence of Athens and Berlin to a theologically and educationally more satisfactory model.

2 Darren Cronshaw: beyond Jerusalem

Darren Cronshaw is professor of missional leadership and head of research at the Australian College of Ministries. Building on the work of Banks among others, his aim has been to find ways of cultivating 'missional spirituality' in the context of a post-Christendom world in which people are attracted by Jesus and by spirituality in general but turned off by the institution of the church. Like Banks but even more explicitly, Cronshaw sees discipleship 'Monday to Saturday as well as Sunday' as part of the mission of God and the foundation on which missional leadership is built.[59]

His approach is eclectic: he accepts the potential of both Athens and Berlin, along with both Banks' Jerusalem model and the 'Geneva' model proposed by Brian Edgar of Asbury Seminary in the United States, under which students engage with the confessional tradition of their denomination. To these Cronshaw adds two other aspects of ministerial formation. The first he names 'Auburn' and refers to his own local context in Sydney, New South Wales to signal the importance of the way formation is shaped by and for a particular context. The second he names 'New Delhi' to acknowledge the multi-cultural nature not only of the local context but of the churches and the mission fields where students are called to serve. New Delhi he pictures as an ashram in terms reminiscent of the ideals of the fresh expressions movement in Britain: small, open communities that are 'located "in the world" without fences; are open to all; offer community living that is engaged in service; emphasize simple living and spiritual maturity; provide a holistic curriculum of intellectual, spiritual, political, aesthetic and relational development; and create time and space for spirituality and self-awareness'.[60]

While Cronshaw sees value in all the models as aspects of formation, he is clear that Jerusalem is at the centre and mission the 'central organizing framework'. He sees the vocation of the pastor as a practical theologian, capable of integrating context, confession, the critical faculty and, above all, love for God and neighbour by means of reflective practice. His concept of missionary spirituality consists of seven elements, which are:

- communal: mission and leadership take place in community where the ministers support and learn from one another
- conversational: training will make use of active and interactive learning methods and teachers will also be learners
- contextual: in that all theology is by its nature contextual; students will learn from the society and culture in which they are set through such media as film as well as from the theological tradition
- cross-cultural: they will be exposed to non-Western theologies and trained in cross-cultural communication
- character-forming: aimed at forming missional and pastoral identity and giving attention to unhealed wounds

- contemplative: rooted in prayer and the knowledge of God
- congregational: training will relate more closely to the local churches than to the academy, faculty and students encouraged to be part of the leadership of local churches and local church members learn along with the students the basics of mission.[61]

Like Banks, therefore, Cronshaw places mission at the heart of ministerial formation, emphasizes the formation of character, looks to good practice in teaching and learning, placing theological reflection at its heart. Like Banks, he sees a role for the local church in formation as well as the seminary and he moves beyond Banks in calling for missionary leaders to be trained as practical theologians, capable of doing theology in context in order to integrate theology with life.

3 Les Ball: formation as transformative learning

While Cronshaw was developing his model of missional and ministerial formation, a major research project was being undertaken into the place of transformative learning in Australian theological education. The research was carried out through the Melbourne College of Divinity on behalf of Council of Deans of Theology and centred on transformative learning. It was noticed that theological training institutions habitually advertised their courses as 'transformative', without being clear as to the nature of the transformation promised or the methods by which it was achieved. The project 'set out to identify the strengths and weaknesses of the undergraduate theological curriculum in providing an increasingly diverse population of theological students with a transformative education'.[62]

In relation to ministerial formation, the picture is complicated by the fact that many ministers in training take their undergraduate theology degree at a higher education institution rather than a theological college. The scope of the project was accordingly extended to more than 50 teaching campuses, not all of which specialized in ministerial formation.

Evaluating the outcome of the survey is also complicated by the concentration of the research question on 'transformative' education despite the recognition that 'the language of transformative learning presents as a vexed issue'.[63] Although the operative definition of 'transformation' rested largely on the work of Jack Mezirow, it was nevertheless necessary to take note of the way in which Mezirow's description of transformation has been subject to continual modification under the pressure of multiple critiques. In effect, the definition of transformative education came to mean for the purposes of the research 'teaching students rather than teaching subjects', or 'learner-centred' rather than 'content-centred' education.[64] If we ask further what these definitions mean in practice, they seem to boil down to an approach that seeks to engage with the whole lives of students in a way that enables them to relate theology to their own and others' life-situations. It is open to question whether the focus of the research was the most appropriate possible, especially given that what the churches look for is 'formation' rather than 'transformation', a 'well-formed church leader with effective ministerial capacities' rather than simply a 'transformed life exhibiting commendable qualities'.[65]

The most striking result of the research is the extent to which theological education in Australia was dominated by a content-centred academic paradigm in which knowledge of the Bible and theology were seen as the most important elements. Ball relates this to the widespread acceptance that the primary task of a theological school was to safeguard the denomination's inheritance of faith. This primary purpose was widely accepted by all the stakeholders consulted.[66] Students enrolling on courses did so in the expectation that they would gain an in-depth understanding of the Bible and the theological tradition. Moreover, this was widely found to be transformative, not only in the way that studying for a university degree ought to be but also in the way students' faith developed. Their understanding of Christian faith was deepened, their facility in theological thinking enlarged and in many cases their faith in God strengthened. Churches were pleased to receive pastors well-versed in the scriptures. On the other hand, graduates frequently remarked that their studies had not engaged sufficiently with their life experience and churches lamented students' lack of preparation for the realities of ministerial life.

As I remarked in *Kingdom Learning*, any programme of education presupposes a vision for human life and an account of the nature of human beings as learners.[67] Unsurprisingly, therefore, Ball points to the importance of institutional aim in achieving transformation. The institution must be guided by a coherent sense of purpose, which must be endorsed by all the relevant stakeholders, not only staff and students but, in the case of ministerial training, the receiving churches. Because the contexts in which institutions are set varies, each will need to work out its own goals and purposes.

However, a key element in any institutional vision aiming at transformation will be a learner-centred approach to education. Here, the research finds a notable lack of experience and expertise, with faculty members overwhelmingly wedded to the traditional academic paradigm. This results in the fragmentation of the curriculum, echoing the usual divisions of academic theology; an emphasis on the transmission of content represented by 'foundationalism', in which introductory modules typically aim at coverage of as much of the subject matter as possible; and a widespread problem of student overload, especially where the ministerial elements of the course, such as fieldwork, are only loosely connected to the academic programme.[68]

Ball suggests that foundationalism can be countered by designing introductory units in such a way as to be considerably lighter on content and instead focus on how to learn, emphasize the main questions of the discipline, and explore the relevance of these to the students' lives and future ministry. In a revealing personal reflection, he recounts the experience of discovering from two of his own former students that they had forgotten virtually all the content he had imparted to them but retained strong memories of the way he had provided a role model of what it meant to think theologically.[69]

Apart from its snapshot of the situation in Australian theological education at the time, the primary outcome of the research consists in the principles offered for curriculum reform. These include the primacy of biblical and theological knowledge, which, as we have seen, is strongly valued by the community for which ministers are being trained; the engagement of theology with culture and society; the integration of learning and life and the intentionality of curriculum design.[70] However, the report is short on the application of educational expertise. Its concrete suggestions for curriculum reform are limited to the use of introductory units, the inclusion of units aimed at transformation at regular points, conversational styles of teaching aimed at drawing students' life experience into the classroom, the incorporation of fieldwork into academic programmes, and the provision of 'capstone' courses enabling students to reflect on the formational and transformational aspects of their learning.[71]

The research portrays a situation in which, despite an aspiration to make courses of theological learning more intentionally transformative, integrating theology with life and providing a solid preparation for ministry, the educational expertise to make this happen is largely lacking. Despite widespread acknowledgement of its limitations, staff, students and receiving churches alike subscribe to an existing paradigm of ministerial formation centred on the inherited divisions of theology and traditional teaching methods. The situation as described by Ball is one in which dissatisfaction with the existing paradigm is beginning to reach a stage at which alternatives are being considered, but where its dominance is still proving a hindrance to renewal. The inherited paradigm provides tangible benefits, with students experiencing a sense of achievement and in many cases transformation as a result of their studies. It also provides the kind of ministers congregations and denominational leaders expect, well-trained in biblical interpretation and knowledgeable about the theological tradition. However, in this post-Christendom age, as Cronshaw is pointing out, something more is required of church leaders, which the existing paradigm is failing to deliver.

4 Perry Shaw: thoroughgoing application of educational principles

In contrast, Perry Shaw presents a situation crying out for paradigm change. In his own life, he experienced a personal crisis in which disillusionment with the world of theological education to which he had devoted his life's energies played a major part. Recovery quickly led to the opportunity to be involved in creative transformation of a programme of ministerial formation as a member of staff at the Arab Baptist Theological Seminary (ABTS) in Lebanon.[72]

In keeping with his experience of disillusionment, Shaw's starting point is a salutary fact: most theological education is counterproductive. A survey as part of the research for Christian Schwarz's book *Natural Church Development* found an inverse correlation between denominational growth and educational expectations: the more training Churches demand of their pastors, the less their churches grow and the more likely they are to decline.[73] Unsurprisingly, Shaw concludes that the traditional curriculum of theological training, based on the fragmentation of academic theology, does not serve ministerial formation. In its place, he proposes a model of integration: of the theological curriculum of theology and context and of theology and the student's self-understanding as a disciple and a minister.

He then brings to the task of devising such a curriculum a thorough knowledge of educational process, starting with intentionality in the language and culture of the institution and going on to intentionality in approaches to teaching and learning. To provide fruitful ministerial formation, institutions need to involve all their stakeholders in formulating a clear vision of what they hope to achieve. He suggests that the ultimate goal of ministerial formation is churches that impact their society and culture for the kingdom of God. This is where 'good theology drives good pedagogy'. The purpose of the church is participation in the mission of God and therefore the purpose of church leadership is to equip churches for mission. The process of goal setting will include a clear picture of the ideal church, of the cultural challenges the church faces in its context and, building on these, a clear picture of the ideal pastor. The ABTS profile of the ideal pastor is a reflective practitioner, with a love for God and others, committed to servant leadership, of which a major element is equipping others for service.[74]

Shaw echoes the priorities of this book as well as those of Banks and Cronshaw in looking for ministers capable of collaborative leadership, with the skills to equip others for service and to lead them in the interpretation of culture, for whom theological reflection is a habitual practice that they pass on to others. This is achieved partly through the integration of learning with ministry: devising learning tasks that require and enable students to integrate their theology with the context in which they are serving. Second, theological reflection is not simply a technique that students learn. Shaw describes a classroom in which *all* learning is theological reflection, integrating theological disciplines; the cognitive, affective and behavioural domains; theology and personal response; theology and practice. 'The curriculum,' Shaw declares, 'has taken seriously the need to bring integration between academic excellence, personal formation and growth, and the development of leadership skills and qualities.'[75] This is achieved by means of sound methods of teaching and learning, for which Shaw provides a handbook more detailed than anything I am attempting in this book and which I will not attempt to describe except to pick out one feature: the 'flipped classroom'. Lecturing is virtually absent. Students are expected to become familiar with the content before the session and to come ready to engage in active learning together based on the required reading.

ABTS thus aims to achieve most of the goals to which Banks, Ball, Cronshaw and, indeed, the Church of England aspire: a collaborative ministry rooted in discipleship, engaging with culture and equipping the whole church for ministry, which implies that the whole church becomes a discipling community. Context is integrated with classroom learning by means of intentionally designed learning tasks which take place both in the classroom and in the form of assessment assignments. On the other hand, although the aspiration that the local church become a learning community is present, there is little emphasis on the local church as a formational community for ministerial training. Most if not all relating of theology to context takes place in the classroom and there is no mention of partnership with supervisors located in the ministry context itself. Moreover, the programme Shaw describes is a three-year programme of initial training for church leadership, rather than a life-long programme of formation for discipleship and ministry, although the aspiration is there that seminary graduates will be equipped to provide this in the churches they go on to lead. Nevertheless, in a situation where the need is for a new paradigm in place of inherited models, Shaw's work is both salutary and enlightening.

5 The United States: pastoral imagination and practical wisdom

Like Robert Banks, the study of theological education in the United States has also moved beyond Kelsey's models, though in a different way. The volume *Educating Clergy* is the outcome of a collaboration between the Carnegie Foundation for the Advancement of Teaching as part of its ongoing programme of research into professional education and the Lilly Endowment, whose research focussed on the way religious leadership functions in American life.[76] The focus of the research is on the pedagogy or teaching methods used in clergy and rabbinical education. While some schools and educators teach for theological scholarship and others for practical competence, still others teach for 'pastoral imagination', which integrates the two.

The term 'pastoral imagination' is taken from the work of Craig Dykstra, then president of the Lilly Foundation and latterly Senior Fellow in Leadership Education at Duke Divinity School. Dykstra describes pastoral imagination as a way of seeing and interpreting situations through the eyes of faith which acts as an 'internal gyroscope', enabling the pastor to respond with integrity, creativity and wisdom to a given situation.[77] The word 'imagination' points to the ability to see deeply into situations, the possession of a world-view enabling the pastor to comprehend and respond to situations in the light of their accumulated pastoral wisdom. The elements of pastoral imagination include:

- an understanding of scripture and theology, and the ability to interpret these in the context of contemporary life
- 'an accurate sense of what makes human beings tick'
- 'a complex understanding of how congregations and other institutions actually work'
- a clear awareness of the world that the church exists to serve.

Pastoral imagination is the ability to bring all these together in specific situations. It is rooted in the 'wisdom and godly habit of life' that resources, guides and enables the practice of ministry.

Pastoral imagination is related to 'ecclesial' imagination: 'the way of seeing and being that emerges when a community of faith, together as a community, comes increasingly to share the knowledge of God and live a way of abundant life'. Ecclesial imagination therefore describes what happens when, in Lesslie Newbigin's words, a congregation 'believes the gospel and lives by it'.[78] Moreover, declares Dykstra, just as it is the pastor's role to teach and enable ecclesial imagination, 'it is the congregation's ecclesial imagination that over time gives rise to the pastor's pastoral imagination'. 'It is the quality and depth of their people's worship that makes it possible for them as their pastors to lead worship with integrity. It is the people's care for one another that makes it possible for them to be caregivers as pastors. It is the people's engagement in the church's mission that enables the pastors to lead the congregation in mission.'[79] In describing the function of the clergy, the Church of England's ACCM 22 report referred to the 'interanimative' nature of ministry: the way the ministry of the ordained and the ministry of the whole church '"bring each other to be" in the way in which the mission of God requires'.[80] This description of the way pastoral and ecclesial imagination animate each other is one of the deepest descriptions I have seen of this aspect of collaborative ministry.[81]

Dykstra's description of pastoral imagination relates specifically to the leadership of a Christian congregation. This should not lead us to fall back into a 'one-size-fits-all' understanding of ministry. In any and all of the diverse fields of Christian ministry, competence takes the form of a similar holistic vision of the situation, the human dynamics at work and God's place in it. The 'pastoral imagination' of the congregational leader is matched by the 'missional imagination' of the pioneer or church planter, the 'pedagogical imagination' of the teacher, the awareness of a chaplain of the pastoral and spiritual needs of the people she encounters, and many more beside.

Pastoral imagination is formed as a result of reflection on practice. Along with the contributors to *Educating Clergy*, Dykstra and his collaborators accept the definition of a practice advanced by Alastair MacIntyre. Pastoral imagination might therefore be understood in relation to the Dreyfus brothers' stages of learning as a description of 'proficiency' or 'expertise' in ministry: the ability to call on a wide range of experience to interpret and respond to the present situation.

Given that education is itself a practice, and that a practice includes methods and strategies for achieving its goal, *Educating Clergy* asks whether it is possible to identify and describe the 'signature pedagogies' used in ministerial formation through which students are enabled to participate in the communities of practice represented by rabbinical or denominational ministry. The pedagogies they observed 'seemed to reflect what these seminary educators view as counting most in preparing students for clergy practice':

- the facility for *interpreting* texts, situations and relationships
- nurturing dispositions or habits integral to spiritual or religious *formation*
- heightening student consciousness of *contexts*
- cultivating student *performance* in clergy roles and ways of thinking.

Since the culture of the various institutions and the expectations of its stakeholders varied with respect to their religious and cultural assumptions, in the manner we have observed through the Australian research reported by Ball, the research was able to identify not simply signature pedagogies deployed by individual educators but 'signature pedagogical frameworks' applying to institutions and reflecting the differing value placed on the four elements listed above.[82] The research was thus able to describe the landscape of clergy education in the institutions studied and was able to relate this to the variation in theology and culture surrounding the work of clergy but did not advance to normative suggestions based on the ways in which people most effectively learn.

However, Craig Dykstra and his colleagues have continued to think together about the kind of knowing represented by pastoral imagination.[83] As the knowledge that arises from engagement in a practice, it is rooted in practical know-how, which, as Michael Polanyi shows, underlies all explicit knowing. Bonnie Miller-McLemore quotes Rodney Hunter's description of practical know-how as 'a contextually embodied, forward-moving, problem-solving activity'. 'This kind of knowing,' she goes on, 'stands behind a seemingly endless variety of activities – how to be a friend, how to be creative with a sermon, how to make a decision, how to be a leader or follower ...'[84] Miller-McLemore is particularly damning about the way theology is in thrall to intellectualism. The fact that theological training has been confined to the clergy has created the illusion of a 'clerical paradigm' excluding the laity from the territory of theology. In fact, she claims, it is the division and specialism within theology that excludes by taking theology away from the congregation and making it a field for experts. The 'academic paradigm' is, in her words, 'as virulent and problematic as the clerical paradigm'. Both practical and systematic theologians, she claims, 'underestimated the intelligence involved in practice and overlooked the limitations of merely academic knowledge'.[85]

At the heart of the practical know-how that underlies pastoral imagination, these authors suggest, lies the Aristotelian virtue of *phronesis* or 'practical wisdom'. This is a kind of knowing that is 'morally attuned, rooted in a tradition that affirms the good, and driven toward aims that seek the good … Most of all, this knowledge is practical, grounded in ordinary experience and learned over time in the company of others and for the sake of others.'[86] As we have seen, practical wisdom emerges from participation in communities of practice and is both embodied and affective rather than purely intellectual.

It may be that these writers are tending to romanticize practical wisdom. After all, there are some communities of practice in which shared practical know-how and habitual responses to situations tend towards the bad and imprison people in a downward spiral. However, the ideal they are seeking is the expression of Christian faith and practice as a community's common life, the reflected practice of discipleship in everyday life, and of ministry in the life of the church and the wider community: a congregation that 'believes the gospel and lives by it'.

In the light of our earlier discussion of the stages by which people learn a practice, it is possible to give more precise definition to the role of practical wisdom. Through disciplined reflection on their gradually increasing store of experienced situations the minister acquires and develops the ability to discern the salient features of a given situation and to respond in a flexible way on the basis of plans and goals that express a relatively stable set of dispositions. It is precisely the ability to hold together the particular and the general, to see both the big picture and the unique features of a situation, that lies at the heart of practical wisdom. As Joseph Dunne puts it:

> To be practically wise or a person of good judgement is to be able to recognise situations, cases or problems as perhaps standard or typical – that is to say, of a type that has been met previously and for which there is already an established and well-rehearsed rule, recipe or formula – or as deviating from the standard and conventional, and in either case, to be capable of dealing with them adequately and appropriately.[87]

This capacity to discern the nature of a situation, the way it corresponds to other similar situations and the ways in which it is unique, and to interpret that situation by placing it in an appropriate framework of understanding, situates *phronesis* as the intellectual virtue that enables us to apply the virtues of character to specific situations. Within the practical know-how that emerges from and guides a practice, *phronesis* or practical wisdom unites theory and practice. We may be courageous, generous or compassionate, but we need to be able to discern in any given situation just what courage, or generosity or compassion requires of us. *Phronesis* is, therefore, the capacity of 'right seeing' or 'virtuous perception'.

Christian Scharen and Eileen Campbell-Reed of the Auburn Theological Seminary are engaged in a longitudinal study investigating the way in which ministers learn 'pastoral imagination', which they describe as the capacity for 'seeing a situation in all its holy and relational depths and responding with wise and fitting judgement and action'. It is a 'capacity for situational perceptions that are skilled and make use of multiple kinds of knowledge about self, context, relationships of power, and ritual practices ... to take risks and act with responsibility'.[88]

Five years into their study, Scharen and Campbell-Reed have been able to distil their research into six major findings:

1 Pastoral imagination is learned best in formation for ministry that is integrative, embodied and relational. By this they do not mean simply situations that bring together insights from different sub-disciplines of theology, but immersion in practical situations in which ministers are required to formulate goals drawing on these insights: situations in which they move from novices or beginners to 'competence' or 'proficiency'. In other words, ministers learn best in real contexts, where learning and practice are not separated, where learning emerges from practice and feeds back into it.

2 Ministers learn best from teachers who have themselves been practitioners and are able to relate what they teach to the practice of ministry.

3 Learning pastoral imagination requires the 'long haul' of regular practice but also emerges from critical moments of crisis or clarity. In other words, it emerges from the 'critical incidents' that become the subject of theological reflection in the midst of daily ministry.

4 Pastoral imagination is most effectively learned in mentoring relationships in which the mentor both shares their own wisdom and engages in shared reflection. In other words, the mentor is not simply telling

the new minister how to do it but helping them to learn for themselves through both advice and reflection.

5 Learning is complicated or inhibited by situations of injustice.

6 Learning pastoral imagination enables the minister to inhabit ministry as a spiritual practice, opening themselves and their communities to the presence and power of God. As a 'wisdom and godly habit of life', pastoral imagination naturally discerns the presence and action of God in situations and enables the minister to cooperate with the work of the Holy Spirit.

The Auburn study thus points towards a different style of learning, in which practitioners learn 'godly wisdom' through techniques of reflection in community and with the support of experienced mentors. This style of learning assumes that learning is concrete and situational, that theory and practice are integrally connected, that learning is essentially relational and integrates intellect, emotion and values.

Theological reflective practice

In the words of Rowan Williams, quoted in the Introduction:

> A theologically educated person is someone who has acquired the skill of reading and interpreting the world in the context and framework of Christian belief and Christian worship ... not someone who simply knows a great deal about the Bible or history of doctrine but somebody who is able to engage in some quite risky and innovative interpretation and ... to recognize holy lives.[89]

It will readily be observed that Williams is describing 'pastoral imagination', the stage of 'proficiency' in the learning of ministry as a practice. As Scharen and Campbell-Reid conclude from their research, pastoral imagination is best developed through shared reflection in context with the help of experienced mentors who are also practitioners. What, then, is the alternative, experiential learning approach?

The complete learning process, of which academic theology is only a small slice, is experiential learning. As described by David Kolb, experiential learning has four elements.[90]

- It begins with the learner's own experience in all its infinite variety. It includes the experiences that take place in the course of life: a casual conversation that may provide cause for thought, a major decision, starting out in a new job, all the way to major life-changing experiences like bereavement or the birth of a child. It also includes a variety of 'formal' or deliberately structured learning experiences: reading a book, or an instruction manual; watching a video or TV documentary; attending a course.
- The learner then reflects on this experience, a process that has the potential to unearth and make explicit the tacit structures of stored experience though which she ascribes meaning to situations. These will include affections and values as well as prior knowledge and opinions.
- Reflection may take place relatively rapidly or last a considerable period of time. Eventually, it leads the learner to conceptualize the new learning by relating it to her existing knowledge. Sometimes new learning is assimilated to existing understanding, sometimes the learner develops new concepts through which her ability to interpret the world becomes richer and more flexible.
- Finally, the learning cycle returns to the outward dimension. It requires the learner to try out her new insights in action. The learner has gained a new perspective on the situation in which the experience arose, enabling her to approach future situations of the same type with a wider variety of possible responses and greater wisdom in deploying them.

Reflective practice is a specific type of experiential learning, which focusses on the experience gained in the course of a given practice in order to generate new learning for future action. Donald Schön distinguishes between 'reflection-in-action', in which the cycle of learning takes place in the course of an activity, enabling the practitioner to adjust her plans and responses at the time; and 'reflection-on-action', which may be informal but may also be planned, structured and deliberate, through which she reviews and evaluates her experience, recognizes and names key features of the situation, enabling her to develop a more complex overall vision and a more adequate set of skills.[91]

Theological reflection (TR) is a specific type of reflective practice, in which space is created for the resources of scripture and Christian tradition to inform the process of reflection. As we have seen, the outcome of theological reflection is 'pastoral imagination' or its equivalent for one of the diverse fields of Christian ministry, in which the virtue of *phronesis* or 'practical wisdom' plays a key part. Pastoral imagination is the 'situational know-how' of the competent practitioner: the ability to see situations whole, to recognize the influence of the various factors at play and, most important, to recognize the presence and activity of God. How then does theological reflection enable the development of this capacity?

- TR involves focussed attention to the specifics of a given situation. It requires the ability to give a 'thick description' of an incident or situation, to describe it not only in detail but from more than one point of view, drawing out the features that appear to be most significant, but without overlooking the details that give this situation its unique character; recognizing the features it shares with other similar situations, but also the ways in which it differs from these. It teaches both 'practical wisdom' and the ability to comprehend and describe life in all its complexity and particularity.
- It draws on a variety of non-theological resources, such as principles of effective leadership, the characteristics of children or of older people, the process of bereavement, and tools for 'exegeting' or reading local culture. It also requires the ability to place these in a dialogue with theology: to recognize those approaches to leadership that echo a Christian understanding of the purpose of human life and those that fail to do so; to correlate the understanding of identity in child development with theological approaches to personal identity; to place bereavement in the context of the importance of relationships for human life generally.
- It draws on the resources of Christian tradition. It requires the ability to interpret scripture intelligently, knowledge of the doctrines of the Christian faith, and experience as a member of the Christian community. It therefore utilizes the resources of academic theology in the context of a much richer process of learning.
- It also stimulates the learning of these things. It requires the learner to delve more deeply into the meaning of Bible passages, to clarify their understanding of Christian doctrine, to appreciate the lessons to be drawn from the history of the church, and so on. Moreover, in reflective learning, the learner's apprehension of 'academic theology' is not only richer and more secure but also more likely to become part of their 'operant theology' because it is applied to their context and life experience.
- It is integrative: it involves considering situations from a variety of different points of view; it makes connections between the various divisions of theology – interpretation of the Bible, church history, systematic theology and so on – as well as making links between theology and other disciplines.

- It looks for patterns of continuity and discontinuity: it aims to provide theologically grounded interpretations of situations or, alternatively, to take note of where situations challenge conventional theological interpretations.
- It is geared to application: it asks how the insights gained from the process of reflection may be taken forward in concrete ways.
- It is reflexive or self-involving. Not only does theological reflection challenge the practitioner to evaluate his existing interpretation of the situation, it asks him to become aware of his feelings, values, motives, assumptions and dispositions. It points to future learning needs, such as unanswered questions and inadequate responses.[92]

It is frequently asserted by members of the academic community, almost as if it were a truism, that it is necessary *first* to be exposed to academic theology and study of the Bible *before* engaging in theological reflection. Nothing could be further from the truth. The assertion is a product of the 'theory-to-practice' mentality, which treats 'theology' as the production of an educated elite and ignores the 'everyday' theology of 'ordinary' believers.[93] As Jeff Astley insists, the conversation between the 'ordinary theology' of believers with no formal theological training and the 'academic' theology of the professionals must begin with 'ordinary theology' and the Christian educator needs to be a 'mediator', who is fluent in both 'languages'. Moreover, like any competent educator, the Christian teacher needs the wisdom to begin with the learners' existing experience and understanding. Only so will learners be enabled to make the connection between theology and everyday life. Any new insights gained must build on this existing understanding and so become part of the learner's operative understanding. In contrast, 'much Christian and academic theological teaching', Astley writes,

> seeks wholly to raze people's pre-existing theological fabrications to the ground, trampling their personal narratives and imaginative images, before attempting (often unsuccessfully) to build something entirely new and unrelated on the bulldozed site.[94]

In *Kingdom Learning* I give examples of people bringing their ordinary theology to corporate theological reflection and as a result growing in faith and being resourced for faithful Christian practice.[95] 'Setting God's People Free' includes a vignette in which reflection with others provides the 'theological imagination' for a security guard to view his role as a 'ministry of reconciliation'.[96] Moreover, as I mentioned in the Preface, Elizabeth Jordan found that the 'ordinary theology' of church members who understood the local church as 'family' was in some ways more sophisticated and more faithful to scripture than that of their clergy.[97]

Theological reflection is the way the resources of academic theology may be fruitfully deployed in the service of formation for ministry. In the Diocese of Oxford research described in the Introduction, all the TEI representatives and most of the focus group participants identified theological reflection as the primary means of enabling ministers to make the connection between theology and everyday life. However, the ministers' response to theological reflection varied. Some welcomed it as a transformational tool, enabling them to make theological sense of the challenges of ministry:

> [TR] was something that absolutely stunned me and I've been a pew-sitter for years and years; that I'd never heard of it; ... and I was like, wow, this is amazing ... I know an awful lot about conveying and teaching and how you communicate, but I'd never done any of that. And I was like, why isn't this being preached? Why aren't we teaching anyone to do this?

Others saw it as 'natural', as what they had been doing anyway in their desire to live a faithful Christian life:

> I was amazed, when I started training, that actually I do it quite naturally. And I think probably most people do. When I had to submit my personal reflections ... I just picked the one that was closest to what I do naturally ...

> I think it's a skill, once you've learnt, you tend to have at the back of your mind ... And every time you go through that cycle, it kind of sparks you off again. I've explained it a little bit to my colleague; she actually understood how powerful it can be ... because she was a Muslim.

Others were left cold:

> I remember the pastoral cycle; I know there are others, but I found that module really boring ...

> I was put off theological reflection big-time by the way it was taught. I'd never done a formal theological reflection before, although I'd done

a lot of informal theological reflection. And the problem was that then we then had to go away and 'do' one … You had to come up with something that fit the structure for a two thousand word [essay].

One of the main reasons that TR had failed to 'land' for these ministers was they had been introduced to it as an academic exercise in the context of an academically oriented course of study. In this context, the transformative potential of TR had passed them by. It is part of the pattern whereby, while equipping them as religious professionals to lead the gathered church, their training had disabled them for the task of enabling the everyday faith of their congregations, arguably the more important element of licensed and ordained ministry in a post-Christendom age.

Quentin Chandler's earlier research with his students on the Diocese of Peterborough's Lay Ministry Training Course offers some further insights into the learning of theological reflection. Chandler found that, in order to master TR, students needed to acquire certain 'threshold concepts'. Drawing on the work of Meyer and Land, Chandler explains that threshold concepts have five characteristics:

> Their negotiation is (1) *transformative* in that it changes learners' perspective of subject matter, discipline or world view; (2) likely to be irreversible in that the transformed understanding will only be unlearned with considerable difficulty; (3) *integrative* in that it uncovers the previously hidden interrelatedness of subject matter; (4) *bounded* in that it delineates the conceptual boundaries of the subject discipline or captures its essence; and (5) *troublesome* because it often involves dealing with knowledge that may be counterintuitive, alien or even absurd on a common sense level.[98]

The troublesome transitions that some students needed to negotiate included:

- the pervasive threshold concept: the realization that *all* experience is potentially material for reflection and that it is possible to draw on *any* subject discipline in reflecting on it
- the interpretive threshold concept: the recognition that when using the Bible in reflection the meaning of the text is subject to interpretation
- the complexifying threshold concept: the realization that, far from providing a straightforward answer to a perplexing question the outcome of reflection was likely to be an awareness of deeper levels of complexity than previously recognized.

The need for students to cross these 'thresholds' in order to acquire the skills of theological reflection reflects a deeper, pedagogical transition: from dependence on the codified knowledge of a self-contained academic discipline conveyed by an authoritative teacher to the confidence to reflect on everyday experience and engage with the Christian tradition in order to arrive at a deeper understanding of the presence and call of God in a given situation. The students were being asked not simply to learn theology as an academic discipline but to learn how to bring their experience and Christian faith together in the service of ministry, while their teachers played the role of both guardians of the tradition and facilitators of learning.

Moreover, Chandler discovered, some students failed to engage with the processes of theological reflection to which they were introduced on the course because they were already familiar with another mode of reflection, namely prayer. These students were used to responding to perplexing and challenging situations by seeking God's guidance in prayer. Moreover, Chandler observed, their ability to interpret the insights they arrived at in this way depended on their accumulated past reading of scripture and their prior experience of prayer and reflection. The outcome was an 'internal voice' which 'represented an internally held "text" brought into dialogue with experience'. Although in many cases the way they were using prayer to discern God's presence and call in a situation might have been quite naïve, these students were becoming used to exercising their developing 'wisdom and godly habit of life' in the course of their reflection on experience. Chandler's conclusion echoes the understanding of theological reflection I develop in *Kingdom Learning*, namely that TR is to be understood as an aspect of prayer in which we consciously seek the participation of the Holy Spirit. It is, moreover, an activity to which we need to bring our whole selves.

Like the students for whom prayer played a central role, all Christians regularly engage in theological reflection in an informal way. And since reflection is an example of experiential learning, their reflections will have involved the four phases of the learning cycle:

- the experiences that raise questions
- the 'internal voice' of their previous experiences, their knowledge of scripture and Christian tradition, the knowledge and expertise they draw from other areas of their lives, which together provide the matrix within which the puzzling experience is considered from a variety of angles

- a conclusion as to how this experience is to be interpreted
- the consequence in terms of changed thinking, affections and actions.

The value of formal models of TR as an element in ministerial formation is that they help to discipline and develop the reflective ability. It is thus in a real and direct way, 'learning how to learn', using a formal process to educate the natural subconscious processes of reflection that we all use to manage our lives. Or to put it another way, learning TR is like sports coaching: taking apart the tennis shot or golf swing and focussing on the parts so that in the context of the game the shot may be more effective.[99]

Rather than introduced as an academic exercise in an otherwise academically based course, theological reflection needs to be integrated with standards of good practice in adult education to shape the way in which theology is taught and learned at every stage of ministerial formation. The study of scripture, the tradition of Christian doctrine, the exploration of ethics and church history, and practical skills such as attentive listening, leading worship, preaching, giving an evangelistic address, are all best learned through reflection in the context of practice and integrated with the learner's existing experience. Theological reflection is good pedagogy and good pedagogy is reflective.

Learning for ministry

To return to the questions with which this chapter began: What exactly is meant by the idea that ministerial training is 'too academic'? What are the shortcomings of the academic model? What are the characteristics of the alternative approach, and how do they reflect the new paradigm of ministerial formation?

The reason that ministerial training is widely seen as 'too academic' is that until the relatively recent past there has been no attempt to distinguish between the distinct though related practices of ministry and theological scholarship. As a result, courses of training for ministry have been dominated by the traditional divisions of the theology of the academy, often taught in a manner more suitable to theology undergraduates than ministerial trainees. By introducing this distinction, the shortcomings of this model become readily apparent:

- The tendency to divide the tradition into self-contained compartments, whereas what is required for ministry is the ability to integrate these and apply them to experience.
- The danger of the training becoming side-tracked by the surrender of some academic theologians to the immanent frame created by the Enlightenment's insistence on the sovereignty of human reason and the epistemological mistakes also deriving from Enlightenment thinking.
- The theory-to-practice model of much academic teaching and with it a 'core belief in the value of codified knowledge, and a strict adherence to the clear division of roles and responsibilities between teacher as knower and student as recipient of teacher knowledge of theology, scripture and tradition'.[100] The outcome of such an approach is that too often the attempt to encourage students in a risky engagement with a deep level of learning – of using their theology to interpret live situations and critique their own practice – and thus to experience theology as inhabited wisdom, is undermined by the easy accessibility and relatively less demanding approach to theology as intellectual pursuit.
- The academy typically fails to connect theology with life experience. The ordinary theology learners bring with them is ignored and may be 'razed to the ground' and the learning made to begin (and often end) with theoretical generalizations drawn from the academic tradition.
- Finally, the academy has so far been unable to extend its assessment procedures to cover the complex range of skills required for the practice of ministry.

In contrast, the characteristics of the alternative approach I have been exploring in this chapter are these:

- It recognizes the task as the formation of the whole person, their intellect, affections and practices. It sees ministry not primarily as a professional task but as an aspect of discipleship so that formation for ministry is continuous with formation for discipleship.
- It recognizes that all God's people have a unique call to cooperate with the Holy Spirit in the renewal of creation and the coming of God's kingdom. This call develops over time so that officially recognized roles such as ordination and licensed lay ministry grow out of a prior call to serve God in other capacities. Accordingly, this approach embraces a 'just-in-time' model, which concentrates on training people for the ministry to which God is calling them now.
- Ministry is understood as a practice, or in some cases a family of prac-

tices: complex shared activities each with a history and goal, whose standards of excellence are internal and continually developing.

- As a result, formation for ministry is geared to practice. The context in which the ministry is to be exercised and the people who share it become an important element in the learning process. A premium is placed on 'inventive ways of involving students in meaningful practices, of providing access to resources that enhance that participation … and of involving them in actions, discussion, and reflections that make a difference to the communities they value'.[101]

- Local churches are encouraged and enabled to become learning communities in which all are formed for discipleship and ministry. Wherever possible, learning is collaborative. Some training for ministry will take place in the context of the local church. Those training for ordination or licensed ministry will become part of a training community but should never lose touch with the life of the local church.

- The goal of formation is understood to be that form of 'pastoral imagination' relevant to the ministry being exercised. Pastoral imagination is seen as practical and situational know-how, the equivalent of the stages of 'proficiency' and 'expertise' in the Dreyfus brothers' description of the way a practice is learned. At the heart of pastoral imagination is the ability to discern God's presence and activity in the ministry situation.

- Pastoral imagination is learned through theologically informed reflective practice. Methods of teaching and learning should be informed by the cycle of experiential learning and recognized good practice in adult education. Formal models of theological reflection play a role in helping the learner to develop the habit of reflection in the context of their everyday lives and ministry and thus discern the shape of a faithful response to God in any given situation.

- Theological reflective practice is rooted in prayer and guided and empowered by the Holy Spirit.

Despite its explicit adoption of the 'Athens' model, the embrace of *paideia* by the Preface to the Common Awards, and the requirement of reflective practice as an element in ministerial training, the Church of England, in common with many other Churches, has been slow to recognize the life-long nature of formation or to move away from the 'theory-to-practice' approach to learning embodied in the practice of theological scholarship. Instead, it has frequently confused formation for ministry with formation for theological scholarship. The next chapter, therefore, looks at the standards of good practice embodied by the experiential learning approach and asks what changes in the Church's current practice are required to meet these.

Notes

1 ACCM 22, §42.

2 www.independent.co.uk/news/education/education-news/ey-firm-says-it-will-not-longer-consider-degrees-or-a-level-results-when-assessing-employees-10 436355.html. The current position is outlined at www.ey.com/en_uk/careers/how-to-join-us, where Michael Bertolino, EY Global People Advisory Services Leader, is quoted as saying: 'Lateral thinking, judgement, empathy, adaptability and creativity are becoming critical in job roles – these are the skills that will bridge human and digital value creation in the future workplace.'

3 See, for example, David Pendleton and Adrian Furnham, *Leadership: All You Need to Know*, Basingstoke: Macmillan, 2012, pp. 118–35.

4 The Robbins Report of 1961 quoted in Stephen Heap, *What Are Universities Good for?* Cambridge: Grove, 2012, p. 12.

5 Lord Browne of Madingley, *Securing a Sustainable Future for Higher Education: An Independent Review of Higher Education Funding and Student Finance*, 2010, p. 14. I explore this trend in slightly greater detail in *Kingdom Learning*, pp. 45–8.

6 Kathleen M. Quinlan, 'Developing the whole student: leading higher education initiatives that integrate heart and mind', Oxford Learning Institute, University of Oxford, 2011, pp. 2–4.

7 David Ford, 'An interdisciplinary wisdom: knowledge, formation and collegiality in the negotiable university' in *Christian Wisdom: Desiring God and Learning in Love*, Cambridge: Cambridge University Press, 2007, p. 305.

8 *Christian Wisdom*, pp. 322–3.

9 Michael Polanyi, 'The logic of tacit inference', *Philosophy* 41, 1966, p. 7, reprinted in *Knowing and Being*, Routledge and Kegan Paul, 1969, p. 144.

10 Donald Schön, *The Reflective Practitioner*, Farnham: Ashgate, 1991, p. vii (emphasis original). For a fuller account of the argument of this paragraph see David Heywood, *Divine Revelation and Human Learning*, Farnham: Ashgate, 2004, pp. 15–32.

11 'Preface to the Common Awards', pp. 1–2, www.dur.ac.uk/common.awards/programmes/.

12 Ford, *Christian Wisdom*, pp. 336–45.

13 Alasdair MacIntyre, *After Virtue*, 2nd edition, London: Duckworth, 1985, pp. 187f.

14 Hubert and Stuart Dreyfus, 'From Socrates to expert systems: the limits of calculative rationality' in *Skillful Coping*, ed. Mark A. Wrathall, Oxford: Oxford University Press, 2014, pp. 25–46, p. 34 (emphasis original).

15 John Adair, *Effective Teambuilding*, London: Pan Books, 1987, pp. 70–6.

16 For team roles, see www.belbin.com/about/belbin-team-roles/ accessed 10 December 2020.

17 Jenny Rogers, *Facilitating Groups*, Maidenhead: Open University Press, 2010, pp. 27–54.

18 See David Heywood, *Transforming Preaching*, London: SPCK, 2013, pp. 61–133.

19 Etienne Wenger, *Communities of Practice*, Cambridge: Cambridge University Press, 1998, pp. 9–10.

20 Wenger, *Communities*, p. 4.

21 Heywood, *Revelation*, pp. 137–44.

22 Miroslav Volf, *Exclusion and Embrace*, Nashville, TN: Abingdon Press, 1996, p. 256.

23 Edward Farley, *Theologia*, Philadelphia, PA: Fortress Press, 1983.

24 David Kelsey, *To Understand God Truly: What's Theological about a Theological School*, Louisville, KY: Westminster/John Knox Press, 1992; and *Between Athens and Berlin: The Theological Education Debate*, Eugene, OR: Wipf and Stock, 1993.

25 Kelsey, *To Understand God Truly*, pp. 63–77.

26 His approach is summed up in his *Brief Outline on the Study of Theology*, translated by Terence N. Tice, Atlanta, GA: John Knox Press, 1966. A summary of his thought is given in Farley, *Theologia*, pp. 84–94.

27 Farley, *Theologia*, p. 86 (emphasis original).

28 Friedrich Schleiermacher, *Brief Outline*, §32 and 33.

29 Kelsey, *To Understand God Truly*, p. 97.

30 See, for example, Gary Wilton, 'From ACCM 22 to Hind via Athens and Berlin: A Critical Analysis of Key Documents Shaping Contemporary Church of England Theological Education with Reference to the Work of David Kelsey', *Journal of Adult Theological Education* 4.1 (2007), pp. 31–47; Kyle J. A. Small, 'Missional theology for schools of theology: re-engaging the question "What is theological about a theological school?"' in Craig van Gelder (ed.), *The Missional Church and Leadership Formation*, Grand Rapids, MI: Eerdmans, 2009; David Hilborn, 'Beyond Athens and Berlin: Past, Present and Future Models of Theological Education', paper given at a colloquium at St John's College, Nottingham, 18 April 2012; John Williams, 'Conflicting paradigms in theological education for public ministry in the Church of England: issues for church and academy', *International Journal of Public Theology* 7 (2013), pp. 275–96. Taking up a remark of Kelsey's, Robert Banks proposed a 'Jerusalem' model, in which mission would play a central part, in *Reenvisioning Theological Education: Exploring a Missional Alternative to Current Models*, Grand Rapids, MI: Eerdmans, 1999. Brian Edgar proposed the addition of 'Geneva' as a confessional model of training in 'The theology of theological education', *Evangelical Review of Theology* 29.3 (2005), pp. 208–17. Darren Cronshaw takes an eclectic approach to all four models, adding a contextual element in 'Reenvisioning theological education and missional spirituality', *Journal of Adult Theological Education* 9.1 (2012), pp. 9–27. In the United States itself, the debate has advanced beyond the comparison of different models: Charles Foster et al., the authors of *Educating Clergy*, San Francisco, CA:

Jossey-Bass, 2006, acknowledge the influence of Kelsey's models but set out to study and reflect on examples of pedagogical practice in theological training.

31 Kelsey, *To Understand God Truly*, p. 2.

32 Farley, *Theologia*, pp. 156–9; Charles Wood, *Vision and Discernment: An Orientation in Theological Study*, Eugene, OR: Wipf and Stock, 1985, pp. 57–77.

33 Kelsey, *To Understand God Truly*, p. 63.

34 See *Reimagining Ministry*, pp. 91–108 for a treatment of the 'powers' drawing on the work of George Caird, John Howard Yoder and Walter Wink, among others. In brief, they are to be seen as idolatrous corporate mindsets with the power to blind people to the truth.

35 Ann Morisy, *Journeying Out*, London: Continuum, 2004, pp. 26–41, and *Bothered and Bewildered*, London: Continuum, 2009, pp. 22–48. See also Paul Ballard and Lesley Husselbee, *Community and Ministry*, London: SPCK, 2007, pp. 21–5.

36 Charles Taylor, *A Secular Age*, Cambridge, MA: Belknap Press, 2007, especially pp. 539–93.

37 Gavin d'Costa, 'On Theology's Babylonian Captivity within the Secular University' in Jeff Astley et al. (eds), *The Idea of a Christian University*, Milton Keynes: Paternoster Press, 2004, p. 184.

38 Leopold von Ranke, *Geschichte der romanischen und germanishen Völker*, Berlin: Reimer, 1824, p. vii, translated and quoted by Volf, *Exclusion and Embrace*, p. 240.

39 A summary and typology of the various 'searches' is given in Tom Wright, *Jesus and the Victory of God*, London: SPCK, 1996, pp. 3–124.

40 Richard Bauckham, *Jesus and the Eyewitnesses*, Grand Rapids, MI: Eerdmans, 2006; Tom Wright, *Victory of God*.

41 Mark McIntosh, *Divine Teaching*, Oxford: Blackwell, 2008, p. 7.

42 Stephen Lyon, 'A Working Party is Formed' in Malcolm Torry and Jeffrey Heskins (eds), *Ordained Local Ministry: A New Shape for Ministry in the Church of England*, Norwich: Canterbury Press, 2006, p. 44.

43 Nigel Godfrey, 'Training Ordained Local Ministers' in Torry and Heskins, *Ordained Local Ministry*, p. 139.

44 Lyon, 'Working Party', p. 51.

45 Godfrey, 'Training', p. 138.

46 Kelsey, *To Understand God Truly*, p. 5.

47 Robert Banks, *Reenivisioning Theological Education*, Grand Rapids, MI: Eerdmans, 1999.

48 Banks, *Reenvisioning*, p. 74.

49 Sylvia Wilkie Collinson, *Making Disciples: The Significance of Jesus' Educational Methods for Today's Church*, Eugene, OR: Wipf and Stock, 2006 (originally Milton Keynes: Paternoster Press, 2004), pp. 103–4. For a further discussion of Collinson's work, see *Kingdom Learning*, pp. 26–30.

50 Banks, *Reenvisioning*, pp. 139–41 and 169–71; see Thomas Groome, *Christian Religious Education: Sharing our Story and Vision*, San Francisco, CA: Jossey-Bass, 1980 (Banks cites Groome, 'Theology on our Feet: a Revisionist Pedagogy for Healing the Gap between Academia and Ecclesia' in Lewis S. Mudge and James N. Poling, *Formation and Reflection: The Promise of Practical The-*

ology, Philadelphia, PA: Fortress Press, 1987, pp. 55–78); Don S. Browning, *A Fundamental Practical Theology*, Minneapolis, MN: Fortress Press, 1992 (Banks cites 'Practical theology and religious education' in *Formation and Reflection*, pp. 79–102).

51 Banks, *Reenivisioning*, pp. 208–14.

52 Banks, *Reenivisioning*, pp. 131–41.

53 Banks, *Reenivisioning*, pp. 218–22.

54 Banks, *Reenivisioning*, pp. 226–7.

55 Banks, *Reenivisioning*, pp. 159–60.

56 Banks, *Reenivisioning*, pp. 169–76, 185–6.

57 Banks, *Reenivisioning*, pp. 229–33.

58 Banks, *Reenivisioning*, pp. 214–18.

59 Darren Cronshaw, 'Reenvisioning theological education, mission and local church', *Mission Studies* 28.1 (2011), pp. 91–115.

60 Cronshaw, 'Reenvisioning', p. 10.

61 Cronshaw, 'Reenvisioning', p. 12.

62 Les Ball, *Transforming Theology*, Eugene, OR: Wipf and Stock, 2012, p. 6.

63 Ball, *Theology*, p. 122.

64 Ball, *Theology*, pp. 21, 127–37.

65 Ball, *Theology*, p. 92.

66 Ball, *Theology*, pp. 66–86.

67 Heywood, *Kingdom Learning*, p. 39.

68 Ball, *Theology*, pp. 21–2, 33–49.

69 Ball, *Theology*, pp. 29–32.

70 Ball, *Theology*, pp. 2–3, 124–7.

71 Ball, *Theology*, pp. 87–103.

72 Perry Shaw, *Transforming Theological Education: A Practical Handbook for Integrative Learning*, Carlisle: Langham Global Library, 2014, p. vii.

73 Shaw, *Transforming*, p. 17.

74 Shaw, *Transforming*, pp. 17–33.

75 Shaw, *Transforming*, p. 4.

76 Charles R. Foster et al., *Educating Clergy*, San Francisco, CA: Jossey-Bass, 2006.

77 Dykstra presents both 'pastoral imagination' and 'ecclesial imagination' in many places. See especially 'Pastoral and ecclesial imagination' in Dorothy C. Bass and Craig Dykstra (eds), *For Life Abundant; Practical Theology, Theological Education and Christian Ministry*, Grand Rapids, MI: Eerdmans, 2008, pp. 41–61. See also Foster et al., *Educating Clergy*, pp. 22–3, from where the quotations in this paragraph and the next are taken.

78 Lesslie Newbigin, *The Gospel in a Pluralist Society*, London: SPCK, 1989, p. 227.

79 Dykstra, 'Pastoral and Ecclesial Imagination', pp. 56–7.

80 ACCM 22, §29.

81 The other is found in Vincent Donovan's book, *Christianity Rediscovered*, London: SCM Press, 1978. Exploring the role of the priest with those Masai kinship groups that had accepted baptism, Donovan arrives at a role the Masai referred to as *ilaretok*, literally a 'helper' but with connotations of 'servant to the community'.

The Masai saw the priest as 'the one who can bring a community into existence, call it together, hold it together, enable the community to function as a community, and enable each member to carry out his or her Christian task in the community. Without this *helper* the Christian community can neither exist nor function. With him it becomes a eucharistic community with a mission' (p. 158).

82 Foster et al., *Educating Clergy*, pp. 33–4.

83 In particular Dorothy Bass, Kathleen Cahalan, Bonnie Miller McLemore, James Nieman and Christian Scharen, who are all contributors to *For Life Abundant* and co-authors of *Christian Practical Wisdom: What it Is and Why it Matters*, Grand Rapids, MI: Eerdmans, 2016.

84 Bonnie Miller-McLemore, 'Academic theology and practical knowledge' in *Christian Practical Wisdom*, pp. 175–231; quote from p. 188.

85 Bonnie Miller-McLemore, *Christian Theology in Practice: Discovering a Discipline*, Grand Rapids, MI: Eerdmans, pp. 171–2.

86 *Christian Practical Wisdom*, p. 5.

87 Joseph Dunne, '"Professional wisdom" in practice' in Liz Bondi et al., *Towards Professional Wisdom*, Farnham: Ashgate, 2011, p. 17.

88 Christian A. B. Scharen and Eileen R. Campbell-Reed, 'Learning Pastoral Imagination: A Five-Year Report on How New Ministers Learn in Practice', Auburn Studies No. 21, 2016, p. 7.

89 Rowan Williams, CEFACS Lecture, Birmingham – Centre for Anglican Communion Studies, 3 November 2004, available at http://rowanwilliams.archbishop ofcanterbury.org/articles.php/1847/cefacs-lecture-birmingham-centre-for-anglican-communion-studies.html accessed 20 February 2021.

90 David Kolb, *Experiential Learning*, Englewood Cliffs, NJ: Prentice-Hall, 1984.

91 Donald Schön, *The Reflective Practitioner*, New York: Basic Books, 1983.

92 In her book *Reordering Theological Reflection*, London: SCM Press, 2020, Helen Collins questions the propriety of starting theological reflection from experience and proposes a new model beginning with scripture. She is rightly critical of writers whose account of TR ignores or downplays the place of the Bible in TR. But it is not true to claim that 'religious experiences of encounter with God' are the 'only experiences of truly theological significance' (p. 119). The discipline of practical theology is founded on the premise that God is at work in the whole of life and TR, whose role is central to practical theology, takes as its purpose the discovery of God's presence and action in the warp and weft of everyday life. While I agree with Collins that scripture is central to TR and authoritative for Christian tradition, I believe she overlooks the importance of what Quentin Chandler calls the 'interpretative threshold': the need for students, when practising TR, to recognize that their understanding of the Bible, like their account of everyday experience, is an interpretation. One of the most important and valuable functions of TR is to subject the ways in which we interpret both the Bible and experience to critical questioning as an integral part of the learning process. Moreover, as I argue in *Kingdom Learning*, the Bible itself is TR. Each passage and book originated as an attempt to discern the character of a faithful response to God in the situation in which it arose. Since our operative knowledge takes the form of practical and situation-related know-how, the quest of the biblical writers to discern the presence and action of God in their

own situations speaks directly and relevantly to Christians who desire to follow him faithfully in their own context – but not without the necessary disciplines of interpretation. Forms of TR that begin with the Bible rather than experience are to be welcomed as ways of applying scripture to everyday life. The ancient practice of *lectio divina* and the Seven Step process, originating with the Lumko Institute in South Africa (The Seven Steps of Bible Study – LUMKO Method – Professor Lakshman Madurasinghe, https://madure.net/2008/03/16/the-seven-steps-of-bible-study-lumko-method-2/ accessed 9 March 2021) are examples of such methods. But it is not correct to claim that TR that begins with experience downgrades the importance of scripture or that it is a feature of a more liberal approach to theology.

93 On the significance of 'everyday' or 'ordinary' theology, see Kathryn Tanner, *Theories of Culture*, Minneapolis, MN: Fortress Press, 1997, pp. 61–92; and Jeff Astley, *Ordinary Theology*, Farnham: Ashgate, 2002.

94 Jeff Astley, 'Ordinary theology and the learning conversation with academic theology' in Jeff Astley and Leslie Francis (eds), *Exploring Ordinary Theology*, Farnham: Ashgate, 2013, pp. 47–8, 52.

95 Heywood, *Kingdom Learning*, pp. 128, 148–9, 153–7.

96 'Setting God's People Free', pp. 13–14.

97 Elizabeth Jordan, 'Conversation as a tool of research in practical theology', *Practical Theology* 12.5 (2019), pp. 526–36.

98 Quentin Chandler, 'Cognition or spiritual disposition? Threshold concepts in theological reflection', *Journal of Adult Theological Education* 13.2 (2016), pp. 90–102.

99 See further my article, 'Learning how to learn: theological reflection at Cuddesdon', *Journal of Adult Theological Education* 6.2 (2009), pp. 164–75. At the time of the article, the narrative that saw TR as failing to connect with most students was still powerful. One of the reasons for this, I suspect, is that the way in which people learn, expressed in the learning cycle, was badly understood by some at least of those teaching TR. One of the aims of the article was to demonstrate that it could be taught effectively. Since then, research findings such as those I examine in the text suggest that TR is becoming increasingly understood and accepted.

100 Leona English, 'The theory-practice of learning portfolios', *Journal of Adult Theological Education* 7.2 (2010), pp. 205–13; quotation from p. 207.

101 Wenger, *Communities of Practice*, pp. 9–10.

3

Adopting the New Paradigm

I am suggesting that the Church move to a new paradigm of ministerial formation: a life-long learning approach based on experiential learning for a diverse and collaborative ministry in which ordained and lay people serve God together, the ministry of the ordained animating and animated by the ministry of the whole church. This paradigm shift brings with it several fundamental shifts in the way ministerial formation is conceived:

- It commits the Church to ministerial formation for *all* its members rather than those few selected for licensed or ordained ministry.
- It commits it to formation for the practice of *ministry* rather than the practice of theological scholarship.
- The outcome of formation for the practice of ministry is to be understood as 'pastoral imagination', the ability and disposition to 'read and interpret the world in the context and framework of Christian belief and Christian worship',[1] rather than the pursuit of knowledge about the Bible and Christian theology for its own sake.
- Pastoral imagination is to be understood as 'situational wisdom' rather than theoretical understanding. It may further be understood as the fourth of the stages outlined by the Dreyfus brothers in the learning of a practice, which they call 'proficiency'.[2] This is the ability to recognize and understand the key features of a situation; to discern the presence and action of God in that situation; to draw on a repertoire of responses; and the 'practical wisdom' to choose the responses most likely to be fruitful.
- As the capacity for 'seeing a situation in all its holy and relational depths and responding with wise and fitting judgement and action',[3] pastoral wisdom is rooted in the 'wisdom and godly habit of life', which has been the Church of England's recognized goal of ministerial formation for over three decades.[4] It is as much the expression of character and disposition as it is knowledge and ministerial skill.

- Pastoral imagination is cultivated through theological reflective practice, a specific kind of experiential learning, in which theological reflection lies at the heart of the formational process, not simply as a technique to be applied but as the warp and weft of the learning experience.
- It is best learned in context, from the long haul of ministerial experience punctuated with critical incidents, with the help of mentors, most of whom should be experienced practitioners with skills in adult education.

The purposes of this chapter are to set out the standards of excellence required for this new paradigm and suggest the changes that need to take place to meet them. These are proposed with the Church of England specifically in mind and its current practice as the starting point. I invite members of other Churches to judge how far they might be applicable to their own context.

The adoption of a new paradigm is a radically different process from making adjustments to an existing paradigm. A new paradigm is a whole new way of thinking and acting, based on a transformed vision of the purpose of and requirements for ministry. Some of the changes I suggest in this section may take several years to accomplish. If these proposals are adopted, it will be important to ensure as far as possible that the adoption of the practices associated with the new paradigm is not undermined by the continuation of habitual practices and ways of thinking associated with the old.

What, then, are the standards of excellence the Church needs to adopt and the actions it needs to take to adopt this new paradigm of ministerial formation?

1 Reimagine ministerial formation as a life-long process

The first step is to map the transitions in ministry beginning from confirmation or adult baptism understood as 'lay ordination', a commitment to play one's part in the mission of God through discipleship and ministry. The table on p. 90 was created in partnership with colleagues from Oxford Diocese and here we attempt to map these transitions for the contemporary Church of England, although with our diocese particularly in mind. The table emphasizes the importance of a learning church in which formation for ministry is the province of the whole church rather than the small proportion of its members selected for ordination. The first three rows of the table assume investment to equip the '98% who are not ordained for fruitful ministry and service'.[5] It should also be assumed that this includes young people from the point of confirmation onwards, whose everyday faith may be lived out in school and college and who have a vital role to play alongside the adults in the shared ministry of their local churches.[6]

Initiation / confirmation preparation for discipleship, ministry and mission (i.e. teaching all God's people of their call to be 'missionary disciples')		
Discernment of gifts (e.g. Personal Discipleship Plans, SHAPE courses)[7]	'Whole-life discipleship' or 'everyday faith', ministry in places of work and daily life	
Intentional study for discipleship and/or participation in mission and ministry through the local church (e.g. through locally based training, Bishop's Certificate courses, Wycliffe Hall or St John's Nottingham extension study).		
Authorized ministries (e.g. authorized preachers, funeral ministers etc.)	Licensed ministries (e.g. Licensed lay ministry (LLM), Church Army)	(Lay) ministry in secular employment
Ordained ministry (curacy and associate ministry)	Specialist ministries (chaplaincy, pioneer ministry, church planting, youth and family workers, worship leading, administrators, trainers etc.)	
Incumbency (responsibility for mission and ministry in a local church or group of churches)		
Training incumbent or other involvement in training others for ministry	Safeguarding trainers, spiritual directors, leadership in LLM community	
Oversight ministry (team rector, ministry area leader, area dean etc.)	Trainer, supervisor, mentor, oversight ministry	

In the fifth row of the table, the distinction between lay and ordained ministry is introduced. This distinction is not watertight. We would expect many specialist ministries to be exercised by lay and ordained alike. We would expect lay people to play a part in the ministry of over-sight, especially where this is exercised through a team. There is also a significant degree of overlap between the rows of the table. The call to a specialist ministry may or may not require diocesan authorization or licensing, and the authorized ministries, such as authorized preachers or authorized funeral ministry, are examples of specialized ministries.

For many people, the call to ordained ministry is a life-long journey along the lines of that suggested in the table. They discern a call to ordin-ation as one step on the journey of ministry and discernment. For others, especially young ordinands, the vocation to ordained ministry has more of the nature of a career choice. Even so, it is usual to expect such young ordinands to undertake some course of study or specific preparation, such as an extended parish placement, before beginning their training. The assumption behind the table is that confirmation is recognized as a call to ministry for every confirmand of whatever age, and that it entails commitment to formation for discipleship and the discernment of gifts for service. The implication is that young ordinands will bring to their ministerial training experience of their local church as a learning com-munity, whose members embrace the call to missionary discipleship.[8]

It is also important to make clear that *all* the training for ministry envisaged here is 'just-in-time' training, including training for ordained ministry. What the Church of England refers to as 'IME 1' (Initial Minis-terial Education Phase 1) currently takes place in a concentrated period of two to three years immediately prior to ordination. The idea of life-long learning in a Church committed to collaborative patterns of ministry in which lay ministry is accorded equal status implies that a large part of the formation required for ordination will already have taken place in the context of locally based training and participation in a variety of lay ministries. In this scenario, ordination ceases to be dependent on the completion of a defined period of 'initial' training. In many cases the transition from lay to ordained ministry will be relatively seamless and involve a minimal amount of specific training. The table of formation qualities required at the point of ordination in Appendix 4 will enable the planning of individualized pathways in preparation for this transition.

I have placed this suggestion for the introduction of the new paradigm first in the list of specific changes because it seems necessary to specify how the life-long nature of the formational journey is to be envisaged, fully realizing that the transformation required in the life of many local churches will only take place as a consequence of the other changes I am about to recommend. In my observation, however, the Holy Spirit is already at work in many local churches, encouraging and enabling the transition from religious institution to community of disciples. Extending the Church's vision of ministerial formation from courses of training for ordination or lay ministry to the whole of the Church's ministry recognizes and cooperates with this aspect of the Spirit's work.

2 Enable 'whole-life discipleship' or 'everyday faith'

Every service of confirmation or adult baptism in the Church of England includes a commission, in which the promises made by the confirmand include to 'continue in the apostles' teaching and fellowship, in the breaking of bread, and in the prayers', to 'seek and serve Christ in all people' and to 'acknowledge Christ's authority over human society'. These promises commit all God's people, adults and young people alike, to pursue 'whole-life discipleship', to live out their faith 'in work and school, in gym and shop, in field and factory Monday to Saturday', as 'Setting God's People Free' puts it.

For 'Setting God's People Free', everyday faith is the key to evangelistic effectiveness, a confident church proclaiming the gospel in life and word. In addition, I have argued that it is the essential foundation for genuinely collaborative ministry, since it cultivates a deeper relationship with God, the fruit of the Spirit in a person's life, confidence in God's gifts, discernment of God's presence and submission to God's call. More fundamental than either of these, however, 'everyday faith' is the birthright of every Christian. God's desire is that each person individually grows to maturity in Christ (Colossians 1.28) and that each local church should 'come to maturity, to the measure of the full stature of Christ' (Ephesians 4.13).

One of the Diocese of Oxford's responses to 'Setting God's People Free' takes the form of a 'Personal Discipleship Plan' or PDP.[9] A PDP centres on a meeting with a trained encourager every few months, in which the disciple is offered a framework for thinking about their life and faith based on the acronym CALLED. The initials stand for:

- Core gifts: What are my gifts? Am I sharing my gifts in my everyday life and work?
- Attracted by: Where may God be calling me, in mission, service, prayer, community, care for the world, ministry, social action, evangelism?

- Listening: Where am I being guided to gain experience or insights? Where is the Bible inspiring and leading me?
- Life plan: What is happening in my life now? What would I be doing if I could invent my ideal future?
- Experience: What energizes me from my current and past experience? Where am I challenged and what am I challenged by? How can I use this in God's service?
- Discipleship: How am I deepening my daily spiritual life and faith? How can I become more Christ-like?

After careful listening on the part of the encourager and prayer together, the disciple is asked to identify at least two 'next steps'. One step addresses the inward journey and pays attention to the person's developing relationship with God, the other the outward journey through which faith is expressed in the world.

The idea that whole-life discipleship (or, as the Church of England has come to call it, 'everyday faith') may be an idea whose time has come is encouraged by the rate at which people are responding to the invitation to adopt a PDP and by the high levels of satisfaction being expressed. One person who has been working on her discipleship plan for about a year says it has been 'inspirational, enlightening and confidence building', has 'provided a bigger picture of the Christian life' and helped her to focus. Others describe the experience as 'incredibly helpful and life-affirming', 'liberating: it gets to the heart of who we are', 'the PDP has helped me recognise where God is calling me whilst giving me the practical resources and guidance to explore this'. A priest who has become an encourager says it is one of the most transformational things he has ever been involved in. Moreover, without undue pressure, PDPs are proving a way in which people are enabled to discover and respond to a sense of calling emerging naturally from the circumstances of their daily lives. The outward steps identified overwhelmingly concern God's call in the wider world rather than service to the church. Examples include becoming a foster carer, setting up a community breakfast club, writing a blog, setting up a local gardening project, a housing project for physically disabled young adults, to discussion around what it means to be a Christian in the Civil Service.

The move represented by PDPs from a Christian faith centred on church-going to one whose centre is in everyday faith reflects the 'seismic shift in culture' called for by 'Setting God's People Free'. Neil Hudson describes this culture shift as a move from a pastoral *care* contract to a pastoral *equipping* contract.[10] By 'contract' he means the unspoken assumptions that sustain church membership. Under the 'pastoral care contract', the vision for the local church's mission and ministry is the responsibility of the leadership; the members agree to support this vision on the condition that they are cared for. Church members are allowed and encouraged to be passive recipients and to value their church for the benefits they receive. By contrast, if the shared 'contract' is one of pastoral equipping, members will engage with their local church to be equipped to serve God in their everyday lives. When difficult circumstances arise, rather than receiving 'care' it may be appropriate for them to be challenged about how they discern God at work in their lives. Rather than keep their working and worshipping lives in separate compartments, church members will share the joys and struggles of the week and enable one another to discern God's purpose in their everyday situations. The local church becomes a learning community through which its members are equipped to serve God in the world.

At the time of writing, the Church of England's response to 'Setting God's People Free' is co-ordinated by Nick Shepherd, whose wife Bridget leads the Church of the Good Shepherd and St Peter in Lee, south-east London. Like many others, the church responded to the coronavirus lockdown by taking their weekly meeting for worship online. Unlike many other churches, however, 'GoodPeterLee' did not seek to replicate the pattern of their normal Sunday worship. A Zoom gathering for coffee was followed by a short time of worship together and then by 'This Time Tomorrow', in which several church members shared what God was doing in their daily lives. The gathering closed with another short time of worship and more coffee and chat. In this short period, church members' knowledge and understanding of one another's lives had accelerated. Assessing the impact of the first few weeks, Nick reflected that the 'pastoral care contract' had been reset. The experience had shifted people's expectations of coming to church 'to be fed' and begun to equip them to live out their discipleship in the world. Unsurprisingly, the sharing of stories had been the most powerful element in the transition.

3 Resource locally based training

One of the weaknesses of the Church of England highlighted by 'Setting God's People Free' is the inadequacy of the resources available for locally based training. A survey of people 'at the frontline' highlighted the following needs:

- support for discovering lay vocation and gifting
- opportunities and encouragement to step into these areas
- fit for purpose, easy to access, contextual training
- connections to others to learn and share with
- a framework for local accountability and learning
- appropriate affirmation.[11]

While Personal Discipleship Plans respond to the desire for support in discovering vocation and encouragement to step into new areas of service, locally based training is the context in which the remaining needs may be addressed. The Diocese of Oxford makes all its training for ordination and licensed lay ministry available to 'interested learners' and candidates are encouraged to bring members of their churches with them to the training sessions. However, for many, signing up for training provided by the diocese is too big a leap. Distance of travel is not the only hurdle to be surmounted. For those taking a first step into intentional training for ministry, accessibility means familiarity: a familiar place shared with familiar people where the learning is led by a familiar face. Enabling people to overcome the 'confidence' hurdle and local churches to become learning communities where such a concept is completely unfamiliar requires the encouragement and resourcing of learning hubs, where locally based training can be shared between appropriate groups of churches.

The goals of locally based training will be to equip God's people for ministry in any of three contexts, depending on individual gifts and calling:

- It will equip them to serve God in the place of everyday life and work.
- To play a part in the local church's mission with and for its wider community.
- To play a part in the life of the gathered church.

The training provided by local learning hubs will, of course, be 'just-in-time' training, provided at the time it is relevant to the area of ministry into which a person is being called. Already this is the case with many of the specialist ministries listed in the table above. Churches may form pastoral visiting teams requiring a relatively short course of specialist training. Training courses for the leaders of fresh expressions of church such as Mission-shaped Ministry produced by Fresh Expressions and 'Xplore' produced by the Church Army are of this kind.[12]

At present, however, my conversations with local church leaders suggest that the 'felt needs' for such training overwhelmingly reflect the needs of the gathered church: pastoral care teams, leaders of worship for rural multi-parish benefices, work with children and young people. As increasing numbers of people respond to the call to 'missionary discipleship' through living out everyday faith, it is to be hoped that the 'felt needs' for training will begin to shift to those associated with discipleship and mission. As practically all the area deans and lay chairs I encountered during a diocesan consultation in 2019 agreed, such a move would represent a profound cultural shift.

Working with colleagues in the diocese, I recently attempted to specify a formational framework for the earliest stages of ministry and some specialist ministries. A far from exhaustive list might include:

- everyday faith
- people exercising leadership in their places of work
- ministries of pastoral care, including bereavement visiting
- work with children, young people and families
- liaison with schools, care homes and other institutions offering pastoral care
- community organizing in partnership with other agencies
- informal chaplaincy roles in a variety of contexts, such as schools, shops, sports venues and agriculture
- focal ministry
- members of church planting teams and leaders of fresh expressions of church
- parish administrators
- churchwardens and PCC secretaries.

In contrast to traditional models of lay training, which foreground the needs of the gathered church, such a framework would be built around the shape of lay ministry in places of work and the wider community. It might include the following areas:

- self-understanding, which could include personality, strengths and weaknesses and should certainly include vocation
- empathetic listening skills, expressing the attitude of a listener: the ability to be vulnerably open to others
- team-working skills and the dispositions required for effective team-work

- theological reflection
- understanding of the five marks of mission,[13] the *missio Dei* and the kingdom of God
- ability to 'read' a context, such as a local community
- understanding of collaborative patterns of ministry and their theological rationale
- Christian lifestyle
- grasp of the broad sweep of the Bible's narrative
- a discipline of regular prayer
- adequate safeguarding training for the scope of the ministry to be exercised
- training in any specific skills required for the role (e.g. authorized preacher, work in schools, street pastor, work with older people).

Notice that there is considerable emphasis on the competencies of emotional intelligence, expressed in self-understanding, empathetic listening and team-working skills, but also that these are related to the qualities of character needed in these areas. Theological reflection is included because it is basic to a person's ability to develop 'pastoral' or 'missional' imagination: to inhabit and grow in the practice of ministry, not only to learn the knowledge and skills required but to relate these to an understanding of Christian mission and ministry. The learning involved is conceived as experiential learning, building upon rather than ignoring the 'ordinary theology' the trainees bring with them. The transition into formal theological learning begins with the theology of mission, ministry and the kingdom of God and should build on the learners' implicit understanding of God's ways in the world. More extensive theological learning would be introduced when the ministry to which people are called involves teaching others or taking a formal representative role.

The context in which this learning is to take place is envisaged as the local church or collaborative grouping of local churches, such as a ministry or mission area or Church of England deanery. It is likely that a significant amount of locally based training will take the form of 'blended learning' with learners working partly online and partly in face-to-face groups. Providing it is well-designed, blended learning benefits from the advantages of both online and group learning. Learners can more easily fit their online learning into the pattern of their lives and benefit from the wealth of resources and information the internet provides, while in face-to-face sessions they are stimulated by discussion and debate with fellow-learners and the guidance of the course facilitator. A diocese might combine investing in the design of online learning resources to be used by local groups with providing signposts to the variety of courses covering these areas which may be more accessible or fit the local context better.

The watchword for training and formation at this stage is flexibility. When we agreed the framework above, we did not envisage that anyone training for discipleship and ministry in a local learning hub would be required to cover every one of the 12 elements listed. We assumed that, since this training would be delivered locally, decisions on the most advantageous context for learning and its pace would also be taken locally. We would be offering the framework as a guide along with advice on how best to use it but leaving the decision-making to those responsible for ministry in the local context.

Like the focus on everyday faith, local learning represents a huge cultural shift. It assumes the local church functioning as a learning community and the presence of local trainers familiar with the methods of experiential learning. Like Personal Discipleship Plans, local learning both requires and contributes to an overall shift in the paradigm of ministerial formation. Rather than experiencing training for ordination and licensed lay ministry as utterly different from anything they have undergone before, candidates familiar with 'just-in-time' training in a local context are enabled to make a smooth transition to the next stage of formation. Here again, I discern the Holy Spirit at work in our own and many other dioceses encouraging and enabling a call for local training in the service of a more collaborative pattern of ministry.

4 Develop more flexible patterns of commissioning and authorization

Under the inherited paradigm, ordained ministry is the standard pattern of ministry and episcopal ordination the standard pattern of authorization. Licensing for lay ministries has echoed this pattern, and it is usual for dioceses to conduct licensing services with a similar celebratory approach as for ordinations.

However, this approach to licensing and ordination depends on a clear separation between front-end-loaded training and subsequent ministry. The extension of ministry to the whole people of God and the development of a variety of specialist ministries with training taking place flexibly and locally requires a more flexible pattern of authorization, involving local commissioning alongside episcopal authorization and licensing.

This also requires careful consideration of patterns of accountability. At a local level, these will involve both ordained and lay ministers moving into formal oversight roles.

The following table sets out the responsibilities associated with three types of support and recognition for ministry. It includes a category of 'recognized' ministry, in which locally trained ministers receive local recognition and review. It is based on a framework developed by the Diocese of Canterbury adapted to reflect the situation in the Diocese of Oxford:

Three types of support and permission-giving for lay ministries
'Recognized Ministry' • Local (parish, benefice, chaplaincy, fresh expression, mission) • Recognition by the local minister and people • For a variety of ministries such as visiting, pastoral care, leading worship, home group leading, prayer and listening, chaplaincy assistant etc. • Supervision by the minister or delegated responsible person authorized or licensed to lead an area of work • Training and support in the local context • Regular local review for renewal of recognition • Local responsibility for safeguarding training and checks • Possibility of public recognition by, e.g., area dean, archdeacon, area bishop
'Authorized Ministry' • Diocesan and episcopal • Authorization by the Bishop on advice of diocesan staff • The three current authorized ministries are authorized preacher, eucharistic minister and funeral minister. We favour restricting the use of 'authorization' to those ministries where there is a legal requirement or historical justification • Training provided and overseen by the diocese • Local supervision by the local minister and final accountability to the Bishop • Initial two-year authorization followed by five-year renewal on behalf of the Bishop • Diocesan oversight of safeguarding training and checks carried out locally

'Licensed Ministry' (for canonical lay ministries: Readers and licensed lay workers/ministers, which includes pioneers)

- Episcopal licence as required by canon and nationally recognized
- Diocesan appointment/selection
- Admission and licensing by the Bishop
- The standard qualification is a Common Awards Diploma but we would wish to be flexible, depending on the context
- Local supervision by the local minister and accountability to the Bishop
- Diocesan training, where required. Access to continuing ministerial development comparable to licensed clergy
- Regular ministry review on behalf of the Bishop overseen by archdeaconry advisers
- Diocesan responsibility for safeguarding training and checks

It will also be necessary for decisions to be made on the timing of ordination and licensing. A life-long learning model of formation means that the present 'just-in-case' approach of IME Phase 1 and much formation for lay ministry becomes redundant. Instead, life-long learning based on a reflective practice approach takes place both before and after licensing or ordination. Careful use of the criteria for licensing and ordination is likely to be the key to such decisions.

5 Balance the need for dedicated learning communities with the need for cross-fertilization

Those undertaking specialized ministries, such as street pastors, leaders of Messy Church, youth and children's workers, and pioneer ministers, clearly benefit from dedicated learning communities, in which they can focus on the needs of their mission context and the specialized skills required, share experience and learn from one another and from skilled practitioners. On the other hand, there is equally clearly a benefit in bringing those training for specialized forms of ministry together, especially where the learning consists of areas of theology and ministry common to them all, so that each can learn from one another's different perspectives and contrasting experience. For pioneer ministers, learning the skills of entrepreneurial ministry and the confidence to deconstruct inherited models of church requires dedicated learning communities led by experienced practitioners. However, the skills and dispositions required to work within a mixed economy alongside traditional patterns of church life are best learned in mixed groups. In the same groups, pioneers contribute a measure of challenge through the gift of 'not fitting in'.[14] Children, youth and families workers training alongside candidates for licensed lay or ordained ministry might bring their awareness of young people's spirituality and advocacy of the needs of young people in a situation in which all learn from and alongside one another. When it comes to the study of the Bible and theology, mission and ministry, there are significant advantages in bringing candidates for different forms of ministry together.

There is therefore a balance to be struck: dedicated learning communities to nurture the distinctive gifts required for specific forms of specialist ministry and learning together to build in all the ministers the sense of belonging to one Church and sharing in a common mission. These complementary principles, like the oneness of the Body and the diversity of its gifts (1 Corinthians 12.1–11), do not always fit comfortably together.

Decisions about whether and when pioneers, children's and youth workers and others with specialized ministries join those training for more traditional ministries, such as ordinands and licensed lay ministers, depend largely on their stage of development and growing confidence. As with local training, there is a stage at which training needs to take place in familiar places, with familiar people, and with the teaching provided by familiar faces. There is then a step into the world of the less familiar but wider church, a step in which the minister not only grows in scriptural and theological understanding but learns to understand their own gifts and ministry in the context of the church's history and inherited tradition.

The need for a balance between dedicated learning communities and cross-fertilization applies particularly to ordinands. The role of ordained ministers is to 'animate' the ministry of the whole church. Each is taking a step from the experience of lay discipleship and ministry, in which it will have been possible for many to focus on their own field of mission and service, and learning the skills and dispositions to enable and equip the ministry of the whole church. Central to the pastoral imagination of the ordained is the ability to discern the way God is working in each of his ministers and the way this coheres with the ministry of all; to teach and enable others in their journey of discipleship; to discern and encourage the gifts of others. All this points to the need for a context of training in which the whole church is present in all its diversity. I will address the challenge this poses to the idea of residential training in a subsequent section of this chapter.

6 Bring ministry and training together

A major feature of the old paradigm is that ministerial formation has been separated from ministry. Apart from supervised placements, ordinands and candidates for lay ministry are often expected to withdraw, wholly or partly, from the life of their local churches to concentrate on their training, so that the ministers' training takes little account of the context in which their pastoral imagination might most profitably be developed, while the local church and community are impoverished by the lack of opportunity to share in the minister's learning. The mentality engendered by the separation also means that many complete their training and promptly give up on further learning to concentrate on the ministry.

For some years, the Church's aspiration has been 'formation for ministry within a learning Church'.[15] Such an aspiration requires that the local church becomes a learning community, in which God's people are formed for discipleship and ministry. The inherited paradigm of ministerial formation, in which men and women are removed from their churches to form a learning community, assumes that this has seldom been the case. In the new paradigm, the 'learning church', local as well as national, plays a fundamental role.

As with several of the previous suggestions in this chapter, the Holy Spirit has already been at work. Context-based training is now a recognized third type of training pathway alongside full- and part-time training. If context-based training is to be effective, however, training programmes will need to adapt to the new paradigm. If not, the value of the student's immersion in a ministry context is undermined by a theory-to-practice approach in the classroom. The experiential learning approach makes the most of the student's experience in context while the skills of reflective practice, especially theological reflection, equip them to learn effectively from their experience.

In a recent Grove booklet, Eeva John, Michael Volland and Robin Barden outline what they call a 'PC3' approach to ministerial formation.[16] The four elements that make up PC3 are participation, classroom, context and community. It is a form of training in which learning is intended to take place not only in the classroom but in the context and through interaction in community. Furthermore, this pattern of training is not confined to ordinands. It has been used successfully with lay members of local congregations and licensed ministers as well as those in training for licensed and ordained ministry. Potentially, claim the authors, it is for the whole people of God.

John, Volland and Barden describe an experiential learning approach to learning, showing how this was characteristic of the way Jesus taught his disciples and its appropriateness for context-based training. This highlights the need for learners to be taught how to learn. Although traditional classroom learning is part of the package, formal learning is intended to resource situation-based reflection.

PC3 is also by its nature a collaborative approach, dependent on harmonious relationships between participants, each of whom plays a different role. Not only do the authors differentiate between the learning community and the host community, itself both a learning and a teaching community, but they also name three key facilitator roles: the experienced practitioner, the PC3 facilitator and the theologian. The experienced practitioner plays the mentoring and supervisory role that the Auburn study identified as so important in the formation of pastoral imagination.[17] The PC3 facilitator oversees the life of the training community, setting the 'hidden curriculum' to provide a supportive context for learning. The theologian is named as a separate partner to emphasize that the whole learning process must incorporate theological understanding. Either the experienced practitioner or the PC3 coordinator may play the role of theologian, although the authors see the potential advantage of specialist theological input. Unfortunately, their experiments in inviting a theological specialist to reflection sessions or setting theological reading have not yielded the results they hoped for, perhaps because of the difficulty for theologians familiar with the theory-to-practice approach of adapting to reflective learning.

As described, the PC3 model is an approach to initial 'just-in-case' training. Its principles, however, are capable of adaptation to a life-long learning model of formation. Its recognition of the need to integrate ministry and learning, the role played by formal theology and its espousal of the key role of the host community as a learning community are all easily transferable to a new situation in which candidates and ministers are formed over a longer period.

7 Think strategically about residential training

The life-long nature of ministerial formation, the observation that pastoral imagination is learned primarily through reflective practice with the help of mentors who are mainly experienced practitioners, the importance of bringing ministry and training together, and the advantages of training in context all raise questions about the continuing place of residential training in the formation of candidates for ordained ministry. Historically, residential training has embodied the existing paradigm of training a small minority of the church for a one-size-fits-all ministry as sole practitioners. Despite frequent pleas from the residentially trained and from the institutions themselves, the Church of England currently sends a decreasing proportion of its ordinands to residential colleges. Such research as there is suggests that residential training has no significant advantages over part-time or context-based models of training.[18]

What then do its proponents see as the advantages of residential training? They may be summarized as follows:

- Spiritual formation is the aspect of residential training most frequently mentioned. Ordinands participate in the life of a community that revolves around a rhythm of prayer. Ideally, they internalize and learn to live out this rhythm in their subsequent ministry.
- Second is the amount of time available for biblical and theological study. Residence provides a form of 'stepping back' for deeper reflection. A correspondent to the *Church Times* testifies, 'I was given the time and space that I needed to learn, explore, question and be formed. Without that significant gift, I doubt that I would be even half the minister I am now. Residential study may not be for everyone, but it is definitely needed for some.'[19]
- Third, residence provides a 'worked example' of community life. Especially if ordinands are drawn from across the range of church traditions, it provides a community in which the deep and sustaining relationships formed 'can contribute significantly to mutual understanding and respect across traditions and passions within the church, particularly important as the Church moves towards patterns of ministry which involve far more collaboration between clergy'.[20]
- Ordinands develop close relationships with tutors, who model what it means to think, live and serve as public ministers. 'Tutors become known as "three-dimensional" people – fellow disciples – which can lead to a healthy degree of non-hierarchical mutuality, and tutors functioning in different ways as role-models.'[21]
- The community fosters humility through a shared life geared to the needs of the Church rather than the individual students.
- The community provides a 'spiritual home' from which its members go out to engage in service and mission.

- The availability of tutors and resources such as libraries contributes to the efficiency of training.

Not included in this list is the capacity of some theological colleges to provide formation for ordination within a single church tradition, whether catholic, liberal or evangelical. While some would undoubtedly see this as an advantage, it is questionable whether it is of benefit to the wider Church, since ordinands leaving such colleges are likely immediately to find themselves serving in parishes and benefices that include churches with a variety of traditions. In the longer term, the ability to understand and work with Christians from across the theological spectrum is likely to be a greater advantage.

The residential pattern of training also has some significant drawbacks:

- In a community in which patterns of worship, mealtimes and the teaching timetable are all arranged for them, ordinands may lose touch with the responsibilities of adulthood and become infantilized. Required to let go of the identity and self-esteem provided by the skills they previously exercised in work to be inducted in new and unfamiliar ways of thinking, they become de-skilled. Far from being formative, the 'liminal space' of residential training may become an unnecessary hindrance to learning and growth.
- Theological reflection on experience is separated from the experience itself. The ordinand leaves the residential community for the purposes of placements and returns to the community to reflect on them. The people encountered on placement become objects of reflection rather than partners in the process. The local church or other organization where the placement takes place receives little benefit. Moreover, the focus of assessment is on interpretation rather than action, the ordinand's ability to reflect rather than her ministerial expertise.
- Formation in a context where the laity are not present runs the risk of socializing ordinands into a 'priestly caste'. 'A course may be teaching collaborative ministry, in the sense of collaboration between laity and priest, and the valuing and respect for lay insight, theological wisdom and mutual support. Yet, if it does so in a context in which the laity are not present, they are the "other" being spoken about not with; the medium undermines the message.'[22]
- There is also a shortage of opportunities to practise the activity that ought to be integral to ordained ministry: enabling the ministry of

others. Patterns of training are required in which both ordinands and candidates for lay ministry are regularly required to teach and enable others: acting as mentors for Personal Discipleship Plans, leading confirmation classes, participatory Bible studies, courses such as 'SHAPE', through which people are helped to identify their vocation, or theological reflection. Through such activities, they will also be learning how to facilitate experiential learning.

- Residential training may not be the only place or even the best in which to develop a rhythm of spiritual life. Experience in the residential community may foster a disconnect with real ministry. A correspondent to the *Church Times* testified to the powerful experience of saying the daily office on a crowded commuter train, 'surrounded by many who do not agree or engage with us, rather than in a peaceful college chapel, surrounded by the few who do'.[23] On leaving the college, the minister may find the community's pattern of daily worship to be unrealistic in the context of ministry. Nor is there the opportunity in a residential setting to work out a pattern of work and rest likely to sustain them in the context of ministry.
- Residential training distances ordinands from the joys and challenges of mission. 'It is very difficult for ordinands' lives to be grounded in mission, shaped by the challenge of evangelism, and enthused by the joy of people coming to faith, if the majority of their time and energy is spent within a community of ordinands and tutors.'[24]
- By removing ordinands from their local church and committing a disproportionate percentage of resources compared with those dedicated to locally based training, the Church signals its lack of vision for the potential of the local church as a learning community.

This list has not so far mentioned the impact on families required to move so that the ordinand can train residentially, only to have to move again two or three years later. There are those who argue that residential training 'offers a supportive environment for individuals and families to prepare for a way of life that is likely to involve regular disruption'.[25] On the other hand, it is worth questioning whether this argument takes full account of the cost to spouses of the disruption of their careers or to children of the loss of friendships and the disruption of their schooling.

By forcing all training institutions to come to terms with online learning, the lockdown of 2020 is likely to accelerate the changes overtaking residential training. Moreover, if blended learning comes to play a major role in locally based training, a new generation of ordinands familiar with the online learning environment will expect their TEIs to provide courses with the same advantages of flexibility and breadth.

In a letter to the *Church Times*, Stephen Spencer, an experienced theological educator, suggests that the future for residential colleges lies in 'a broader commitment to theological education of the whole people of God'.[26] If the argument is to be settled and a balanced judgement about the place of residential training arrived at, this can only be in the context of a model of life-long ministerial formation for the ministry of the whole church. In Chapter 4, I suggest a future for residential institutions within a life-long pattern of training that preserves some of their advantages, such as space for reflection, the availability of resources, and opportunities for teaching staff to be mutually enriched and engage in research, while minimizing the disadvantages that accrue from their relative lack of connection with the local church in mission.

8 Ensure that the contexts in which formation takes place model diverse and collaborative patterns of ministry

Under the title 'Questions and Considerations for the Future', the Appendix to the 2014 report on the training of training incumbents raised questions about the contexts in which curates and local lay ministers are trained.[27] A key question concerns the pattern of ministry held up as the model for ministers in training, both lay and ordained. Is this to be the traditional 'general practitioner' model or will the training incumbents and supervising ministers be chosen from among those already exercising a ministry of oversight in which they resource and enable a diverse team of practitioners, including lay ministers, youth workers, administrators and others? Another concerns the relationship between training incumbents and curates: should this continue as 'master and apprentice' or should it be remodelled so that the training incumbent becomes the coordinator of training input from a diverse range of sources?

In a life-long learning model, these questions concern not only curates and training incumbents, but apply to supervising ministers at all stages of formation. As the church gradually moves to a collaborative understanding of ministry, it will become increasingly important that supervising ministers are themselves trained in the skills required to manage another person's training and that the choice of contexts, supervising ministers and training incumbents fits the new model.

9 Incorporate intentional training in the competencies of emotional intelligence (EI) into strategies for teaching and learning

The concept of 'emotional intelligence' came to the fore in the 1990s following the work of Peter Salovey and John D. Mayer. Introducing their work in an article of 1990, they located EI as 'a subset of social intelligence' and defined it as 'the ability to monitor one's own and others' feelings and emotions, to discriminate among them and use this information to guide one's thinking and action'.[28] Empathy, the ability to comprehend another's feelings and to feel them oneself, they saw as the central competence. Despite this, EI is clearly defined as a *cognitive* ability: intelligence about emotions.

Over the next few years, Salovey and Mayer refined their use of the concept, defining it in 1997 as:

- the ability to identify and express emotion
- the ability to use emotion to facilitate thinking
- the ability to understand and analyse emotion
- the ability reflectively to regulate emotion.[29]

The great advantage of restricting their definition in this way is that it becomes possible to predict what the results of these abilities should be and to measure them, thereby testing the validity and value of the concept. In a later article, Salovey, Mayer and John Caruso demonstrated how one manager was able to turn around his performance and job satisfaction through learning the competencies of emotional intelligence in which he had previously performed weakly.[30] The great disadvantage is that in empathy, the central aspect and key to emotional intelligence, abilities other than the cognitive are clearly in play.

While Salovey and Mayer were refining their version of the concept, Daniel Goleman published two books that both popularized and broadened it, returning it to something much closer to social intelligence.[31] In 1998, Goleman described 25 EI 'competencies' in five categories:

- self-awareness: knowing one's internal states, preferences, resources and intuitions
- self-regulation: managing one's internal states, impulses and resources
- motivation: emotional tendencies that guide or facilitate reaching goals

- empathy: awareness of others' feelings, needs and concerns
- social skills: adeptness at inducing desirable responses in others.

As will be apparent, Goleman's expanded concept incorporates the area of motivation, albeit from a particular point of view: the way understanding of our emotional life and that of others enables us to direct our energies purposefully and reflectively. He also includes as 'emotional' competencies a range of social skills that might be better defined as the outcome of emotional intelligence. By so doing, several of his 'competencies' lose precision: for example, 'influence' appears to sum up the ability to manage the mood of a group; rather than a single competence, 'leadership' clearly combines a wide range of abilities, as does 'conflict management'. Moreover, several of his 'competencies', such as 'building bonds' and 'leveraging diversity', reflect culturally desirable orientations rather than specific skills.[32]

On the other hand, Goleman appears to be reaching for a virtue framework to define the qualities that make for personal and business success. The Preface to *Emotional Intelligence* (1995) is entitled 'Aristotle's Challenge' and in its final paragraph he writes:

> In *The Nichomachean Ethics*, Aristotle's philosophical enquiry into virtue, character, and the good life, his challenge is to manage our emotional life with intelligence. Our passions, when well exercised, have wisdom; they guide our thinking, our values, our survival ... As Aristotle saw, the problem is not with emotionality, but with the *appropriateness* of emotion and its expression. The question is, how can we bring intelligence to our emotions – and civility to our streets and caring to our communal life?[33]

Later, he claims, 'There is an old-fashioned word for the body of skills that emotional intelligence represents: *character*.'[34] Although this is a laudable aspiration, it claims too much. A competency is not in itself a consistent habit of life, and several of Goleman's competencies may be deployed for good or ill, to enhance either personal influence or the well-being of others. However, when exercised intentionally and consistently, they may become building blocks for the development of virtue.

In the literature, emotional intelligence is usually defined as one of a variety of 'multiple intelligences', drawing on the work of Howard Gardner and others.[35] In the light of our exploration of knowledge in Chapter 2, it is possible to see that this theory is both confused and confusing. In the words of Etienne Wenger, 'knowledge is competence with respect to valued enterprises'.[36] Knowing is firmly situated in practices and consists of the ability to interpret and respond to situations. 'Proficiency' in a practice requires the ability to perceive situations in depth and detail, drawing on accumulated experience of many similar situations, to weigh the elements of the situation for their relative importance, to deploy a range of possible responses, and the practical wisdom to discern which is likely to be the most fruitful response in this particular situation. Competence in recognizing one's own and others' emotions, regulating one's own and influencing those of others, is clearly a vital element in proficiency in any interpersonal situation. Character or habit of life is the outcome of values consistently followed. While those values provide the motivation for the difficult and demanding task of learning to understand ourselves and others more clearly, competence in this area increases the range of possible responses at our disposal, the skill and wisdom with which we are able to deploy them, and thus enables greater consistency and confidence in a chosen pattern of life. A 'Christian' character is one that consistently chooses to act from love for God and others, is guided by the practical wisdom to discern what that means in any given situation, and attained by the relational skills to put the chosen path into practice.

Building on his work on EI, Goleman went on to describe six 'leadership styles':

- the coercive style, demanding immediate compliance
- the authoritative style, mobilizing people towards a vision
- the affiliative style, creating harmony and building emotional bonds
- the democratic style, forging consensus through participation
- the pacesetting style, setting standards of performance
- the coaching style, developing people for the future.[37]

The important thing to recognize about these styles is that they are not facets of personality but sets of consistent behaviours. As such, they can be learned and deployed flexibly. Leaders build up a repertoire of ways in which each of these styles may be deployed in a variety of situations and good leaders develop the practical wisdom to discern which of the styles is most appropriate. 'Proficiency' in leadership consists of what we might call 'leadership imagination', the ability to discern when and how to deploy the leader's repertoire of leadership behaviours in a variety of circumstances. Moreover, 'leadership imagination' has a virtue component: for example, the choice of democratic or coercive leadership will be influenced by the leader's personal goals, success for themselves or the flourishing of the group; the propensity to deploy the 'coaching style' will largely depend on the leader's concern for the well-being and development of her subordinates. Well attested in research by the Hay Group in the United States and widely used over a long period in the training of headteachers in Britain, Goleman's 'virtue' approach to leadership is well in advance of most Christian writing, in which leadership styles tend to be seen as facets of personality.[38]

If EI has greater influence on business success than intellectual ability, then it is vital for the fruitfulness of Christian ministry. Although EI competencies are implicit in published criteria for ministry, present patterns of training pay little overt attention to the need to incorporate EI into ministerial formation. Appendix 2 provides brief descriptions of Goleman's EI competencies. In the table, I have allocated each competency the equivalent of the academic levels recognized by British universities.[39] I have placed emotional awareness and understanding others at level 3, as competencies without which it would be inappropriate to select people to train for licensed or ordained ministry.

EI competencies build upon one another, so specific competencies are introduced at succeeding levels, as the earliest stage at which focussed attention to these competencies becomes possible and appropriate. Some ideas are presented for the teaching and learning strategies that might encourage or enable learners to grow in each of the competencies. In some cases, such as training in the skills of attentive listening, development in the competency might form the main focus of learning; in others, such as self-confidence, teaching methods might be chosen to enable the development of EI alongside knowledge and skills. In the final column, I have included some observations on the competency itself and its relation to ministerial proficiency or 'pastoral imagination'.

Appendix 3 is a table of grade descriptors setting out expectations for the development of EI at the equivalent of levels 4 to 7. Neither table includes suggestions about means of assessment, but I suggest that this is quite possible through the choice of suitable methods. These might include theological reflections, journals, presentations, group projects, resources for others and even essays with suitable titles.

In Appendix 4 I introduce a further table, in which EI competencies are listed as part of the skills base required for each of the qualities the Church of England looks for as the outcome of formation for ordinands. In this table, I have been cautious about the description of these skills, not wishing to become too reliant on Goleman but rather to present descriptions attuned to the demands of Christian ministry.

10 Assess 'wisdom and godly habit of life'

Writing in the *Journal of Adult Theological Education* in 2007, Gary Wilton drew attention to a watershed moment in the life of the Church Army's Wilson Carlile Training Centre.[40] From 1995, subjects like church history, biblical studies and doctrine were to be assessed through the College of York St John and validated by Leeds University. Retreats, human relations, communication and worship remained as purely in-house units with no external validation. Prior to 1995, the learning community placed most emphasis on vocational and personal development. After that date, students placed most emphasis on the credit-bearing units.

My experience during the 11 years in which I served as a personal tutor at Ripon College Cuddesdon probably echoes that of many others in a similar position. Every student has to come to terms with the fact that some elements of their training receive a numerical mark leading to an academic qualification while others receive no mark but are assessed solely through their final report. Even for the more mature, those with the ability to resolve this tension, the situation provides a major distraction. For the less mature, especially those studying for the more prestigious qualifications, it can seriously impair overall formation, regardless of their eventual classification.

In 2006, in *Shaping the Future*, a task group on the parameters of the curriculum for the Church of England declared:

> Accreditation should be gained for the whole programme, not simply for the 'academic' elements. This is not to say that every element is or ought to be assessed through HE criteria, but that the award takes full account of the vocational nature of the education and training, with the integration of being, knowing and doing as fundamental.[41]

Speaking at the 2019 Theological Educators Network conference, Frances Clemson of the Durham University Common Awards team drew attention to the patterns of elitism in both Churches and universities. Patterns of assessment heavily weighted towards academic ability play their part in perpetuating elitism and exclusion. The world of higher education, she pointed out, is moving towards assessment *for* learning rather than simply *of* learning. Designing assignments to provide quality feedback and so enhance students' learning requires methods of assessment appropriate to the learning outcomes. Although training institutions face considerable challenges in the shape of limited staff time and expertise, student unfamiliarity, institutional resources and stakeholder expectations, the use of creative methods of assessment covering the whole formational process remains a standard of excellence to which to aspire.

If the Church is to take seriously its commitment to 'wisdom and godly habit of life' as the measure of a person's suitability for ministry, it must cease to give mixed messages through the way candidates are assessed. In principle, all the elements of formation are capable of assessment: intellectual grasp, emotional intelligence, practical skill and character development. Theological reflections requiring candidates to demonstrate awareness of their own responses to a given situation and the ability to reflect on these, individual reflections on group tasks, 360-degree assessment by tutors and peers to which the candidate is required to respond, practical ministerial tasks and tasks set with the intention of assessing specific EI competencies are just a few of the possible methods of assessment that might be used.

Although the example of the Southwark OLM training scheme, which I gave in the previous chapter, suggests that some academic institutions may not have the skills necessary for this all-round assessment, as the Church's validating university, Durham is actively encouraging the use of creative means of assessment. All that is needed is for theological educators to be trained to use them.

Appendix 4 consists of a table setting out the qualities of formation to be sought in ministers who expect to become incumbents at the point of ordination in the Church of England. The framework is intended to pay equal attention to godly wisdom as to ministerial skills and theological understanding, and the approach to theological understanding places the emphasis on the developing ability to inhabit the living tradition of Christian faith in company with others. Inhabiting a quality speaks of a life-long process that is ever deepening and resonates with the ancient term 'habitus', which speaks of dispositions lived out through deep immersion in a wide variety of lived contexts and relationships, all of which shape both life and calling.

It will readily be seen that aspects of ministerial formation appear in distinct parts of the grid. For example:

- biblical and theological understanding, seen as the inhabiting of a living tradition, in Love for God/Church
- prayer and the inward journey of discipleship in Love for God/Self
- pastoral care in Love for People/Christ

- collaborative leadership skills in Wisdom/Church
- locating oneself in the context of pluralism in Fruitfulness/Christ
- worship and preaching in Fruitfulness/Church
- mission and the enabling of everyday faith in Fruitfulness/World
- self-care in Fruitfulness/Self.

Moreover, several of the sections build on one another:

- collaborative leadership in Wisdom/Church on Love for People/Church
- exercising representative ministry in Call to Ministry/World on Love for God/World
- both emotional maturity in Wisdom/Self and understanding of the demands of ministry in Call to Ministry/Self on Love for People/Self.

The table incorporates three 'layers': the 'top level', which consists of the qualities of life described in bold in the 28 boxes at the head of each table; the 'middle level' consisting of these headings and the evidence by which the ordinand's attainment of these qualities is to be assessed. The table given is the third and most detailed level. The 'pattern of life' for each quality describes in greater depth and detail the 'wisdom and godly habit of life' corresponding to the quality. Then come the dispositions to be associated with that pattern of life, several of which draw on the Beatitudes as Jesus' definitive description of the way of life to which his followers are called to aspire. Next is the knowledge and skill base required for the pattern of life, including both cognitive understanding and EI competencies. Finally, the evidence lines reflect the knowledge and skills base and are framed as learning outcomes. This more detailed table is intended to serve as a guide for training institutions in the planning of the curriculum and assessment, with the aim of enabling them to incorporate as far as possible every aspect of formation in formal assessment.

11 Assess practice rather than theory

A central issue in any kind of training is the extent to which the learning that takes place in the context of the learning community is transferred into practice. An essay may assess the candidate's grasp of an area of theory, their facility in verbal communication, logical argument and written presentation, but it does not guarantee the transfer of their understanding to the practice of ministry. Alternative written tasks, such as the production of resources for others with a rationale, assess the same strengths and weaknesses but in a situation that is closer to a ministerial context. A portfolio requiring evidence of good practice as well as an extended reflection, such as those used in the modules on Education and the Learning Church, is closer still. Assessed conversation enables the candidate to demonstrate their biblical understanding or grasp of doctrine in a 'live' situation, which models the aspiration that they pass on what they have learned to others.

In a life-long learning model of formation, it is to be expected that candidates for formal qualifications will already have accumulated considerable experience of the practices of ministry. Rather than 'initial training' for those with little experience, the context of formation is closer to continuing ministerial development. It is, therefore, both important and appropriate that the assessment process takes account of this.

12 Broaden learning objectives to include EI competencies and dispositions

The generic grade descriptors currently used by the Quality Assurance Agency for Higher Education (QAA) focus on a relatively narrow range of intellectual competencies. At level 5, the level required for ordination or licensing as a lay minister, these comprise:

- knowledge and critical understanding of the well-established concepts and principles relevant to their area of study and the way these have developed
- ability to apply these principles in a range of contexts, including that of employment
- knowledge of the main methods of enquiry in a subject discipline and ability to choose the best methods of problem-solving
- an understanding of the limits of their knowledge
- ability to communicate accurately, reliably and coherently to a variety of audiences
- the qualities and personal skills necessary for employment requiring some personal responsibility and decision-making.[42]

It will readily be appreciated that these are skewed to intellectual grasp of a subject area and, within that, to the understanding of abstract concepts. The 'practical know-how' necessary for the application of the principles and concepts of the subject receives little attention. Collaboration and group working, creativity and inventiveness, trustworthiness, self-management, ability to resolve conflict, orientation to the needs of others, humility and self-awareness come bundled together under the 'qualities and personal skills required for employment'.

The narrow focus of the QAA, while it serves the goal of comparability between qualifications and hence of commodification, lies at the heart of the swelling chorus of criticism of higher education noted in the previous chapter. On the other hand, a widening of these grade descriptors to make them suitable for the assessment of candidates for ministry might, at the same time, contribute to the reform of higher education required in response to these criticisms.

The detailed level table of formation qualities presented in Appendix 4 points the way towards a suitably revised generic grade descriptor for the exercise of Christian ministry, specifying dispositions and EI competencies, ministerial skills and the appropriate knowledge base for the exercise of these skills and could serve as the basis for a revision of module learning outcomes incorporating all these dimensions.

13 Train theological educators in experiential learning

As the validating university for the Common Awards, Durham University currently requires of all theological educators competence in a specialist academic area at an appropriate level as part of academic validation. Unfortunately, however, many academic subject specialists are not well placed to implement an experiential learning model, being far more familiar with the theory-to-practice mode of teaching and learning in narrow specialist sub-disciplines typical of formation for theological scholarship rather than for ministry.

Moreover, Edward Farley warns of the dangers of what he calls the 'scholarly-guild mindset'. To men and women with this way of thinking, the standards, scope and methods of their chosen discipline have proved their excellence over time. Their instinct is to initiate candidates into these ways of thinking. To have to think in terms of applying the insights of the discipline to ministry does not come naturally and is often resisted.[43]

Beyond a certain point, however, scholarly expertise in Old or New Testament, doctrine, ethics, or any one of the traditional sub-disciplines of theological study becomes less important than the ability to draw on the insights of these disciplines to resource the practice of ministry. This may well be one of the most important reasons why the Auburn study found experienced practitioners to be the most effective teachers of pastoral imagination.

Experiential learning is a well-established discipline, with widely understood methods and criteria of excellence. If it is to move to an experiential model of teaching and learning for ministerial formation, the Church will need to encourage theological educators to undergo training in this field of expertise, such as through the Durham University Excellence in Learning and Teaching Award, and require TEIs as part of their periodic external review to demonstrate that their staff are sufficiently well qualified.

An immediate step would be to review the practice of identifying ordinands as potential theological educators based on their academic ability alone. Over the past two or three years in the Oxford Diocese, we have been gathering a group of recently ordained men and women with a vocation to teach. Only half the members of this group had been 'flagged' by their selection panels. In some cases, their vocation was to be a teacher in a local church context, in others to contribute to diocesan programmes, and others aspired to become staff members of a TEI. As well as providing relevant experience for as many as possible, in some cases our task was to challenge the expectation that academic ability alone equips a person to be an educator of others and in others to build the confidence of those with clear potential but who had not been 'flagged' at selection.

14 Review the aims, content and learning outcomes of existing Common Awards modules and/or encourage the development of new modules

The modules for Common Awards were created by a collaborative process involving a significant proportion of the members of the community of theological educators. To have accomplished so much in such a comparatively short time was a notable achievement. The modules can be assumed to reflect best practice at the time of their creation. They therefore reflect the gradual transition to the new paradigm I am advocating already taking place. They are available as resources with which to create tailor-made programmes reflecting the emphases of the various TEIs.

However, due to the short timescale available for the work, the modules suffer from some significant shortcomings. Subject-specific dispositions were to have figured in the learning outcomes, but this requirement was dropped at an early stage. Integration of subject areas and integration of theory and practice were initial aspirations, but in most cases such integration is dependent on decisions regarding the pattern of formative assessment. After one meeting of the short-lived MA group, I suggested that a set of integrated modules be created, allowing post-graduates to integrate their knowledge and apply it to practice. A colleague responded that he personally would be excited by such a development but that he doubted whether the cross-disciplinary expertise existed to create such modules.

I have already argued that all modules should include dispositions and relevant EI competencies in their learning outcomes. Whether time and expertise are available for such a review to be carried out centrally is doubtful. An alternative would be for individual TEIs to be encouraged to propose revisions to the modules, including revisions of learning out-comes, or to create new ones and to 'road-test' the teaching of these modules using teaching methods that build EI competence and engage dispositions.

A simple question to be applied to existing Common Awards modules would be, 'Does this module take for granted the inherited paradigm of ministry and ministerial formation, or does it look forward to the new paradigm?' Over time, TEIs could be discouraged from using modules that appear to promote a 'sole practitioner' mentality and encouraged to adopt those designed to form candidates for collaborative ministry; just as they would be discouraged from using theory-to-practice methods of teaching in favour of experiential learning.

15 Provide reflective supervision for clergy

In a life-long model of ministerial formation, the provision of support and guidance for ongoing development is crucial. Ordained ministers, whose role is to animate and oversee the ministry of the whole church, both need and deserve regular supervision. In most other 'people profes-sions', supervision is a requirement. Counsellors may receive projections from their clients, which they need to identify and work through. They may find themselves dealing with issues that affect them personally or face situations in which it is difficult to be sure whether their response was the best possible. Ordained ministers meet all these situations and much more besides. They work with groups as well as individuals. They face expectations that are often unreasonable, and maintaining appropriate boundaries is a constant challenge. For all these reasons, ordained ministers need to find the necessary space for supervision as well as being equipped to provide supervision for those, both clergy and lay, whose ministry they are called to oversee.

Frances Ward calls supervision a 'space to play': a place for the minister to step aside from immediate pressures to rerun aspects of ministry in a safe environment.[44] 'In a nutshell,' write Jane Leach and Michael Paterson, 'pastoral supervision is a relationship between two or more disciples who meet to consider the ministry of one or more of them in an intentional and disciplined way.' They go on:

> Pastoral supervision is practised for the sake of the supervisee, providing a space in which their well-being, growth and development are taken seriously, and for the sake of those among whom the supervisee works, providing a realistic point of accountability.[45]

Supervision overlaps with and includes elements of counselling, spiritual direction and work consultancy but it is not the same as these. Its primary method is reflection and, in a Christian context, theological reflection.

Since 2015, under the leadership of Jane Leach, the Methodist Church in Britain has gradually introduced 'reflective supervision' for all its clergy and some lay leaders, using the 'three-legged stool' of supervision based on the work of Francesca Inskipp and Brigid Proctor:[46]

- the restorative: contributing to well-being through the gift of a listening ear
- the formative: enabling a focus on the requirements of ministry, difficult or challenging situations and drawing attention to areas of development
- the normative: paying attention to risks, boundaries and norms of conduct and addressing mistakes.

Careful consideration was given to providing a safe environment in which to retain the normative element while maintaining the distinction between 'reflective' and management supervision. Reflective supervision is a non-coercive relationship whose model is the example of Jesus' self-giving love, which nevertheless retains a focus on the norms of practice that guide both supervisor and supervisee. At the heart of supervision, Leach observes, is the space in which to pay attention to God's call. The centrality of God's voice means that supervision potentially becomes 'a means of grace by which the whole church may be recalled to life'.[47]

Pilot studies of the ministers who have undertaken a discipline of regular supervision have confirmed the benefits that flow to all involved, the ministers and those whom they serve:

- In the restorative dimension, clergy experience a greater sense of well-being. They welcome the gift of time and attention represented by the presence of the supervisor, the awareness of God's presence and the breaking down of isolation. They experience a release of energy (since difficult situations no longer fester), a decrease in stress, better sleeping patterns and greater emotional availability, including to their families.
- In the formative dimension, supervision is experienced as a gift of wisdom. They are enabled to recognize their own and others' unconscious dynamics and drives. New skills become embedded habits. They experience an increase in self-efficacy as they become more confident in handling difficult situations. Their focus moves from solving immediate problems towards ways of being in ministry.
- In the normative dimension, safety is a specific focus of the supervision sessions. However, rather than leading clergy to become risk-averse, supervision has provided greater confidence in taking responsible risks. It has also improved role clarity and the ability to exercise appropriate authority.[48]

Contrary to some expectations, ministers have experienced accountability as a means of grace. The normative dimension of supervision provides a combination of safety and challenge in which growth can take place.[49]

Moreover, Leach observes that the introduction of supervision is beginning to affect the culture of the Methodist Church even at this early stage. Ministers remarked that 'supervision is beginning to change the culture of ministry from an isolated drivenness and anxious need to fix things to a more relaxed and intentional attentiveness to self and other and God'.[50] Comparison with the formational requirements for ministers, on a grid similar to the one for Anglican ministers in Appendix 4, reveals that the dispositions that prove to be required in both supervisors and supervisees align with those the Church looks for in its ministers: non-anxious, alert to the Spirit, dependable, accountable, reflective, collegial, empowering, playful or curious, compassionate and courageous. The practice of these dispositions in supervision embeds them in the lives of ministers. The 'normative' theology of the Church becomes the 'operant' theology of its ministers. As one minister put it, '[Supervision] feels like a blood trans-fusion. The [Methodist] Church is receiving some life-giving and healthy blood into the system at intervals and at defined places/times.'[51]

16 Share good practice

The paradigm I am proposing is already 'emerging' in the life of the church and inspiring renewed practice, from which the whole community of theological educators can learn. In this section, I draw attention to some examples.

'Learning to Inhabit the Kingdom' is the title of the report of a work-shop held in 2016 to explore imaginative approaches to transformational learning for discipleship and ministry. The convenors were Eeva John, then of Westcott House, Cambridge; Naomi Nixon, then of Coventry Dio-cese; and Nick Shepherd, then of Southwark Diocese. In their reflection, the authors explain that they embarked on the project in the conviction that the actual practice of educators is a valid source of theory. Explor-ing the pedagogical approaches that facilitate transformational learning serves as a pointer to the nature of learning itself. Observation of the way the learners' understanding and relationship with God was affected throws light on the nature of our relationships, with God and with one another.[52]

The fruitfulness of the workshop and the extent of the conclusions to be drawn from it confirms the value of the sharing of good practice, not only for building theological educators' practical skills but also the potential for identifying fruitful areas for theological and educational exploration. In this case the experience of those sharing the workshop suggested that transformational learning is learning that:

- engages with the whole person
- involves real encounters
- stimulates the imagination
- crosses thresholds.

As we saw in Chapter 2, a 'threshold concept' is one that is 'akin to pass-ing through a portal'. Having grasped the concept, the student is never the same again. The new concept reinterprets all relevant experience. John, Nixon and Shepherd identified five threshold concepts concerning the experience of learning for discipleship and ministry, each of which is integral to the emerging paradigm of formation I am describing. Students were transformed by realizing that Christian learning:

- involves character as well as knowledge and skills
- is not simply about learning theology but that theology is a lens through which to interpret the whole of experience
- is deeply contextual, a realization that enhances the students' appreciation of experiential learning
- affects the emotions as well as the intellect
- is relational, impacting our relationships with ourselves and others.

In this instance, the sharing of practice also served to highlight some of the challenges associated with promoting transformational learning. The authors record widespread dissatisfaction among theological educators with assignment tasks that are inadequate and inappropriate for assessing transformational learning, another reason for diversifying the range of assessment. Without this, there is a danger that pressure to teach to the assessment can result in the framing of ministerial formation as merely the acquisition of knowledge and skills, ignoring or downplaying the importance of emotional, relational and dispositional change. The value of sharing experience is further emphasized by the fact that the article in *Practical Theology* in which the workshop was reported is followed by three spontaneous responses from theological educators in other parts of the world, each of whom acknowledges the limitations of much educational practice.[53]

An example of a different kind was given in a paper to the British and Irish Association for Practical Theology at its summer conference in 2019. In their paper, Michael West and Richard Hainsworth outlined the philosophy and practice of St Padarn's Institute, the training institution for the Church in Wales. In 2013, the six dioceses of the Church in Wales affirmed their commitment to the development of ministry areas, which would be 'collaborative and team centred, embracing both ordained and lay ministries'. Among the key principles that were to underpin formation for ministry were the requirement that 'training in discipleship and ministry be held together in one integrated process', and that any course be 'both *practical*, focussing on the effective delivery of ministry … and *reflective*, helping participants to integrate theology with ministry and with the life of prayer'.[54] Accordingly, theological reflection was to be at the heart of learning, enabling students to learn in such a way that theology became a resource for both discipleship and ministry.

St Padarn's builds on the practice of several Church in Wales dioceses of providing training for three groups of students: candidates for licensed and ordained ministry; those whose initial desire was to serve in their ministry areas but might at the same time be exploring a vocation for licensed ministry; and those whose primary aim was to deepen their discipleship. The students learn together in four contexts:

- Regional seminar days at the beginning and in the middle of each module serve to build relationships, introduce the topic, introduce the activities that take learners deeper into the topic, and provide the opportunity for advice on assignments.
- Facilitated learning groups of 3–8 learners, led by a volunteer tutor, are at the heart of the learning. The groups work through the 'flipped classroom' approach, so that members first learn the material on their own and then come together for deeper learning through a series of shared group assignments.
- Formational cells for worship for lay and ordained ministerial candidates build up the learning community and enable learners to embed their learning as an element in spiritual formation.
- Candidates for ministry learn through context-based ministerial experience using an apprenticeship model.

West and Hainsworth stressed that the course is to be seen as 'fractal', each separate element echoing the theological and pedagogical philosophy of the whole, with the aim that each learner becomes a confident practical theologian and skilled theological reflector with the ability to interpret not only their ministerial context but their whole experience through the lens of Christian theology.

The challenges faced by St Padarn's in extending this paradigm to the whole of Wales include:

- The historical and cultural differences between the north and south of the province.
- The continuation of residential training for approximately 9% of candidates. This is addressed by Jeremy Duff's paper, which I have quoted above. The continued existence of the college, situated in Cardiff, has tended to echo traditional models and allows the continuation, where it exists, of the prejudice that sees residential training as superior to context-based models.

- The 'fractal' pattern involves bringing all learners together into facilitated learning groups. In practice, this proves a step too far for some, for whom the academic demands have been greater than expected. In the section above on locally based training, I noted the need of many for a familiar context in which to take their first steps before the move to a nationally provided programme.
- Formal assessment is limited to the theological programme and does not yet extend to spiritual formation or the practical placements.
- The framework for the course is a modified approach to 'initial training', in which others may join rather than a fully fledged life-long learning model.
- Other parts of the 'system' are still in the process of change. Despite its ambitious embrace of experiential, context-based learning, St Padarn's draws its learners from, and sends its graduates into, a Church in which the mindset of many of its existing clergy has been formed in the old paradigm of ministry and training.

Despite these hurdles, St Padarn's remains an example of what might be aspired to and what can be achieved in a Church committed to 'whole system change' in its approach to mission, ministry and formation.[55]

A third example is provided by *Anvil: Journal of Theology and Mission*.[56] Beginning its life as a scholarly journal in the Anglican evangelical tradition, *Anvil*'s current incarnation is as a journal of mission based in the work of the Church Mission Society and edited by Cathy Ross, previously general secretary of the International Association for Mission Studies and now head of Pioneer Mission Leadership Training Oxford for CMS. The edition in question is an account of a 'Hui', the Maori word for a gathering for the sharing of ideas in community, a choice of title drawn from Ross's native Aotearoa/New Zealand. The gathering involved mission educators from four continents, who came together to share and reflect on their experiences.

In a short space, it is impossible to do justice to the richness of the insights emerging from the Hui and recorded in the various articles in the journal. In her editorial, Ross rejoices in the untapped potential for theological education, the opportunities for creativity in both delivery and content, and in the range of participants, as well as the way the gathering opened up the fundamental question, 'What is theology?' Among the important themes to emerge are:

- The importance and value of community. The opening session of the gathering featured space for the participants, drawn from several countries, not only to share their experiences but to become vulnerable to one another by acknowledging difference and sharing feelings. In the words of one contributor, 'Who we learn with determines what we learn',[57] and several articles provide examples of fruitful learning from one another in community.

- The use of physical and metaphorical space. The event itself began in a space divided into five 'zones' evoking five contexts: the urban, jungle, river/sea, desert and mountain; and worked with the metaphors associated with each: heat, adaptation and solitude for desert, barriers, adventure and awe for mountain. Subsequent articles include an account of a course in mission theology devised by John and Olive Drane based around ten rooms of a house and a process devised by Anna Ruddick using a variety of postures to focus different aspects of the learning. In the case of Ruddick's use of different stations to frame the learning, her intention was 'to bring into synergy the cognitive mind, the spirit, the body and the emotions in the process of learning'.[58]

- The courses mentioned above are examples of another set of themes running through the gathering: playfulness, creativity and improvisation, which provide space for divergent as well as convergent thinking. A clear sense is conveyed of a shared desire to move away from the constraints of the academic paradigm in order to explore new ways of teaching and learning. One contributor, a member of CMS, reflects several of the emphases of this book: 'CMS approaches theological reflection not as an academic exercise, but as a group activity where real issues and experiences are discussed. Then there are follow-up sessions to see how action has been taken in light of the prior reflection. Also the majority of the teachers at CMS were practitioners themselves, engaged in the work of ministry and mission while being teachers. This meant that they were not divorced from the everyday realities of priestly life.'[59]

- Moreover, the new paradigm of teaching and learning coming into being is mutual, exploratory and non-directive. The same contributor continues: 'Another interesting quirk of CMS was that much of the time people who were teaching in one class would then be a student in another. The learning environment encouraged everyone to learn from one another, rather than a top-down approach. This was refreshing as everybody's opinions and contributions were respected. This in itself helped train people in the realities of ministry where every member of the congregation has an opinion. Perhaps this way of learning teaches people in an "elder" style of leadership, and listening to the whole body of Christ, not just those in power.' This relationship of mutuality between student and teacher, in contrast with the 'expert' style of the academic model, gives value to student experience as the starting point for further learning.

- In the context of exploratory, open-ended learning, as several articles testify, it is the *missio Dei* that provides 'true north': a foundation of stability from which the exploration takes its bearings.[60] In practice, this means that pioneer missioners need to adopt a posture of listening. As one contributor notes, 'One of the key learning challenges for Reformed and European churches is to pay attention to God's agency and integrate a sense of the Spirit across the whole of life. If this is the mission of God then the first act of mission is listening and then learning to walk (not run) with what we are discovering.'[61] The discipline of corporate discernment becomes central to missional learning.

- Finally, the experience of new forms of learning raises the question, 'What is theology?' Students and teachers move from understanding theology as a field of expertise guarded and imparted by qualified experts to something more 'communal and conversational' that connects with real life. 'The students begin to move from a world where theology is a content to be downloaded, learned and imparted – and perhaps defended – to a world where theology is more like a process with which the community engages together.'[62]

I am particularly glad to finish this chapter with reflections on 'Learning to Inhabit the Kingdom', St Padarn's Institute and the CMS 'Hui'. As a manifesto calling for a reshaped paradigm for ministerial formation, the focus of this book is necessarily on what is wrong and needs to change. In contrast, workshop, course and gathering highlight the way in which the new paradigm I have described is already taking shape and the potential not simply for transformational learning but for a transformation of the entire enterprise of ministerial formation.

Notes

1 Rowan Williams, CEFACS Lecture, Birmingham – Centre for Anglican Communion Studies, 3 November 2004, available at http://rowanwilliams.archbishop ofcanterbury.org/articles.php/1847/cefacs-lecture-birmingham-centre-for-anglican-communion-studies.html accessed 20 February 2021.

2 Hubert and Stuart Dreyfus, 'From Socrates to expert systems: the limits of calculative rationality' in *Skillful Coping*, ed. Mark A. Wrathall, Oxford: Oxford University Press, 2014, pp. 25–46, quotation from p. 34.

3 Christian A. B. Scharen and Eileen R. Campbell-Reed, 'Learning pastoral imagination: a five-year report on how new ministers learn in practice', *Auburn Studies* 21 (2016), p. 7.

4 Advisory Council of the Church's Ministry, *Education for the Church's Ministry*, 1987, §46. Archbishops' Council, *Formation for Ministry within a Learning Church*, London: Church House Publishing, 2003, p. 45.

5 Archbishops' Council, 'Setting God's People Free', 2017, p. 1.

6 The report 'Rooted in the Church' from the Church of England Education Office, 2016, lists 'meaningful roles' including leadership and serving opportunities as one of the factors predisposing those who grow up in the church to stay with it into adulthood.

7 For Personal Discipleship Plans, see further below. 'Your Shape for God's Service', originally developed by Amiel Osmaston for the Diocese of Carlisle and now available online from several places, including Carlisle Diocese, CPAS and the Arthur Rank Centre.

8 For more detail on how this can be encouraged, see David Heywood, *Kingdom Learning*, London: SCM Press, 2017, pp. 119–78.

9 Personal Discipleship Plans are the brainchild of the Diocese's Discipleship Enabler, Tina Molyneux, who currently coordinates the work of publicizing them and training mentors. For more details, see www.oxford.anglican.org/personal-discipleship-plan/ accessed 20 December 2020. They also draw extensively on the work of the London Institute of Contemporary Christianity, which has been working in the area of whole-life discipleship for many years. See www.licc.org.uk/about/life/ accessed 11 December 2020.

10 Neil Hudson, *Imagine Church*, Nottingham: IVP, 2012, pp. 116–22.

11 'Setting God's People Free', p. 18.

12 See https://fxresourcing.org/ and www.xplore.org.uk/.

13 The Anglican Communion's 'five marks of mission' are explained at www.anglicancommunion.org/mission/marks-of-mission.aspx accessed 11 December 2020.

14 The phrase is taken from the publicity of the Church Mission Society.

15 The title of the 'Hind' Report: Archbishops' Council, *Formation for Ministry within a Learning Church*, 2003.

16 Eeva John, Michael Volland and Robin Barden, *Context-based Learning for Discipleship and Ministry*, Cambridge: Grove, 2017.

17 Christian A. B. Scharen and Eileen R. Campbell-Reed, 'Learning Pastoral Imagination: A Five-Year Report on How New Ministers Learn in Practice', Auburn Studies, No. 21, 2016, pp. 23–8, 33–7.

18 J. Michael, M. J. Reiss, T. Mujtaba and R. Sheldrake, *Resourcing Ministerial Education*, University of London Institute of Education, 2014; Liz Graveling, 'Vocational Pathways: Perspectives for Initial Ministerial Education Phase 1', Archbishops' Council Ministry Division, 2016; Ruth Perrin, 'Vocational Pathways: Perspectives from Curacy', Archbishops' Council Ministry Division, 2016. In a comparison between residential and online students studying the same undergraduate theology programme at Laidlaw College, New Zealand, Mark Nicholls found that part-time students experienced significantly better overall formation and development: 'A comparison of the spiritual participation of on-campus and theological distance education students,' *Journal of Adult Theological Education* 12.2 (2015), pp. 121–36. In a further article, Nicholls found that the fellowship of their local churches provided the formational context that enabled distance students to flourish. See 'The formational experiences of on-campus and theological distance education students', *Journal of Adult Theological Education* 13.1 (2016), pp. 18–32.

19 Rich Cresswell in the *Church Times*, 13 December 2019, p. 17.

20 Jeremy Duff, 'Formational Excellence in this Generation: The theological basis for St Padarn's approach to full-time ordination training', December 2018, unpublished. I am grateful for permission to quote from this paper.

21 Duff, 'Formational Excellence'.

22 Duff, 'Formational Excellence'.

23 Ben Cahill-Nicholls in *The Church Times*, 31 January 2020, p. 15.

24 Duff, 'Formational Excellence'.

25 Michael Volland in *The Church Times*, 2 March 2018, p. 25.

26 Stephen Spencer in *The Church Times*, 31 January 2020, p. 15.

27 Archbishops' Council Ministry Division, 'Report on Good Practice in the Appointment and Training of Training Incumbents', 2014. This appendix is unfortunately absent from the 2017 revision. The full text is given in Appendix 1.

28 P. Salovey and J. D. Mayer, 'Emotional intelligence', *Imagination, Cognition and Personality* 9.3 (1990), pp. 185–211; reprinted in *Emotional Intelligence*, ed. Peter Salovey, Marc. A. Brackett and John D. Mayer, Katonah, NY: Dude Publishing, 2004, pp. 1–27; quotations from *Emotional Intelligence*, p. 5.

29 John D. Mayer and Peter Salovey, 'What is emotional intelligence?' in *Emotional Development and Emotional Intelligence: Educational Implications*, New York: Basic Books, 1997; reprinted in *Emotional Intelligence*, pp. 29–57; quotations from *Emotional Intelligence*, p. 37.

30 David R. Caruso, Peter Salovey and John D. Mayer, 'Emotional intelligence and emotional leadership' in *Multiple Intelligences and Leadership*, ed. R. E. Riggio and S. E. Murphy, Mahwah, NJ: Laurence Erlbaum, 2003, pp. 55–73; reprinted in *Emotional Intelligence*, pp. 305–25.

31 Daniel Goleman, *Emotional Intelligence*, London: Bloomsbury, 1995; *Working with Emotional Intelligence*, London: Bloomsbury, 1998; combined volume 2004.

32 Salovey and Mayer describe them as, 'the standard competency models of HR professionals'; 'Emotional leadership', p. 312.

33 Goleman, *Emotional Intelligence*, p. xiv (emphasis original).

34 Goleman, *Emotional Intelligence*, p. 285 (emphasis original).

35 See, for example, Howard Gardner, *Frames of Mind*, New York: Basic Books, 1993.

36 Etienne Wenger, *Communities of Practice*, Cambridge: Cambridge University Press, 1998, p. 4.

37 Daniel Goleman, 'Leadership that gets results', *Harvard Business Review* (March–April 2000), pp. 78–90; see also Daniel Goleman, Richard Boyatzis and Annie McKee, *Primal Leadership*, Boston, MA: Harvard Business School Press, 2002; published in Britain as *The New Leaders*.

38 For example, Keith Lamdin, *Finding Your Leadership Style*, London: SPCK, 2012. Simon Walker sets out eight leadership styles, some very similar to the Hay Group styles that figure in Goleman's work. However, Walker connects these to temperament and personal history. Goleman's approach is analogous to cognitive behavioural therapy and emotional intelligence competencies are learned in a similar way to cognitive behaviour change, through practice, reflection and reinforcement. Walker's approach is closer to depth psychology. Simon Walker, *Leading Out of Who You Are*, Carlisle: Piquant Editions, 2007; *Leading with Nothing to Lose*, Carlisle: Piquant Editions, 2007.

39 Level 4, the first year or a degree or 'certificate' level; level 5, the second year of a degree or 'diploma' level; level 6, degree level; and level 7, post-graduate study.

40 Gary Wilton, 'From ACCM 22 to Hind via Athens and Berlin: A Critical Analysis of Key Documents Shaping Contemporary Church of England Theological Education with Reference to the Work of David Kelsey', *Journal of Adult Theological Education* 4.1 (2007).

41 Archbishops' Council, *Shaping the Future: New Patterns of Training for Lay and Ordained*, London: Church House Publishing, 2006, p. 80.

42 Quality Assurance Agency for Higher Education, *UK Quality Code for Higher Education*, date not given, p. 26; www.qaa.ac.uk/docs/qaa/quality-code/qualifications-frameworks.pdf.

43 Edward Farley, *Theologia*, Philadelphia, PA: Fortress Press, 1983, p. 19.

44 Frances Ward, *Lifelong Learning*, London: SCM Press, 2005, p. 88–95.

45 Jane Leach and Michael Paterson, *Pastoral Supervision: A Handbook*, London: SCM Press, 2010, p. 1.

46 Francesca Inskipp and Brigid Proctor, *Making the Most of Supervision, Part 1: The Art, Craft and Tasks of Counselling Supervision*, 2nd edition, Bend, OR: Cascade Publications, 1995.

47 Jane Leach, *A Charge to Keep*, Nashville, TN: United Methodist Church General Board of Higher Education and Ministry, 2020, p. 15.

48 Leach, *Charge*, pp. 58–72.

49 Leach, *Charge*, pp. 74, 109.

50 Leach, *Charge*, p. 73.

51 Leach, *Charge*, pp. 117–23, 138–42, 189–95.

52 Eeva John, Naomi Nixon and Nick Shepherd, 'Life-changing learning for Christian discipleship and ministry: a practical exploration', *Practical Theology* 11.4 (2018), pp. 300–14.

53 'Forum: transformational learning in theological schools', *Practical Theology* 11.4 (2018), pp. 315–19.

54 *Ministry in the Church in Wales: A Position Paper by the Bench of Bishops,* Cardiff: Church in Wales, 2013.

55 I am grateful to Manon Ceridwen James, Richard Hainsworth's successor, for her advice in writing this section.

56 Volume 36, edition 2, available from: https://churchmissionsociety.org/wp-content/uploads/2020/07/Anvil-Volume-36_Issue-2-FINAL-VERSION.pdf.

57 René August on p. 36.

58 Anna Ruddick on p. 31.

59 'J' on p. 28.

60 Jonny Baker and Cathy Ross on p. 27.

61 Mark Johnston on p. 46.

62 Jonny Baker and Cathy Ross on p. 24.

4

A Different World

What might the new paradigm look like in practice? It is not easy to say. To embark on a process of adaptive change such as a change of paradigm requires is to undertake a journey into the unknown. Moreover, adaptive change requires the wisdom of a whole community and no single voice can be expected to provide all the insight required. Nevertheless, without some concrete sense of what might be involved in a whole new way of teaching and learning for life-long ministerial formation, the new paradigm remains a set of abstract principles. Since 'operative' knowledge is practical and situational, some account of how the new situation might take shape is important.

There is another vitally important caveat. Ministerial formation is only one part of a wider system: the church's whole approach to mission and ministry embedded in its structures of ministry and governance. The new paradigm will only take root as part of 'whole system change', which requires a renewed theology of mission, church and ministry as well as for ministerial training. In the case of the Church of England, the 'system' is at present an extremely anxious one, dominated by the fear of declining numbers and influence. Within this anxious system, clergy play the role of the 'designated patient': 'a lightning rod for the negative energy of the system'.[1] There is thus a great temptation to assume that 'fixing' the training of the clergy will fix the system. In contrast, I have tried to show, and this chapter assumes, that the Church will only be renewed by a deep-rooted and thoroughgoing change to its whole approach to ministry.

The chapter takes the form of a retrospect from a point of view some 20 years from the writing of the book. The reader is invited to dream with me.

As I look back, on this last day of the year 2040, I can only offer profound thanks to God for the transformation that has taken place in the life of the church over the past 50 to 60 years. Back then, in the mid-1980s, it was rare to read of a new church opening. Now, for the past ten years or more, on average at least one new church has been opening every day somewhere in the country. Then the churchgoing population was ageing; church closures were already taking place and the pace was beginning to accelerate. Now, with our younger demographic and the decline in the number of children and young people in our churches reversed, there is genuine hope for the future.

Not only is the Church growing, but we are beginning to have an impact on society. Even the media are beginning to sit up and take notice. Until well into this century it was rare for any story about the Church of England not to include a routine passage about the Church's decline. Now the story is about the Church as a force for good. Compassion and care for neighbours are becoming fashionable. No longer do politicians proudly proclaim that they 'don't do God'. Instead, the possibility of God is a factor in the 'public square'.

How has this taken place? Of course, it is a move of God's Holy Spirit. Without the Spirit's sovereign influence nothing could have changed. However, as we are now more aware than ever, God calls us to cooperate with the Spirit as partners in his mission. Our prayers and obedience play a vital role. More than that, it is about the Church's corporate heart and vision. To my mind, it is possible to sum up the difference in the word 'repentance': repentance as recognition and turning from the errors of the past and repentance as a change of mindset, a new vision of God and his will for the church. Peter Senge writes that 'metanoia' or 'shift of mind' is what it takes to change a system, and system change is what the Church of 50 years ago desperately needed.[2]

The bishops' call to repentance of 2023 was undoubtedly a milestone. In the light of the work on 'Setting God's People Free', it was becoming clear that clericalism was not just an unfortunate habit of thought but a sinful mindset embedded in every part of the Church's structures, affecting clergy and laity alike. We needed to name our tendency consistently to privilege the ministry of the clergy over that of the whole church and express publicly our determination to turn away from clericalism in all its forms.

Stephen Covey writes of the need to balance attention to 'P' with 'PC', production with productive capacity.[3] In our case, we needed to balance the energy we put into 'mission' with resources devoted to increasing our 'mission capacity'. We needed measures to promote generous giving and smarter fundraising. We needed to invest in parish administrators to free the clergy from the increasing burden of administration that began to surround all charities in the early years of the century. Above all, we needed to invest in discipleship and training for the whole church and to ensure that training was effective not only in equipping God's people with skills for mission, but in enabling that deep reliance on God, in the words of John's Gospel that 'abiding in Christ' without which we could accomplish nothing.

Changing a whole system is no easy task. If you try to change one part of the system in isolation, the rest of the system will frustrate the change.[4] Only a change to the whole system at once will succeed. Since the heart of any system is the shared assumptions on which it is based, change could only take place by consistently applying a new way of thinking to each element: patterns of mission, ministry, training, selection, governance, finance and administration. Thankfully, circumstances combined in our diocese to allow us to pioneer a series of changes all based on a consistent vision of mission, ministry and training, which, when supported by the diocesan administration, its bishops and elected bodies, proved a catalyst to changes already under way in the national Church and so contributed to the new life and growth we are at last beginning to see and rejoice in.

Local training for local ministry

Although we were seeing an encouraging number of candidates for licensed lay ministry on our diocesan School of Mission, we were aware of a call from churches throughout the diocese for a more flexible and locally accessible pattern of training. Combined with the impetus from the work on 'Setting God's People Free', this led us to consider a pattern of training to resource lay people for the practice of everyday faith and equip them for ministry in their local churches and communities. The framework we eventually adopted had several complementary elements:

- A network of encouragers to facilitate Personal Discipleship Plans.
- A network of local trainers in deaneries, towns and cities.
- A 'just-in-time' approach to training, in which small groups and learning communities came together to train and encourage each other for the ministry in which they were already engaged.
- A shared outline for the people skills, theological themes, biblical understanding and spiritual practices that formed the core of the training.
- The flexibility to use resources that best suited the context, whether from the diocese or parachurch organizations.

REIMAGINING MINISTERIAL FORMATION

- A blended learning approach, in which online resources from the diocese or other providers combined with small group learning in the
localities.
- As part of their ongoing learning, all newly ordained ministers received
training in the skills of adult education and were encouraged to develop
an orientation to equipping others for ministry through leading SHAPE
courses,[5] catechesis or basic Christian nurture, and theological reflection
groups.

With the diocese acting to ensure good communication, equip the local
trainers and provide resources for learning, the outcome was a gradual
change in culture. Local churches gained the confidence to take responsibility for their own training needs, in response to God's call to mission
in their own contexts and the gifts and passions of their members. As the
churches became increasingly equipped to respond, so the invitations and
opportunities for mission began to arise. Not only were local churches
becoming increasingly influential in their communities, but the trend of
church leaving began to be reversed. The many mature Christians previously frustrated at their churches' lack of vision and courage began to
find avenues for fruitful service without having to leave the church to do
so.[6]

Ministerial Development Review

Ministerial Development Review (MDR) requires every lay minister and
member of the clergy to review their ministry at regular intervals. But
what model of ministry will the preparation material and subsequent
interviews take for granted: the traditional clergy-centred sole practitioner
model or the model of clergy as animators of the ministry of the whole
church? A review of MDR in the diocese provided the opportunity
radically to reshape the process so that the preparation material required
each member of the clergy to review the ministry of the whole church and
their place within it.

Moreover, our bishop was clear that the review should be develop-
mental, so that the objectives set for each review cycle would be learning
objectives rather than ministry objectives. Through the preparation material and the development interview, clergy would be helped to consider
the learning and development they would need to fulfil their role in the
church's mission.

Once the new shape of clergy MDR was well-established, we started to think about how to bring licensed lay ministry into alignment. The preparation material was revised to help lay ministers to think about their place in the team and their role as teachers of the faith, enablers of everyday faith and representatives of Christ in the community.[7]

As with the local ministry initiative, the result was a gradual change in culture, as clergy and lay ministers were helped to rethink their role and to recognize ministerial development as an aspect of life-long learning.

Reimagining ministry

As we know, the encouraging upturn in the number of ordinands following Resourcing Ministerial Education[8] began to stall in the early 2020s. The well of potential vocations to ordained ministry waiting to be tapped by the effort and energy expended in the early days began to run dry. Throughout the Church, the question that had been put off by the initial success of RME now had to be faced. Was the challenge insufficient clergy to fulfil the Church's mission? Or was it that our understanding and approach to ministry was over-reliant on the clergy? Belatedly, it was realized that the real problem, to which we should have given priority all along, was the second of these. At a conference I attended in 2018, a diocesan bishop declared that reimagining ministry could not take place in the southern dioceses because people were not ready for it. In the prosperous south, the church continued to survive despite the decline in clergy numbers. The closure of churches due to Covid-19 in 2020 put paid to such complacency. A few years later, I was glad to hear that same bishop concede that a process of adaptive change, such as reimagining ministry, requires leaders to *create and manage* the disequilibrium needed for change.[9]

In our diocese, it was a crisis that led to the decisive step forward. In one of our episcopal areas, more than 20 parishes fell vacant within a short space of time. People began to realize that even in the south of England, the days of readily available clergy were coming to an end. The prospect of some vacancies lasting for a considerable time led to a recognition of the need for a strategic approach to pastoral reorganization. The diocesan leadership was courageous enough to base its approach on local rather than full-time stipendiary ministry. Instead of asking how to reallocate parishes between the declining number of stipendiary clergy, the diocese began to base its pastoral reorganization initiatives around the question as to how local ministries could be raised up and overseen.

After a great deal of consultation, ministry areas entrusted to a minister with oversight and led by collaborative ministry teams of local lay and ordained ministers began to be formed. The teams were given the task of discerning together the shape of God's mission in each of the localities and networks of the ministry area and promoting cooperation between the churches in each locality, each helping the others to fulfil their God-given callings.[10]

Along with the move to ministry areas, the diocese recognized the need for effective administrative support for the ministry teams. Some areas agreed to forgo the attempt to recruit further clergy in favour of recruiting an administrator to facilitate communication and free the other members of the team for their function. In others, the diocese agreed to match-fund bids for administrative support from its Growth Fund, recognizing its vital contribution to mission. As ministry areas have developed, it has become normal for them to include lay people in full-time stipendiary posts: administrators, church planters, children and families workers, schools workers, community organizers, chaplains, and a host of other specialist ministries have taken their place alongside the clergy. Most ministry areas either run their own local learning hub, or are linked to a neighbouring hub, sometimes run by a 'resourcing church', through which ongoing formation for discipleship and mission is easily accessible. Most significant of all, at Synods and in diocesan communications, the word 'ministry' now routinely means the ministry of the whole church rather than that of the clergy alone. Our underlying mindset and, with it, our language has changed.

Clergy as supervised overseers

In partnership with neighbouring dioceses, we were already providing residential consultations at key stages of ministerial development: for new incumbents, change of posts, area deans, the need to refocus in mid-ministry and preparation for retirement. However, we realized that another important transition was less well covered: the transition to a ministry of oversight. Incumbents in multi-parish benefices, team rectors and vicars of larger churches increasingly require the skills and dispositions to create and maintain ministry teams and to oversee the ministry of others.

From the early 2020s, we developed a programme of leadership training with three strands:

- It provided the hard skills required by clergy and lay leaders in these situations, such as team building and team leadership, volunteer management, leadership development, coaching and conflict mediation.
- Second, the programme placed these firmly in a framework of key theological themes including the Trinity and the mission of God, the relational nature of human beings, the local church as the people of God, Jesus as image of God, atonement and resurrection, the kingdom of God and the Servant of the Lord as a model for ministry.
- Finally, the programme aimed to equip church leaders to grow in their personal relationship with God and the ability to manage their lives and vocations through 'watching over themselves'.

The roll-out of supervision, providing the high-quality support they had previously been lacking, further reinforced the gradual change of culture. The affirmation they lost through the step away from pastoral ministry into an oversight role was now provided more reliably and in a more focussed way through regular supervision. With decreasing dependence on the expectations of their congregations and the gradual acceptance of a culture in which they were required regularly to pause and reflect on their ministry, clergy began to resist the pressure to overwork with enormous benefits to their health and well-being.

Increasingly, clergy and lay church leaders found themselves able to give more time to 'prayer and the ministry of the Word' (Acts 6.4, NIV) as the local training initiative provided more church members with the vision, understanding and skills required for ministry.

Reconfiguring curacy

The 'Report on Good Practice in the Appointment and Training of Training Incumbents' of 2014 had already raised most of the issues we had to face surrounding the place of curacy in the emerging shape of ministry and ministerial formation.[11] The existence of a leadership programme training clergy and lay leaders for a ministry of oversight meant that it soon became possible to assume that all potential training incumbents would be engaged in this training and to allocate curates accordingly. The development of flexible local training for recognized ministry meant that all newly licensed and ordained ministers could expect to work alongside lay people exercising a diverse range of specialist ministries. Together, these began to provide the opportunity for curates to experience a wide variety of ministry situations, further explore their own specialist gifts, play their part in training and equipping others and learn the ministry of oversight from their training incumbents. The relationship between curate and training incumbent moved from 'master' and 'apprentice' to the training incumbent as supervising minister and coordinator of a variety of training opportunities, both within and beyond the training parish or ministry area.

The School for Mission

The diocese's ministerial training scheme initially arose as a development from locally based training and was well placed to respond to its further extension. Theological educators based in the diocese played a leading role in resourcing the network of local trainers and providing web-based materials for local training groups.

Nevertheless, the growth of locally trained ministers required the School for Mission to adapt to new circumstances. There was now a threefold pattern of locally trained and recognized ministry; diocesan trained and episcopally authorized ministries, including authorized preacher, eucharistic minister and funeral minister; and diocesan trained licensed lay and ordained ministry. With more and more people experiencing a pattern of locally based 'just-in-time' training in which ministry and training were thoroughly integrated, the School for Mission had to follow suit. Training for licensed lay and ordained ministry became fully contextual, with congregations as learning communities and supervising ministers playing key roles in the training.

The stage was set for experimentation with a variety of forms of learning. Blended learning, combining web-based material with local groups was a relatively easy starting point. Group learning, in which groups of trainee ministers engaged in shared tasks based in their different contexts was a logical next step. Integrated modules emerged naturally from group learning, providing a framework within which learners could bring together their knowledge of the Bible and theological tradition with a range of other disciplines to analyse and reflect on a ministry context. Finally, we took the plunge into enquiry-based learning, with the aim of helping learners to become self-directed explorers, capable of reflecting theologically on their everyday as well as ministry experience and equipped for life-long learning and development. The results were even more encouraging than we had expected. Through engagement with the basic questions 'What do I know?', 'What do I need to know?' and 'How will I find out?' members of the collaborative study groups were able effectively to integrate their 'ordinary' theology with life, ministry and new theological learning while at the same time training themselves to become life-long learners.

Integration with locally based learning also resulted in a lengthening of the timescale. The distinction between initial training and continuing development gradually broke down as learners grew familiar with 'on-the-job' training and the disciplines of reflective practice. For most learners, the pattern of 'initial training' began to conform to that of continuing development, with periods of involvement in intentional learning alternating with periods in which they continued to learn through reflection and supervision in their localities rather than through formal courses or group projects. On the one hand, the flexibility required to allow learners to progress at their own pace caused administrative headaches for the training team, but on the other it almost entirely removed the stress on families associated with a pattern of 'initial training', in which everything deemed necessary for ministry had to be crammed into two or three years.

These developments, as well as the roll-out of the new framework for formation qualities in the early 2020s, necessitated a flexible and creative approach to assessment. The training team adopted a range of creative assessment methods, including assessed conversation, presentations and group projects, for most modules. This made it much easier to devise assignments arising from practice and requiring shared reflection in the ministry context, thus effectively integrating theology with practice. With assessment arising naturally from their ministry contexts, it became less onerous for candidates. It provided space for personal reflection through which it is possible to assess reflexivity and disposition. It meant that facility in abstract reasoning became less important as a factor in assessment while practical skills and fruitfulness in ministry gained greater salience.

Another potential headache, but in fact a source of great joy, was the massive increase in the number of people in training. Some had feared that the availability of local training would lead to a decrease in the number of people offering for licensed and ordained ministry. As it turned out, familiarity with a flexible and contextually appropriate training environment helped to reduce the fears associated with training. The excitement of ministry, the joy of being enabled to connect everyday life with Christian faith, the discovery of God-given vocation and the love of learning encouraged more and more to offer for licensed ministry. Throughout the diocese it became the norm for a small team of full- or part-time lay and ordained ministers to co-ordinate the efforts of a much larger team of volunteers, each engaged in a specialist ministry of one kind or another. Local ministry was now visibly and in experience the standard form of ministry, with ordained ministers the supervisors and 'spiritual leaders' of ministry increasingly co-ordinated by lay volunteers.[12]

Moreover, because of the increasing number of stipendiary clergy trained in oversight and supervision, it became much easier for people to grow from locally recognized ministry through contextually based training for ordination and into curacy without the severe disruption to marriage and family life caused by continual changes in context. More and more clergy could be expected to be competent to act as supervisors and training incumbents. Continuity between context-based training and curacy became the norm, though the distinction between the two is now so blurred as to be almost non-existent, while the use of short- and longer-term placements ensured that those going on to stipendiary and incumbent-focussed ministry continued to benefit from a range of challenging ministry contexts. The pattern of assessment through reflective practice assignments also continued from 'initial' training into curacy, with the addition in curacy that most modules also require the candidate to teach or equip the ministry of others.

'Initial training' in the life-long learning model

As a populous and relatively resource-rich diocese, ours was well placed to influence progress in the national Church. As it turned out, however, little overt influence was required. The changes we had worked on were part of a larger move of the Spirit. In several areas, other dioceses were moving ahead of us. More and more people involved in initial training began to realize that the most vexing questions in fact arose from the limitations of the traditional model and disappeared with the adoption of the new paradigm. The problem of 'IME 0' – what candidates need to know before beginning 'IME 1'[13] – answered itself as more and more dioceses put in place schemes to equip the laity for the practice of every-day faith and local ministry. More and more candidates began to enter initial training with a basic grounding in biblical and theological knowledge, familiar with ministry in a variety of contexts and with experiential learning methods.

By the mid-2020s it became possible for the Ministry Team to allow a longer period for 'initial' training. The limitations of front-end-loaded 'just-in-case' training even for younger candidates in residential training became ever more apparent, especially when compared to the outcome of context-based training where a longer timescale had been allowed for. Moreover, as the expectation of continuing life-long learning and development became more widely accepted, the 'problem' of what to include in the initial two or three years similarly disappeared. Specific content became much less important than the development of theological curiosity, the ability to bring theology to bear on situations in life and ministry and the development of 'pastoral imagination' and 'practical wisdom'. It was not that training became watered down; but that it ceased to be a pre-packaged curriculum and became a journey of exploration. 'Initial training' had become one step in a journey of life-long learning.

Common Awards

All this was greatly helped by the guidance and encouragement of the Common Awards staff at Durham University. Moreover, with the Churches' ministerial candidates forming one of their largest and most committed cohorts, the university could easily see the advantages of flexibility. Unsurprisingly, with academics trained in rigorous patterns of thought, each new development had to be justified in detail and argued with patience and persistence. It took time, but eventually all the most important developments were agreed:

- A relaxation of the timescales allowed for the completion of each formational level (what we used to call 'academic' level, the change of name following the integration of cognitive with affective and dispositional learning outcomes).
- Inclusion of cognitive ability, emotional intelligence and dispositions in the generic grade descriptors for each level of the qualifications in Theology, Mission and Ministry and in the learning outcomes for each individual module.
- The appropriate weighting of practice, reflection and reflexivity in assignments.

One of the disappointments at the outset of the Common Awards had been the reluctance of theological educators to try their hands at designing integrated modules. Trained in their specialist disciplines, it appeared there was not the confidence to venture outside these areas of expertise.

However, with the increasing prevalence of experiential learning methods and context-based training came the confidence to design integrated modules. By the late 2020s it became possible to attempt a complete MA through group learning using modules that integrated a range of disciplines, theology and reflective practice, and theological understanding with growth in maturity, character and spirituality. Assessment for 'wisdom and godly habit of life' was becoming a reality.

Theological Education Institutions (TEIs)

Residential training for ordained ministry emerged in the mid-nineteenth century as an integral element in the professionalization of the ministry. To have undergone a period of initial training helped to cement the status of the minister as a member of the upper middle class. It was also a means to the 'formation of Clerical character', as the original rules of Cuddesdon College, still displayed on the library wall, put it. Young men went to college to be socialized into the newly emerging clerical mentality and manner of life.

Despite its commitment to residential training and the enormous expense it requires, 'The rationale of theological education in the Church of England has never been made explicit.'[14] Despite the fact that for many older clergy, including many bishops, a period of residential training constituted a kind of 'gold standard' for ministerial formation, there has never at any time been agreement as to precisely what should be studied during this period in order to form the candidate for ministry. Diocese by diocese, as more forward-thinking bishops and Directors of Ordinands sought to implement the new paradigm of ministerial formation, life-long learning, often in context, became the standard pattern for formation. Already under pressure to justify the extra cost of residence, the colleges found it difficult to sustain their place in the emerging scheme of things.

Their survival depended on successfully adapting to a new role. As the life-long learning model of formation became the standard pattern, not only was licensing and ordination decoupled from academic qualification but the boundary between 'initial training' and 'continuing development' increasingly lost its relevance. Candidates were licensed and ordained at the bishops' discretion with the firm expectation that training would continue rather than cease. Residentials and training days designed to address challenges currently being faced by the learners, which had previously been the pattern of 'Continuing Ministerial Development' (CMD), became the norm for both initial and continuing training.

In place of continuous training with a termly pattern, most TEIs began to adopt a pattern of online and blended learning through a mixture of training days, weekend and week-long study units, residential courses and summer schools, allowing candidates to pursue tailor-made courses at their own pace. A weekend or longer period given over to the study of a biblical book or theme, wrestling with the theology of the Trinity, experimenting with creative approaches to liturgy or working towards a deeper understanding of bereavement while engaging with colleagues from across a region regularly provided both refreshing time away from the daily challenges of ministry for candidates and licensed ministers alike and challenging learning to take back into the ministry context. Alongside these, clergy and others with specialist skills and interests regularly contribute to TEI training programmes and TEI staff members travel to take training days and evening courses to the localities, or to train and mentor the many part-time and volunteer tutors throughout the region in good adult education practice.

Not all TEIs found the transition easy. Some, either wedded to a specific theological tradition or taking their stand on traditional academic pedagogy, resisted and a small number of colleges inevitably closed. But others successfully adapted, and some were even newly founded as regional training centres. There proved still to be a place for the small number of, mainly younger, candidates for whom continuous residence proved a necessity, following an accelerated pattern of training interspersed with immersive placements. But most colleges were able to adapt their business models, letting their rooms for bed and breakfast whenever courses were not in session and even making what had previously been student accommodation available as affordable housing.

The use of college buildings as regional centres complementing the pattern of dispersed blended learning has allowed a reduction in the number of TEIs even while the numbers in training have continued to rise. TEI staffs have thus increased in number, strengthening still further the diversity and interchange between theological educators. Since each staff member is now required to hold or be working towards a qualification in experiential learning, the focus in TEIs has shifted from academic specialization to innovative and creative ways of making the Church's traditions of theology, spirituality and ministerial practice available to candidates to support them in ministry. The collegiality of larger TEI staffs, the majority of whom are now experienced practitioners as well as scholars, has provided an immense boost to their research potential. As theology in the universities continues to atrophy, theology in the TEIs has gained a new lease of life. Working in an ecclesial rather than academic context, the Churches' theologians can begin to work together to unpick the errors of the past while engaging creatively with the challenges of the present and future.

With returning confidence, we now find ourselves in a position to play a role in the rescue of the universities. The Common Awards cohort now models what every university is coming to realize that it needs: communities of learning committed to a shared task; mutuality and collegiality in shared learning and research; a rich and diverse tradition of learning and practice on which to draw for guidance and inspiration; and an approach to learning that marries interpersonal skills and character development with scholarly rigour.

The Servant of the Lord

By freeing itself from the academic tradition, the Church and its TEIs have become a 'light to the nations'. As a result of the renewal of ministerial formation, articulate Christians equipped for everyday faith and ministry are found in virtually every area of the nation's life, from the cabinet table to the outer urban estates where those who suffered most from the economic collapse of 2020–21 are to be found, working for the coming of God's kingdom in the power of the Holy Spirit.

The journey of the past 50 years, from a declining Church hampered by the professional model of ministry and ministerial formation, over-reliant on an increasingly over-burdened clergy, to a Church in which every member is enabled to serve, confident in its mission and humble in its engagement with society, has not been an easy one. There has been fierce opposition from within, especially from scholars wedded to the various traditions of theology to have emerged from modernism and clergy fearful of stepping outside the safety of their familiar church traditions. There has been opposition from without, especially from those threatened by the church's growth in numbers and increasing influence in society.

Moreover, the journey is still fragile. Just as the move of what we used to call 'fresh expressions' of church to the mainstream took time and suffered from lack of comprehension in the traditional church, so there are many whose understanding of ministry and ministerial formation is still instinctively clericalist and academic and who see the profound changes that have taken place as merely cosmetic.

However, the momentum is undeniable. Clergy and laity in a variety of ministries are not only being trained but assessed for 'wisdom and godly habit of life'. Through their influence, the Church is increasingly marked by confidence and humility, love and compassion, patience and resilience. More and more, its ministry manifests the church's essential nature as *koinonia*, called to friendship with God and one another in the service of a common task. The commitment to life-long experiential learning within a diverse and collaborative Church is bearing fruit.

Notes

1 Nigel Rooms and Patrick Keifert, *Spiritual Leadership in the Missional Church*, Cambridge: Grove, 2019, p. 6. Rooms and Keifert are drawing on family systems theory and cite Edwin Friedman, *Generation to Generation: Family Process in Church and Synagogue*, New York: Guilford, 1985.

2 Peter Senge, *The Fifth Discipline*, London: Random House, revised edition 2006, pp. 13–14, 163–252, 283–316.

3 Stephen Covey, *The Seven Habits of Highly Effective People*, London: Simon and Schuster, 1992, pp. 52–64.

4 Senge, *Fifth Discipline*, pp. 83–8.

5 See https://arthurrankcentre.org.uk/church-life/your-shape-for-gods-service-2/.

6 Steve Aisthorpe has interviewed more than 800 Scottish Christians who have left their churches, many after long periods during which they were among those most active in the churches' life. In more than half of the accounts, 'a sense of commitment to God's mission was prominent'. He found a significant number of people who had left precisely because they saw their churches as blind to the opportunities for mission on their doorstep. Aisthorpe, *The Invisible Church*, Edinburgh, St Andrew Press, 2016, pp. 167–84.

7 See 'Book Review: Resourcing Sunday to Saturday Faith', the renewed vision of the Central Readers Council of the Church of England and the Church in Wales, https://transformingministry.co.uk/2019/12/11/resourcing-sunday-to-satur day-faith/ accessed 11 December 2020.

8 In 2015, General Synod Paper 1979, 'Resourcing Ministerial Education in the Church of England', recommended the Church to aim at a 50% increase in the number of ordinands over the level in 2013. It also recommended 'a rapid development of lay ministries' but 11 of its 12 recommendations were about ordained ministry and in contrast to the focus on vocations to the ordained ministry, which received enormous resources of time and money, the recommendation about lay ministry received virtually none. Report available from www.churchofengland.org/sites/default/files/2017-12/gs%201979%20-%20resourcing%20ministerial%20 education%20task%20group%20report.pdf accessed 11 December 2020.

9 See Ron Heifetz, *Leadership without Easy Answers*, Cambridge, MA: Har-

vard University Press, 1994; and Ronald Heifetz, Alexander Grashow and Marty Linsky, *The Practice of Adaptive Leadership*, Boston, MA: Harvard Business Press, 2009.

10 Martyn Snow, *Mission Partnerships: Churches Working Together in Mission*, Cambridge: Grove P133, 2013. Snow sets out four possible shapes of inter-change working undergirded by a theology of partnership.

11 See Appendix 1.

12 The reference to 'spiritual leaders' is intended to point to the similarity between the role of ordained leaders in the Partnership for Missional Church process and the ministry of oversight described here and in Chapter 3. See https://churchmission society.org/churches/partnership-missional-church/ accessed 11 December 2020.

13 In the Church of England, 'IME 1' stands for Initial Ministerial Education Phase 1 and refers to the training of ordinands and candidates for licensed lay ministry. 'IME 0' is not a training programme: it refers to the question, irresolvable under the old paradigm, as to what knowledge, skills and experience candidates need to bring with them to initial training.

14 ACCM Occasional Paper 22, 'Education for the Church's Ministry: The Report of the Working Party on Assessment', 1987, §21.

Appendix 1
Questions and Considerations
for the Future

[The Appendix to the original version of the 'Report on Good Practice in the Appointment and Training of Training Incumbents', Archbishops' Council, 2014.]

In producing this report, the working group has been acutely aware of a wider context that raises a number of issues, theological, educational and practical, that should be actively monitored and considered further over the next five years.

- The actual practice of ministry curates can expect to observe in their supervising ministers is becoming increasingly *varied and unpredictable*.
- The use and meaning of *episcope* in the context of parish ministry is still emerging but is widely recognized as important in future patterns of ministry. New models of ministry, with fewer full-time clergy, will require new ways of working.
- The experience of curates in *contexts other than traditional parish ministry*, e.g. pioneers and chaplains, is a developing area of practice that is not yet fully understood.
- The experience and training required to enable the *transition from assistant to incumbent status ministry by curates* who may have had a limited self-supporting curacy, undertaken alongside a secular post, needs further consideration.

The nature of the local church

1 The first set of questions has to do with *locality* and emerges from the context in which the title post is located. The traditional single parish benefice is becoming increasingly rare. Recent years have seen increasing numbers of multi-parish benefices and some dioceses are grouping parishes into mission communities, beginning to experiment with minster models or placing greater emphasis on the deanery. These moves result in both practical challenges, e.g. the availability of curate housing stock, to more profound questions about the required flexibility in the way the clergy carry out their ministry. Increasingly clergy are required to be familiar with team working and to be able to animate and supervise the ministry of lay people in a variety of roles. This means that the actual practice of ministry curates can expect to observe in their supervising ministers is becoming increasingly varied and unpredictable.

2 Whilst recognising this complexity we also recognise the importance of place and belonging in the training of public ministers: churches are communities, located in specific places. The curacy enables the immersion of a new minister over a reasonable length of time in the faith-community, in its context. This is about learning to understand that context, the ministry and mission of the Church in relation to it, and about the time it takes to develop meaningful relationships within the worshipping congregation and local community. This location over time remains essential to any genuine experience of and training for public ordained ministry. If other approaches to training are used to supplement this, e.g. placements or some other elements of wider deployment, there still needs to be this core working in a specific location for the bulk of the curacy.

Developing models of parish ministry

3 A second, overlapping set of issues surrounds *models of ministry*, specifically the degree and type of collaboration to which the minister in training is likely to be exposed. Depending on their circumstances, a training incumbent may already occupy a supervisory role in relation to lay ministers, youth workers, parish administrator and music director. In addition, he or she may be concerned to resource and enable the ministry of members of the congregation in their places of life and

work. In contexts where the supervising minister works across several congregations he or she may be seeking to animate the ministry of a local minister or local ministry team for each congregation. Alternatively, he or she may, by temperament and training or because of the expectations of the churches, be attempting to play a more traditional clergy role, but in multiple congregations. The choices the minister makes in this increasingly common situation will in turn affect the degree to which the curate under their supervision is provided with experience in animating and supervising the ministry of others.

4 The desirability of the relationship between curate and supervising minister being located in the broader context of collaborative ministry opens up a further question of the meaning of *episcope* in the context of parish ministry. Although the *episcope* of the minister in the local church is recognised in the Hind Report (4.12) and this recognition is becoming increasingly common in the literature, the Church has no common definition or understanding of *episcope* in this context, especially in relation to parish ministry. In view of developments on the ground, this would seem to be an urgent piece of theological work. In the context of the training of training incumbents, the fact that both 'supervision' and 'oversight' share the same derivation may provide some help in approaching this task.

Developing ministries

5 Further questions arise from the experience of trainee ministers in *contexts other than traditional parish ministry*. In relation to ordained pioneer ministers, research by Beth Keith of the Church Army demonstrates a significant difference in the experience of those ministers expected to find support and supervision within existing 'modal' church structures and those working outside existing church structures, developing new ways of being church within specific communities or contexts and connected to a 'sodal' organisation such as the Church Army or CMS. Specifically, when based in a traditional parish context and supervised by clergy without experience of pioneer ministry, pioneer ministers frequently lack the support required to help them to imagine the way Christian community and eventually worship might be expressed in a particular culture (other than the supervising minister's).

6 Despite its considerably longer history than pioneer ministry, the

issues surrounding the supervision of trainee ministers in the context of chaplaincy are, if anything, less well understood. Alongside those contexts with clear institutional requirements for chaplains, such as the NHS, the Armed Forces and the prison services, are the many less formal contexts in which chaplaincy is offered: nursing and care homes, schools, town centres, local authorities, sporting venues and many others. Since a great deal of this more informal chaplaincy ministry is undertaken by parochially based clergy, it is increasingly likely that a curate in training will have some exposure to it, but precisely how likely this is and what differences exist between parishes remains, as yet, unresearched. There may be important parallels with the experience of pioneer ministers. Uncertainty over the extent to which trainee clergy can be expected to be equipped for chaplaincy roles thus poses important questions.

Assumptions about ministry and training

7 These questions and areas of uncertainty emerging from the need to specify good practice in the training of supervising clergy clearly point to the need to address the Church's implicit assumptions about ministry and training. Some of these inherited working assumptions, such as that each curate will be attached to a training incumbent based in a single parish and operating in a way that is broadly comparable with all other training incumbents, can already clearly be seen to be erroneous and in need of revision. Similarly, the idea that a suitable training incumbent or housing will be available when and where needed. What follows is an attempt to articulate some of these basic assumptions and suggest alternatives.

The 'general practitioner' model of ministry

8 One set of assumptions seems to come together in what might be called the 'general practitioner' model of parish ministry. In this model, ministry is based in a given location, and it devolves on a single, professionally trained individual, who may or may not be assisted by a variety of lay ministries but is ultimately responsible for all the leadership, pastoral care, teaching, leadership of worship, occasional offices, evangelism and administration that is required, as well as much else

besides. Ideally, this minister will be full-time and stipendiary, and every other form of ministry – lay ministry, self-supporting ordained ministry, pioneer ministry and so on – are seen by extension as auxiliary optional extras. Selection and training for ordained ministry are carried out on the assumption that this 'one-size-fits-all' model is the standard form of ordained ministry from which every other form is a deviation.

Ministry – collaborative in essence

9 In contrast, experience on the ground clearly points to the need to reimagine ministry as *diverse and collaborative* in its very essence. Such a concept of ministry goes far deeper than merely providing the ordained minister with auxiliary help of various kinds. It sees ministry arising from the common life of the church in a given location or network. It sees ministry as belonging to the whole church and the essential role of the ordained as animating and in turn being animated by the ministry of the whole. It sees ministry as infinitely diverse, flowing from the variety of humanity and the diverse gifts bestowed by Christ on the church through the Holy Spirit. In this model 'ministry' is the church's participation in the mission of God and the church, in the words of Lesslie Newbigin, the 'foretaste, sign and agent' of God's kingdom.

Ministry – local and contextual

10 Moreover, since the mission of God is by its very nature incarnational and therefore local and contextual, *ministry is essentially local and contextual*. That is to say, the 'standard' form of ministry is not a general practitioner who has a wide range of skills to do everything but the local minister sufficiently skilled and broadly experienced to enable others. Full-time stipendiary ministry emerges from the local not in order to take it over but to resource and equip the local and to help provide that essential connection to the wider church. This ministry of resourcing, equipping, guiding and overseeing is, moreover, best approached collaboratively, since no one person can expect to have all the gifts and human capacity necessary for such a demanding task. Ministry is also essentially relational as arising out

of and being part of Christian community. For this reason, secular management models based upon efficiency of task performance will not fully translate to ministry.

Ministry – life-long learning

11 A further set of assumptions, arising from the general practitioner model, surround training for ministry. The Church's inherited focus on initial training originated in the nineteenth century; it not only reflected the aspiration of clergy to professional status but played a key role in securing it. The outcome of this focus has been investment in high-quality and high cost initial training, and this investment has, until recently, carried with it the assumption that every other aspect of training for ministry is auxiliary and even optional. In contrast, we are coming increasingly to recognise that *we live in an age of life-long learning* in which continuing ministerial development is of equal importance with initial training.

Risks associated with the present model

12 This questioning of assumptions raises questions about the dominant model of ministry to which the trainee minister is to be exposed: inherited 'general practitioner' or mission-focussed and collaborative; about the most appropriate contexts for training: a single parish or benefice or a wider grouping of churches and parishes; about the selection of supervising ministers, the extent to which they require proven collaborative experience; and about their training, whether this is to focus narrowly on the relationship between incumbent and curate or take account of the wider context in which both incumbent and curate act as animators of the ministry of the whole church. It also prompts the question as to whether our current model for IME 4–7 is overly dependent on the role of the training incumbent: whether the advantages when the relationship is good are outweighed by the potentially disastrous outcome for the curate at a crucial stage of ministry when it is not (although it is important that the training model is not driven by a failure to exercise proper control or the failure to deliver adequate training). A model of ministry and train-ing based on diversity and collaboration and envisaged as part of

life-long learning might place the supervising minister in a somewhat different role, as co-ordinator of the input available from a variety of sources rather than as 'master' to an 'apprentice'. However, this model should not be considered at the expense of training in episcope or in a way that effectively reduces IME 4–7 to a number of consecutive or concurrent placements.

13 In relation to pioneer ministry, a focus on local contextual ministry rather than a parish-based general practitioner model may allow the Church to view pioneer ministers in the way they ask, namely as a unique gift to the Church: one of a rich variety of ministries rather than a deviation from the norm. This further allows the Church to view contextually based training, as recommended by *Mission-shaped Church*, rather than residential training as the norm even for those under 32 and the mission community rather than parish as appropriate support structure. It may also be that some such sodality might prove appropriate for the support and supervision of trainee ministers in chaplaincy situations. However, we must be clear about what we are doing. If we are creating specific training contexts we should understand that we are training 'pioneers' or 'chaplains' and not 'incumbents', any subsequent desire for transition should recognise this through clear selection and training.

Not just clergy

14 Many of the questions surrounding the facilitation of the training and formation of self-supporting and pioneer ministers apply equally to formation for Reader ministry, both in the IME and CMD stages. Whilst the approach to Reader training is determined at diocesan level, generally speaking the inherited focus makes heavy use of a dispersed 'apprenticeship model', particularly for ministerial and spiritual formation. Funding and geographical constraints, work and family commitments make it, in many cases, impossible for this to be undertaken anywhere other than the 'home' parish or benefice for the vast majority of the time. By default, therefore, training is contextually based, often without conscious assessment of the suitability of the context in question. Whilst considerable emphasis has been given to the curate/training incumbent relationship and to their needs and expectations less attention has been paid to the Reader/training facilitator relationship and training expectations, or to the need to

assess the gifts of and to equip those tasked with supervising and supporting a Reader in their developing ministry, pre and post licensing. Many of the questions which arise mirror the wider questions of this Section and the approach to formation for Reader ministry may both inform and develop from this wider debate. Specifically there is scope to consider the particular skills required in someone facilitating the development of licensed, lay, voluntary ministers and who (lay or ordained) might be in the best position to do this, given the diverse manifestations of Reader ministry at the current time. In addition, in the same way that taking on the responsibility for training curates will contribute to the CMD of training ministers, so participating in or taking responsibility for a Reader's development could contribute to the CMD and sense of value of particularly gifted or more experienced Readers.

A more strategic approach?

15 Increasing recognition of the importance of training for training incumbents against the background of the growing importance of CMD generally invites a question as to whether such training is better offered at diocesan or regional level. Already there are examples of dioceses combining resources and following common programmes. With the additional consideration that some at least of the training is appropriately at Masters level (whether or not it is formally accredited) the question arises as to whether a sufficiently high quality of provision is possible on a diocese by diocese basis. Moreover the shift to life-long rather than sporadic or episodic learning as the norm with ministerial development increasingly seen as integral to ministry rather than optional would appear to call for a more strategic approach to CMD in general and invites consideration as to whether the idea of a national staff college, considered and rejected in the Hind Report (6.25) in favour of the development of RTPs,[1] might now supplement the work of the Regions specifically in the area of CMD.

Note

1 RTP is an abbreviation for the Regional Training Partnerships recommended by the Hind Report in 2003.

Appendix 2: Incorporating EI competencies into the formation curriculum

Level	Category Self-awareness; self-regulation; motivation; empathy; social skills	Competency	Goleman remarks	Teaching methods	Comments
3	S-A	Emotional awareness	knowing what emotions I am feeling and why basic to all EI competencies cultivated through contemplative discipline required to align work with values and goals	training in listening skills name feelings arising from event in theological reflection regular contemplative discipline	basic to all other EI competencies vital to cultivating healthy work–life balance in relation to higher competencies, self-awareness becomes knowing one's own *values*, not just feelings, and is thus related to aligning work with values and goals
3	E	Understanding others	ability to listen well ability to take perspective of others requires genuine care for others	basic listening skills training some TR models verbatim role play	basic to all other-oriented EI competencies Goleman notes there is usually a power gradient: those in power are not expected to empathize with those less powerful – servant leadership reverses this gradient
4	S-A	Accurate self-assessment	awareness of strengths and weaknesses ability to learn from experience open to feedback from others	group work, involving regular peer feedback; shared project with tasks divided out; opportunities to work in areas of weakness coaching in giving and receiving feedback; counselling/mentoring/supervision	openness to feedback is key here, requiring vulnerability, and leading to humility (appreciation and celebration of self and others' strengths); thus, this ability underlies and provides the building block for disposition
4	S-R	Self-control	builds on emotional awareness ability to manage emotions ability to 'turn off' or 'turn down' amygdala threat warning results in resilience	regular contemplative discipline role play supervision and reflection training in conflict management	research suggests resilience is a key competency enabling flourishing in ministry (resilience does not appear as a separate competency in Goleman's list)

Level	Category Self-awareness; self-regulation; motivation; empathy; social skills	Competency	Goleman remarks	Teaching methods	Comments
4	E	Service orientation	understand the needs of others understand perspective of others readiness to offer assistance	intermediate listening skills placement experience and journaling basic research techniques, e.g. interview design and lead creative worship TR on situations	this is a value that requires the relevant EI competencies for its practice we tend to assume this in all candidates for ministry, but is it really the case? some candidates may be offering for ministry largely to meet personal need
4	E	Leveraging diversity	understand diverse world-views understand and relate well to people from diverse backgrounds challenges bias and intolerance; avoids stereotyping	diverse training cohort placement experience, especially in unfamiliar situations study weeks on, e.g. children, ageing, inter-faith work in pairs or groups unconscious bias training	like service orientation, a culturally desirable value, which with practice and familiarity becomes part of pastoral imagination spiritual writers talk about the ability to create 'hospitable space'
4	SS	Building bonds	maintaining informal networks building rapport making and maintaining friendships seeking out beneficial relationships	relationship games group projects	builds on self-awareness, empathy, service orientation crucial for success in interpersonal work; the goal is trusting relationships
5	S-A	Self-confidence	builds on self-assessment contributes to self-confidence and 'presence' contributes to self-efficacy contributes to courage	presentations case studies role play supervision peer feedback	research shows self-efficacy is key competency or disposition enabling resilience in ministry contributes to courage

Level	Category Self-awareness; self-regulation; motivation; empathy; social skills	Competency	Goleman remarks	Teaching methods	Comments
5	S-R	Innovation and Adaptability	builds on self-confidence and self-control, i.e. resilience under threat / ability to cope with change / ability to initiate change	brainstorming / group projects / problem-solving / coloured hats	placed at level 5 as necessary for ordained ministry, but to be nurtured in curacy / change management not included in the competencies, but relies on management of both self and others
5	SS	Communication	active, accurate listening / fostering open communication / ability to pick up emotional clues / dealing with issues persuasively	listening skills, building beyond basic to include asking good questions, picking up tacit clues, owning one's own emotions / persuasive writing, concentrating on emotional quality / verbatim with analysis of underlying feelings and assumptions	builds on both empathy and self-awareness, since effective communication requires other-understanding / placed at level 5 because the description involves some higher level listening and responding skills but could be level 4
5	SS	Influence	appears to sum up as ability to influence shared mood or emotions / includes effective listening and communication / relies on empathy, self-awareness, self-confidence / may be less effective with lack of political awareness	relationship and simulation games / group exercise + peer and supervisor feedback	Goleman has to distinguish it from mere self-interested manipulation: best performers 'respect others and put the organization first'
5	SS	Collaboration and cooperation	balancing task and relationship promoting cooperative climate requires 'team awareness' and willingness to share plans, information and resources, plus ability to spot opportunities for cooperation	group projects	at this point social skills begin to become vague because so many competencies are involved / at least one person with this competency needed to act as 'glue' for any successful team

Level	Category Self-awareness; self-regulation; motivation; empathy; social skills	Competency	Goleman remarks	Teaching methods	Comments
5	E	Developing others	requires empathy and self-assessment ability to affirm others ability to offer useful, relevant feedback also essential in managing upwards	training in helping others to learn, especially framing objectives relevant to the learner group settings requiring peer feedback in group learning, role play exercises in coaching and mentoring	placed at level 5 because of the importance of managing upwards plus readiness to develop others in curacy servant leadership gives feedback when and how the other needs it, rather than to secure compliance
6	S-R	Trustworthiness	builds on self-awareness, self-assessment and self-control requires courage faithfulness to personal values: having a rudder steering the ship	group work case studies supervision	EI competencies are here shading into the territory of virtue through alignment with self-chosen goals
6	S-R	Conscientious-ness	twin to trustworthiness rooted in values related to self rather than task avoids criticism and competitiveness	group work case studies supervision	EI competencies shading into the territory of virtue through alignment with self-chosen goals
6	M	Commitment	alignment with organization's goals requires self-awareness as knowledge of own values maintains work–life balance by balancing organization's values with own values identification with organization's goals means orientation to adopt long-term perspective requires affiliation with fellow-workers, based on other-competencies	supervision	relates to Lencioni's model of well-functioning teams, in which each member is prepared to sacrifice personal goals to the shared goal of the team[1]

Level	Category Self-awareness; self-regulation; motivation; empathy; social skills	Competency	Goleman remarks	Teaching methods	Comments
6	M	Initiative	based on commitment ability to spot and readiness to seize opportunities in line with goals must be balanced with social awareness	simulation games competitive (group) projects, in context of overall affiliative and collaborative training	must be aligned with commitment to the organization's goals in Erik Erikson's theory of development, initiative is a fundamental psycho-social ability developed in childhood[2]
6	E	Political awareness	accurately read power relationships understand forces that shape others' views and actions accurately read organizational culture and context	some models of TR conflict management training unconscious bias training	conflict management expected in curacy political awareness particularly valuable for incumbency roles
6	SS	Conflict management	handling people and situations with diplomacy and tact de-escalating potential conflicts encouraging discussion and debate orchestrating win-win solutions	simulation exercises case studies	a high-level skill rather than a single competence requires communication, self-awareness, self-confidence, self-control, empathy; improved with leveraging diversity and political awareness
6	SS	Leadership	setting an emotional tone communicating vision ability to make decisions and require compliance leadership by example	group leadership and task leadership with peer and supervisor feedback	rather vague, since effective leadership is an amalgam of competencies, including several under achievement motivation, plus influence, political awareness etc. placed at level 6 since this is 'basic' leadership; level 7 competencies improve it
6	SS	Change catalyst	recognizing need for change challenging the status quo championing the change modelling the change	simulation exercises case studies	requires a variety of competencies, but falls short of change management, especially management of adaptive change

Level	Category Self-awareness; self-regulation; motivation; empathy; social skills	Competency	Goleman remarks	Teaching methods	Comments
7	M	Optimism	ability to interpret setback in context (not as personal failure) requires desire for success rather than fear of failure	simulation games competitive (group) projects, in context of overall affiliative and collaborative training supervision	Goleman concedes this may be culture-specific to the US and come across as arrogance in Europe but it also aligns with higher levels of reflective ability described by Hawkins and Shohet, i.e. context-oriented viewpoint[3]
7	M	Achievement drive	motivated to achieve challenging goals, desire to improve based on self-confidence, builds on conscientiousness	reflection on practice SMART objectives research skills / project mission action planning continuing ministerial development	Goleman writes in relation to business effectiveness; for ministry this should be reframed in terms of passion for God's mission and *compassion* towards people it also relates to knowing one's own values and passions
7	SS	Team capabilities	modelling the qualities of good team working drawing others into participation building team identity and commitment protecting the group, sharing the credit	this is when the *team* as a collective displays the competencies; the team itself becomes a learning laboratory within which people learn the abilities required to work together	requires at least one person with the competency of collaboration to act as 'glue' within the team teams only achieve this with the ability to engage in healthy debate, which requires self-awareness, empathy and communication from all

1 See Patrick Lencioni, *The Five Dysfunctions of a Team*, San Francisco, CA: Jossey-Bass, 2002.
2 See, for example, Erik H. Erikson, *Childhood and Society*, Harmondsworth: Penguin, 1965, pp. 239–66. For an overview of the theory, see Gordon R. Lowe, *The Growth of Personality*, Harmondsworth, Penguin, 1972.
3 See Peter Hawkins and Robin Shohet, *Supervision in the Helping Professions*, Maidenhead: Open University Press, 2006, p. 56–103.

Appendix 3: Grade descriptors for emotional intelligence

Level	Personal Competence			Social Competence	
	Self-awareness	Self-regulation	Motivation	Empathy	Social skills
4	• adequate emotional awareness • adequate assessment of strengths and weaknesses • limited self-confidence	• aware of disruptive impulses • limited trustworthiness • limited openness to change • limited comfort with new ideas	• limited drive • limited commitment to group goals • limited initiative in a few areas • reacts poorly to setbacks	• adequate understanding of others • adequate anticipation of the needs of others • adequate understanding of diversity • little development of others • little understanding of group power and process	• adequate ability in building relationships • basic understanding of team working • limited communication • limited ability to influence others • limited ability to catalyse change • limited conflict management • limited ability in collaboration
5	• realistic emotional awareness • realistic assessment of strengths and weaknesses • growing self-confidence	• limited control of disruptive impulses • basic trustworthiness • growing openness to change • growing comfort with new ideas	• growing drive to achievement of goals • growing commitment to group goals • growing initiative in a wider context • deals with setbacks adequately	• growing understanding of others • growing anticipation of the needs of others • growing understanding of diversity • beginning to help develop others • beginning understanding of group power and process	• growing ability to build and maintain relationships • growing communication • growing ability to influence others • growing ability to catalyse change • growing conflict management • growing ability in collaboration • growing understanding of team working
6	• clear emotional awareness • clear assessment of strengths and weaknesses • confident and courageous	• good control of disruptive impulses • conscientious in a range of contexts • trustworthy in a number of contexts • positive openness to change	• able to energize drive for particular goals • able to help set group goals • able to operate confidently with initiative • deals with setbacks confidently	• clear understanding of others • regularly responds to the needs of others • regularly helps develop others • welcomes diversity • beginning to analyse group power and process	• confident in building and maintaining relationships • confident and able to influence others • communicating in a variety of mediums • able to catalyse change • manages conflict adequately • able to collaborate and cooperate • able to form and lead teams
7	• thorough and habitual practice of emotional awareness • can help others assess strengths and weaknesses • self-confident and helps others in self-confidence	• helps others with control of disruptive impulses • trustworthy in complex contexts • helps others in openness to change • advanced comfort with new ideas • constructs flexible and appropriate personal goals	• able to energize others and oneself • able to interact and develop group goals • oversees a range of initiatives • learns and grows from setbacks	• helps others understand themselves • enables others to help others • enables others to anticipate the needs of others • fosters a climate of diversity • competent in relation to group power and process	• helps others to build relationships • helps others in clear communication • helps others to influence others • able to catalyse change and help others in change • helps others to manage conflict • able to foster collaboration and cooperation • able to form and lead teams in a variety of contexts

Appendix 4: The Church of England's formation qualities for ordinands with incumbent focus

Priest (Incumbent) IME 1	Christ	Church	World	Self
Love for God The ordinand …	… is reliant on God – Father, Son and Holy Spirit – and lives out an infectious, life-transforming faith	… is rooted in Scripture, the worship of the Church and the living traditions of faith	… whole-heartedly, generously and attractively engages with God's world	… is prayerful and studies the Bible
Pattern of Life The ordinand …	… is reliant on God the Trinity and lives out an infectious, life-transforming faith	… is committed to shaping their life according to the living tradition of Christian faith	… whole-heartedly, generously and attractively engages with the world	… is committed to being 'diligent in prayer, in reading Holy Scripture, and in all studies that will deepen your faith and fit you to bear witness to the truth of the gospel'[1]
Dispositions	• poverty of spirit (recognition of their dependence on God's grace) • gratitude towards God in all circumstances • ever-increasing dependence on the grace of the Holy Spirit	• meekness (obedience to their apprehension of God's purpose for themselves and the world) • love for the Bible • desire for ever-closer relationship with God • desire to know and respond to an apprehension of truth in relation to God • willingness to shape their life in obedience to their interpretation of Christian tradition	• purity of heart (the desire to make God's will their first and overriding priority) • desire for the coming of God's kingdom	• purity of heart • desire to develop an ever-closer relationship with God
Knowledge and skills base	• knowledge of the four texts (Jesus' summary of the Law; Lord's prayer; apostles' creed; Beatitudes) and well-developed pattern of life based on these	• understands the significance of the Bible for the Church and the world through critical engagement with the Old and New Testament text and issues relating to their interpretation • understands Christian beliefs and practices: how they have developed in historical and cultural contexts and are interpreted today	• is able to 'lead Christ's people in proclaiming his glorious gospel, so that the good news of salvation may be heard in every place' • can draw on the resources of Scripture and theology in a critical manner to explore issues of ethics at personal and systemic level	• understands different Christian approaches to, and traditions of, personal and corporate prayer, and that different practices appropriately sustain different people and communities • understands and uses a variety of approaches to personal Bible reading

		• is developing skills in reflecting critically on how Christian doctrine and ethics relates to discipleship, church and society • familiarity with approaches to theological reflection • understanding and ability to communicate a Christian understanding of creation, sin, salvation and future hope	• can draw on the resources of disciplines other than theology and integrate these with the insights of theology and experience • has experience of engaging in mission, evangelism and apologetics appropriate to specific contexts, both inside and outside the Church	• nurtures their private prayer life with regular spiritual practices (e.g. spiritual accompaniment, quiet days, retreat, cell group, prayer triplet) and is developing a capacity to speak about the accountability and challenge experienced in such relationships • is developing a commitment to study of scripture and theology which will resource them for ministry • can engage with the ongoing Anglican tradition of different approaches to prayer and spirituality • is committed to the Daily Office or other forms of public daily prayer • is able to evidence how the study of scripture has deepened their personal study of the Bible and the growth of their faith • can show how they teach others how to pray, or to deepen their prayer lives using a range of approaches
	• shows a love for scripture and is learning to inhabit the living tradition of faith more deeply, interpreting it in different contexts and especially as they explore issues of faith in preaching • participates in a worshipping community and can make the connections between this community and the history and tradition of liturgical belief and practice • can understand and engage with the tradition of Christian beliefs and practices as they have developed across a range of contexts to enable them to interpret that tradition today • demonstrates the ability to apply the Bible and tradition of faith to specific issues in the contemporary Church and society critically and reflectively • demonstrates willingness to shape their life in response to the Church's tradition of faith in specific ways		• is developing skills in articulating responsibly God's saving purpose for Creation and humanity in the context of major issues facing the world and local community • is developing skills in drawing on the resources of scripture and theology to explore issues of ethics at the personal and systemic level • can share the good news of Jesus Christ and has experience of mission and evangelism and of watching for the signs of God's kingdom • is actively engaged with, and has a capacity to inspire others to be engaged with, issues of justice, peace and the integrity of creation • can draw on the resources of disciplines other than theology and integrate these with the insights of theology and experience
Evidence	• can describe how their faith is maturing through IME 1 • is growing in Christlike character in daily living, e.g. love, patience, prayerfulness, obedience • shows a vibrant faith that can speak about their own disappointments, experience of change or failure as they prepare for ordained ministry with an understanding of how grace is at work in their life • has a well-developed pattern of life based on the four foundational texts (Jesus' summary of the Law; Lord's prayer; apostles' creed; Beatitudes)		

Priest (Incumbent) IME 1	Christ	Church	World	Self
Love for People The ordinand ...	... welcomes Christ in others, listens, values and respects; cares for those in poverty and the marginalized	... builds relationships which are collaborative and enabling	... shows God's compassion for the world	... has empathy and is aware of how others receive them
Pattern of Life The ordinand ...	... discerns and welcomes the presence of Christ in others and extends respect and love to all regardless of status and circumstances	... values the uniqueness, gifts and points of view of others	... shows God's compassion for the world	... loves others as they love themselves
Dispositions	• commitment to the Christian imperative to 'resist evil, support the weak, defend the poor, and intercede for all in need' • willingness to share empathetically in the suffering of others • desire for justice and righteousness	• humility • values the uniqueness of others • looks for the gifts of others • willingness to subordinate personal interests to those of the group to which they are committed	• values the uniqueness of others • compassion for those in need • desire to share the good news of Christ • hungers and thirsts for righteousness (the realization of God's kingdom) • knowing themselves to be reconciled to God in Christ, desires to be an instrument of God's peace in the Church and in the world	• humility • values the uniqueness of others • compassion for those in need • appropriate self-respect and care for self
Knowledge and skills base	• understanding of the historical, psychological and theological foundations of Christian pastoral care • empathetic understanding of others • capacity to understand the needs and perspectives of others	• skills of attentive and empathetic listening • ability to take the perspective of others • skills of clear and appropriate communication • ability to notice and encourage the gifts of others • trustworthiness (faithfulness to personal values)	• skills of attentive and empathetic listening • ability to take the perspective of others • skills of clear and appropriate communication	• emotional awareness • accurate understanding of self • empathetic understanding of others

164

Evidence	• is developing empathy and wisdom in pastoral relationships especially with those who are different from themselves • can build healthy pastoral relationships that go beyond the superficial while respecting boundaries • can understand and articulate the importance of Safeguarding and knows what good practice in managing the care of children and vulnerable adults looks like • demonstrates the disposition to resist evil, support the weak, defend the poor and intercede for the world	• demonstrates good listening skills in relationships with those inside and outside the Church, including their own peers • can build professional and trusting relationships with colleagues within IME contexts that enable mutual respect, flourishing and learning • can show reflective practice and learning from a range of pastoral and professional relationships • is alert to the existence of various forms of prejudice, including racism, in the Church, and is learning how to challenge them and to support those who suffer from them • is developing skills in enabling others to assume roles of responsibility, in drawing teams of volunteers together, mentoring and supervising others	• is evidencing a capacity for engaging compassionately with people in the wider world that shows a capacity to put people at their ease • can demonstrate how their faith is shared in a specific act of missional engagement, and how they might go about enabling others to engage in thought, prayer and action • evidences the desire and ability to work for peace and reconciliation in the world • is aware that they are part of the worldwide Anglican Communion and is learning from their sisters and brothers around the world in order to develop and strengthen their own faith understanding	• is aware of how others see them and is aware of the need to manage expectations appropriately in forthcoming ministry • is growing in self-awareness and able to reflect on their strengths and vulnerabilities with honesty and openness • shows maturity and resilience in balancing the demands of formation, family and friends, drawing on supportive and healthy relationships to support them in the joys and challenges of life • is developing capacity to work with others in voluntary and professional settings, articulating their understanding of their own working style and respect for others who differ

Priest (Incumbent) IME 1	Christ	Church	World	Self
Wisdom The ordinand …	… is inquisitive, (curious) and open to new learning	… shows leadership that enables thriving and healthy churches, handles conflict and can lead in mission	… is robust and courageous and prepared to take risks	… is a mature and integrated person of stability and integrity
Pattern of life The ordinand …	… is committed to ongoing personal development and actively seeks new learning	… consistently leads in a way that enables the flourishing of individual gifts and shared commitment to agreed goals	… consistently takes well-judged initiatives in the pursuit of community well-being and mission	… exercises a high degree of reflexivity, enabling them to mitigate their vulnerabilities and manage strong emotional reactions
Dispositions	• humility • scholarly rigour • diligence • desire to learn and grow in order to serve	• humility • self-efficacy • desire for the flourishing of others • hungers and thirsts for righteousness (the realization of God's kingdom) • actively seeks for harmony and well-being	• self-efficacy • hungers and thirsts for righteousness and justice (the realization of God's kingdom) • seeks for harmony and well-being • willingness to defend unpopular decisions	• purity of heart (desire to make love of God and serving God's kingdom their first and overriding priority) • humility • self-discipline • desire to learn and grow in order to serve
Knowledge and skills base	• the methodologies of theological reflection and reflective practice • tools for life-long learning • creativity and innovation • ability to cope with change • ability to spot and readiness to seize opportunities in line with goals	• understanding of biblically and theologically informed perspectives on discipleship, leadership and community formation especially in the changing and diverse contexts of the Church of England • understanding of contemporary perspectives on leadership and organizations • ability to affirm the gifts of self and others • empathy and ability to build relationships • effective communication skills • practical wisdom in decision-making • ability to 'hold the space' to enable mutuality and the development of others • (ability accurately to read power relationships in a group)[2]	• understands the character (economic, social, cultural) of the setting in which they are called to serve and can respond in ways corresponding to the five marks of mission • has self-confidence based on accurate assessment of own strengths • conscientious (able to be guided by their own values without criticism or competitiveness) • able to spot and ready to seize opportunities in line with goals	• emotional awareness • accurate awareness of one's own strengths and weaknesses • appropriate self-confidence • high degree of personal organization • (ability to manage conflict)

Evidence			
• demonstrates a capacity to live with unanswered questions and open-ended situations • demonstrates a commitment to life-long learning, whether through academic study, reflective practice or engagement with personal development • is able to reflect alone, and with others, on their experiences in ministerial formation, to articulate their learning and demonstrate its impact in changed behaviours • has demonstrated learning in a new and different context which has been outside their comfort zone, such as a placement • is developing skills in enabling others to learn in both informal and formal settings	• can make creative use of the resources of scripture, theology and contemporary perspectives on leadership and organizations to inform discipleship, leadership and community formation in the changing contexts of the Church of England • is developing visionary leadership gifts within a church setting with integrity and is able to reflect on their own leadership preferences and demonstrate flexibility in adapting their leadership style to the context • can see the bigger picture and has the capacity to develop a strategy for growth that takes people with them • shows initiative, drive and creativity in implementing growth so as to encourage, enable and develop the leadership of others • can demonstrate the part they have played in collaborative leadership, showing awareness of the challenges and tensions of working in teams • is developing the capacity to learn from having difficult conversations and disagreement and to make any necessary changes to their behaviour as leader or member of a group • is developing the ability to read power relationships in a group	• can understand the character (economic, social, cultural) of a context in which they have been placed and can respond in ways which correspond to the *Missio Dei* and the five marks of mission • demonstrates the capacity to reflect for themselves and to act in accordance with their convictions • is able to articulate their own stance on issues facing society, and to demonstrate how this is formed by their understanding of Christian faith • is developing qualities of leadership such that they can defend unpopular decisions if needed to • can gather evidence of where they have seen others take well-judged initiatives in their leadership and respond appropriately	• demonstrates maturity in the relationship with their TEI Principal, supervisors and tutors, balancing accountability with personal integrity • can accept fair criticism with maturity and respond appropriately, with humility and good grace • can demonstrate the ability to love their vulnerabilities and to manage strong emotional reactions • demonstrates integrity in their dealings with others, including those in authority over them • demonstrates the capacity to hold the ring in terms of decision-making when the buck stops with them

Priest (Incumbent) IME 1	Christ	Church	World	Self
Fruitfulness The ordinand ...	... embraces the different and enables others to be witnesses and servants	... shows the capacity to exercise sacramental, liturgical and an effective and enabling teaching ministry	... shares faith in Christ and can accompany others in their faith	... has resilience and stamina
Pattern of Life The ordinand ...	... consistently conducts relationships in a manner that promotes the growth and flourishing of others	... exercises God-centred leadership in the gathered church with humility and integrity	... exercises leadership in the community in a manner that speaks of Christ and enables other Christians to live out their faith in the context of everyday life	... consistently relies on God's strength and comfort in times of difficulty
Dispositions	• humility • values the gifts and uniqueness of others • commitment to personal views and values • desire for wholeness and harmony in relationships	• purity of heart (the desire to make God's will their first and overriding priority) • desire for the flourishing of the Church • desire for the spiritual growth of themselves and others	• desire for the coming of God's kingdom • desire to see others share faith in God • desire for the fruitfulness of the Church • willingness to suffer persecution for Christ	• self-efficacy • willingness to face difficult situations, to be stretched and to go beyond their comfort zone when called upon • proper respect and care for self • willingness to work within God-given boundaries
Knowledge and skills base	• understanding of the perspectives and practices of the wider Anglican community, other Christian churches and other faith communities and the nature of Christian mission in a multi-faith context • ability to apply and communicate personal position and values in a situation of difference	• understanding of the history of the theological basis for the Church's tradition of liturgy • is able to faithfully minister the doctrine and sacraments of Christ as the Church of England has received them, so that the people committed to their charge may be defended against error and flourish in the faith • ability to conduct worship with reverence • skills of communication, especially in teaching and preaching • skills of adult education	• ability to discern the presence and activity of the Holy Spirit in the community beyond the Church • skills of attentive listening to individuals and the community • ability to communicate the gospel sensitively and appropriately using a variety of media, both inside and outside the Church	• self-confidence based on accurate assessment of their own gifts and capacity • self-control and adequate organizational skills • ability to apply and communicate personal position and values in a situation of difference • trustworthiness (ability to articulate and live faithfully to one's values) • ability to interpret setbacks in context (not as personal failure)

Evidence			
• demonstrates appreciation of and willingness to engage with the views of others (both within the Church of England and ecumenically) that differ in theological position • shows evidence of respectful engagement with the beliefs, practices and spirituality of a world faith community • gives evidence of developing skills in enabling growth in faith of others	• can make creative use of scripture and theology to resource their understanding of worship, especially sacramental worship in its various forms across the breadth of the Church • is developing aptitude in planning services and liturgy that is nurturing and can lead worship with confidence across a limited range of services and contexts • is developing gifts in preaching which draw on the resources of scripture and theology and that are growing in effectiveness in teaching the faith and discipleship • is developing aptitude in communicating the faith to children and adults and enabling children and adults to grow in faith • evidences capacity to communicate faith and practice in a new setting, with sensitivity to their audience	• can speak with confidence and infectious enthusiasm about their own journey of faith and discipleship • is able to listen attentively to individuals and the community so that they can discern the presence and activity of the Holy Spirit • shows how their IME 1 training is preparing them to encourage others in their everyday faith, in the school, workplace or family • has had experience of evangelism and mission and can reflect on lessons learned, both from activities that were fruitful, and those that were not and how all of this connects to the mission of God • has engaged with how children and adults learn and the implications for preparing children and adults for rites of initiation	• is working on a rhythm of life that has space for rest and re-creation • understands their own conscious and unconscious bias and has strategies to mitigate them • can tell a story of their capacity to bounce back after disappointment • can manage their time, showing the ability to prioritize under pressure

REIMAGINING MINISTERIAL FORMATION

Priest (Incumbent) IME 1	Christ	Church	World	Self
Call to Ministry The ordinand ...	... responds to the call of Christ to be a disciple	... understands the distinctive nature of ordained priestly ministry	... is committed to being a public and representative person	... articulates an inner sense of call grounded in priestly service
Pattern of Life The ordinand ...	... relates every part of their life to their commitment to be a follower of Christ	... lives out of the call to build the Church as a community of discipleship and mission	... consistently seeks to allow their outward behaviour to be guided by the responsibility of representing God's people in the wider community	... is guided by an inner sense of call grounded in priestly service
Dispositions	• poverty of spirit (recognition of their dependence on God's grace) • love for Jesus and desire to serve him • willingness to sacrifice and suffer for his sake • motivated by the promise of future glory • committed to their own growth as a disciple • committed to 'fashion their own life and that of their household according to the way of Christ, that they may be a pattern and example to Christ's people'	• 'delighting in the beauty of the Church and rejoicing in its well-being' • desire to serve and facilitate the mission of God	• respect and love for the people of God and for the Anglican Communion in particular • concern for the well-being of the wider community in which they are to exercise their ministry	• willingness, 'in the strength of the Holy Spirit, continually to stir up the gift of God that is in you, to make Christ known among all whom you serve'
Knowledge and skills base	• understands the impact of a vocation to ordained ministry on every aspect of their life [and that of their family]	• understands the theological underpinning of different ministries in the Church of England and of the ordained ministry to which they are called within the breadth and diversity of a mixed economy of traditional and fresh expressions of church • understands how Christian beliefs and practices shape the moral life of individuals and communities	• knowledge of important aspects of the history, diversity and contemporary challenges of the Church of England and the Anglican Communion worldwide • skills in managing themselves and their family relationships in the context of the gifts and pressures of public ministry	• understanding of the nature, joys and costs of priestly service • self-confidence, based on accurate assessment of one's strengths and weaknesses • trustworthiness (ability to articulate and live faithfully to one's values)

	understanding of a ministerial context and discernment of the work of the Spirit in that context • self-confidence, based on accurate assessment of their strengths and weaknesses • commitment (ability to align the organization's goals with their own and orientation to a long-term perspective)	• can speak of the joys and challenges of ministry, and the way in which ministerial formation has promoted their flourishing and their developing relationship with Christ, while being able to speak honestly when this has been hard • continues to discern the call on their life and on what being a priest will entail in the future • displays a willingness to accept the costliness of ordained ministry, while growing in awareness of the proper limits to that costliness and of the support they can expect as they face it
	• can articulate the emerging shape of their ministry and the way they are being formed as a priest during IME 1 • understands the practices of their own tradition within the Church of England which will enable them to engage generously and with respect for those whose tradition and practice are different • can engage with the living tradition and breadth of ministries in the Church and articulate the theological underpinnings to these ministries • is developing the capacity to discern and foster the gifts of all God's people as part of a commitment to the whole people of God • understands the ongoing conversation around the history, diversity and contemporary challenges of the Church of England and the Anglican Communion and is willing to engage in it	• is developing an informed appreciation of the representative role of a minister in the Church of England and has had experience of this across a range of public settings • is developing skills to communicate the hope of the gospel afresh to a wide audience • is developing understanding and skills to manage themselves and their family relationships in the context of the gifts and pressures of public ministry
Evidence	• is committed to their own growth as a disciple and to forming new disciples • can speak about the call of Christ on their life and that of their household as it is emerging in IME 1 and its impact in daily decision-making • can tell a story of personal growth in discipleship during training	

Priest (Incumbent) IME 1	Christ	Church	World	Self
Potential The ordinand has potential to...	... grow in faith and be open to navigating the future in the company of Christ and guided by the Holy Spirit	... manage change, and see the big picture	... see where God is working in the world and respond with missionary imagination	... be adaptable and agile
Pattern of life The ordinand ...	... habitually seeks to discern the way their calling is developing in obedience to Christ	... holds lightly to the present; sees the present shape of ministry as one possibility among many	... habitually looks for the signs of God's presence and activity in the world	... habitually identifies and responds with discernment to new challenges
Dispositions	• poverty of spirit (recognition of their dependence on God's grace) • self-efficacy • desire for continuing growth and development • openness to feedback	• desire for the flourishing of the Church and the effectiveness of God's mission • willingness to 'be the change you want to see'	• desire for the flourishing of the Church and of God's mission • hunger and thirst for righteousness (the flourishing of God's kingdom) • desire for harmony and well-being	• readiness for growth and change • hunger and thirst for righteousness (the flourishing of God's kingdom) • willingness to face the costs of change and growth, • (motivation to achieve challenging goals and to improve)
Knowledge and skills base	• accurate self-assessment • skills of life-long learning • ability to cope with change • flexibility • ability to spot and readiness to seize opportunities in line with goals	• ability to manage appropriately issues of authority, responsibility, power and group dynamics in relation to leadership and communities • (ability accurately to read power dynamics of a situation, organizational culture and context) • ability to discern the presence and activity of God in situations • ability to envision church communities for their future, and to discern what needs to change to grow into that vision • responsible initiative in seeing and grasping opportunities for mission • ability to evaluate risk and know when a risky venture is justified and appropriate	• ability to discern God's presence and activity within and beyond the Church • skills in evangelism and apologetics in the public arena • (ability as a change catalyst, motivating and inspiring others) • responsible initiative in seeing and grasping opportunities for mission • ability to evaluate risk and know when a risky venture is justified and appropriate • (enable others in mission and evangelism in contexts where the Church has little presence, and in contextually appropriate ways)	• ability to cope with and initiate change • skills of life-long learning • ability to maintain satisfactory integration between work and personal life

Evidence			
• reflect on their experience of a variety of fields of ministry • enter IME 2 with trust, realism and to grow into the new opportunities and places which ministry will call them to • enable and inspire others to grow in faith and discipleship.	• manage their own and others' use of authority, responding appropriately to the dynamics operating within the local church • support both traditional and new Christian communities, showing an appreciation of the role that each can play in the mission of God • identify where there needs to be change in the life of a church community, reflect on the implications for themselves and to have the negotiating skills to manage change effectively • pursue, in partnership with others, new opportunities for being the Church, evaluating wisely the risks involved while being appropriately courageous	• discern the presence and activity of God in situations • be an articulate apologist and interpreter of the faith in the public arena • enable and to lead the Church's mission and evangelism in contexts where the Church has little presence • make good use of social media in mission	• grow in self-awareness as a reflective practitioner, able to change their mind in the light of experience and practice • assess their own personality, strengths and weaknesses • demonstrate integration between discipleship and ministry, work and personal life • face the challenges of ministry, including its disappointments, with equanimity

Priest (Incumbent) IME I	Christ	Church	World	Self
Trustworthiness The ordinand...	... follows Christ in every part of their life	... leads maturely which promotes safe and harmonious Christian communities	... lives out their life as a representative of God's people	... has a high degree of self-awareness
Pattern of Life The ordinand ...	... relates every part of their life to their commitment to be a follower of Christ	... leads the Christian community in a manner that promotes mature relationships and the flourishing of safe and harmonious community	... consistently seeks to allow their outward behaviour to be guided by the responsibility of representing God's people in the wider community	... exercises a high degree of reflexivity, enabling them to mitigate their vulnerabilities and manage strong emotional reactions
Dispositions	• poverty of spirit (recognition of their dependence on God's grace) • love for Jesus and desire to serve him • committed to their own growth as a disciple • committed to 'fashion their own life and that of their household according to the way of Christ, that they may be a pattern and example to Christ's people'	• places a high value on their own and others' integrity • compassion for those in situations of need and suffering • desire for the flourishing and well-being of others • hungers and thirsts for righteousness (the realization of God's kingdom) • actively seeks for harmony and well-being	• respect and love for the people of God and for the Anglican communion in particular • concern for the well-being of the wider community in which they are to exercise their ministry	• purity of heart (desire to make love of God and serving God's kingdom their first and overriding priority) • self-discipline • self-discipline in relationships, including sexual relationships • desire to honour the discipline required to live with diversity
Knowledge and skills base	• knowledge of the four texts (Jesus' summary of the Law; Lord's prayer; apostles' creed; Beatitudes) and well-developed pattern of life based on these • understanding of the impact of a vocation to ordained ministry on every aspect of their life [and that of their family]	• understanding of the legal and administrative responsibilities of an ordained minister • understanding of the Guidelines for the Professional Conduct of the Clergy • understanding of the safeguarding requirements of leadership in the Christian community • empathy and ability to build relationships • effective communication skills • practical wisdom in decision-making	• ability to discern God's presence and activity within and beyond the Church • skills in evangelism and apologetics in the public arena • responsible initiative in seeing and grasping opportunities for mission • ability to evaluate risk and know when a risky venture is justified and appropriate	• emotional awareness • accurate awareness of one's own strengths and weaknesses • appropriate self-confidence • high degree of personal organization • understanding of the demands of confidentiality • understanding of the bishops' guidelines on human sexuality • understanding of the five guiding principles[3] • understanding of the Church's fitness to practise framework

Evidence				
• can show that they are able to accept the holy Scriptures as revealing all things necessary for eternal salvation through faith in Jesus Christ • has knowledge of the four foundational texts (Jesus' summary of the Law; Lord's prayer; apostles' creed; Beatitudes) and well-developed pattern of life based on these • has demonstrated personal and scholarly integrity in fulfilling the requirements of their training	• can show that they are ready to accept and minister the discipline of the Church and respect authority duly exercised within it • can demonstrate developing skills in managing relationships • demonstrates awareness of what knowledge and skills are required to fulfil the legal and administrative responsibilities of an ordained minister • demonstrates a willingness to engage with the vision and values of the diocese in which they will be placed • demonstrates understanding of the Guidelines for the Professional Conduct of the Clergy • can understand and articulate the importance of safeguarding and knows what good practice in managing the care of children and vulnerable adults looks like • demonstrates a concern and the ability to create safe environments in which sensitive issues and concerns can be raised honestly and openly • demonstrates a capacity to be a charity trustee	• ability to 'hold the space' to enable mutuality and the development of others • ability to recognize and mitigate situations of risk • (ability accurately to read power relationships in a group)	• demonstrates the ability to communicate Christian faith in a credible way that respects the context in which that witness takes place • exercises care and integrity in using social media • has ability to evaluate risk and to know when a risky venture is justified or appropriate	• demonstrates the ability to manage confidentiality • demonstrates ability to live within the House of Bishops guidelines on human sexuality • demonstrates the willingness to honour the five guiding principles • demonstrates understanding of the Church's fitness to practise framework and how this affects ongoing ministry • is able to describe the accountability mechanisms in place for the next stage of their ministry • can speak of the joys and challenges of ministry, and the way in which ministerial formation has promoted their flourishing and their developing relationship with Christ, whilst being able to speak honestly when this has been hard

1 Text in quotation marks are quotations from or allusions to the Church's Ordinal.
2 Aspects of knowledge and skill in brackets are desirable at this stage of ministry.
3 The five guiding principles are those by which the ministry of women as priests and bishops in the Church of England is understood and guided.

Index

ACCM 22, *see Education for the Church's Ministry*
Adair, John 44–5
Aisthorpe, Steve 29, 145 n6
anti-intellectualism 13–14
Anvil: Journal of Theology and Mission 124–6
Arab Baptist Theological Seminary 65–7
Aristotle 70, 109
assessment 55–6, 112–16, 122, 124, 139, 141–2
Astley, Jeff xii–xiii, 75
Athens model of ministerial formation 48–50, 58, 60, 61, 81
authorization for ministry 16, 90, 91, 98–100
authorized ministries 90

Ball, Les 62–5, 66, 69
Banks, Robert 58–60, 62, 66, 67
Baptism, Eucharist and Ministry 17 n1
Barden, Robin 102–3
Bauckham, Richard 53–4
Beatitudes 32–3, 114
Belbin team roles 44–5
Berlin model of ministerial formation 48–54, 58, 60, 61
Berlin, University of 25, 39, 48
'Beyond the Fringe' research 29

blended learning 97, 134, 138, 143–4
Bonhoeffer, Dietrich xiv–xv
British and Irish Association for Practical Theology (BIAPT) 122
Brown, Malcolm 28
Browning, Don 59

Calvin, Jean 4
Cameron, Helen 18 n21
Campbell-Reid, Eileen 71–2
Carnegie Foundation for the Advancement of Teaching 67
Caruso, John 108
Chandler, Quentin 9, 77–8, 86–7 n92
chaplaincy 90, 96, 136, 147, 149–50, 153
Christendom 4, 15, 27–31
Church Army 90, 95, 112, 149
Church in Wales 24, 122–4
Church Mission Society (CMS) 124–6, 149
Church of England xv, 28, 66
church planting 90, 96
Church Times 103–7
Clark, Jonathan 1
Clement of Alexandria 48
Clemson, Frances 112
clericalism x–xii, xvii n6, 132, 145

collaborative learning 55–7, 81,
103, 122–4, 139
collaborative ministry ix, 1, 6,
11, 15, 16, 20–4, 31–2, 66, 68,
91, 92, 97, 101, 104, 105, 107,
114, 122–4, 136, 145, 148–52
College of York St John 112
Collins, Helen 86–7 n92
Common Awards 16, 26, 41–2,
81, 100, 112, 116–17, 117–18,
141–2
communities of practice 46–7,
56–7, 70
confirmation 89–91, 92
context-based training 102–4,
123, 138–40, 141, 142, 153–4
contextualization 30
Continuing Ministerial
Development 100, 139, 141,
143, 152, 153–4, 160
Coventry, Diocese of 29
Covey, Stephen 132
Croft, Steven 24
Cronshaw, Darren 61–2, 65, 66
curacy 107, 137–8, 147–54

d'Costa, Gavin 52
'Developing Discipleship' (General
Synod document 1977) 7
discipleship, *see* 'everyday faith'
*Divine Revelation and Human
Learning* x
Donovan, Vincent 85–6 n81
Drane, John 125
Drane, Olive 125
Dreyfus, Hubert 43–5, 68, 88
Dreyfus, Stuart 43–5, 68, 88
Duff, Jeremy 104–7, 123,
128 n20
Duke Divinity School 67

Dunne, Joseph 70
Durham, University of 116, 141–2
Durham University Excellence in
Teaching Award (DULTA) 117
Dykstra, Craig 19, 34 n1, 50,
66–70

Edgar, Brian 61
Education for Discipleship 6–7
Educating Clergy 67–9
*Education for the Church's
Ministry* 26–7, 38, 68
emotional intelligence 16, 39, 97,
108–11, 113–14, 115–16, 118,
133, 155–61
empathy 96, 108, 155, 156, 157,
159, 161
Enlightenment 26, 27, 40–1, 47,
48–54, 80
Enlightenment university 15,
25–6, 38, 39, 40–1, 48–50
enquiry-based learning 138
Ernst and Young 38
everyday faith ix, x–xi, xii, 3–14,
15, 16, 22, 30–1, 61, 66, 70,
77, 89, 90, 91, 92–4, 95, 96,
123, 133–4, 140
experiential learning ix–x, 16,
25–7, 46–7, 55, 72–9, 97, 103,
116–17, 141–2, 143–4, 145

Farley, Edward 48–50, 116
flipped classroom 66, 123
focal ministry 23, 96
Ford, David 39, 42
*Formation for Ministry within a
Learning Church* xii, 149, 154
Frensdorff, Wesley 60
Fresh Expressions 95
funeral ministry 43–4

178

Gardner, Howard 109
Geneva model of ministerial
   formation 61
Goleman, Daniel 108–11, 155–61
Green, Laurie xvii n6
Groome, Thomas 59

habitus 113
Hainsworth, Richard 122–4
Hardy, Daniel 1, 34
Hay, David 36, n19
Hay Group 111
hidden curriculum 49, 59, 103
Hind Report, *see Formation for
   Ministry within a Learning
   Church*
Holy Spirit x, xii, xiii, xiv,
   xvii n16, 1, 3, 4, 17, 20, 21, 24,
   25, 32, 47, 58, 78, 80, 81, 92,
   98, 102, 126, 132, 140, 144,
   151
House of Lords 28
Hudson, Neil 93–4
Hunter, Rodney 69

'immanent frame' 27, 50, 80
Initial Ministerial Education
   (IME) Phase 1 25, 91, 140–1,
   153
Inskipp, Francesca 119

Jackson, Bob 23
Jerusalem model of ministerial
   formation 58–60
'Jesus of history' 52, 54
John, Eeva 102–3, 121–2
Jordan, Elizabeth xiii, 76
'just-in-case' training 19–20
'just-in-time' training 19–20, 80,
   91, 95, 98, 133, 138

Kelsey, David 48–50, 58, 67
Kendal Project 36 n22
Kingdom Learning ix, x, xi, 6,
   40, 42, 43, 63, 75, 78, 86 n92
kingdom of God ix, xiii, xiv, 1,
   22, 24, 31, 32, 33, 51, 52, 80,
   97, 144, 151
koinonia ix, xiii, 22, 145
Kolb, David 55, 72–3

lay ministry 1, 2, 3, 6, 19, 22–4,
   25, 44–5, 89–91, 94–100,
   122–4, 134, 136, 137–8,
   139–40, 151, 153–4
Leach, Jane 119–21
leadership styles 110–11
learning communities 100–1, 103,
   125, 133, 138, 144
learning cycle ix–x, 72–3, 78
'Learning to Inhabit the Kingdom'
   121–2
Leeds, University of 112
Lessing, Gotthold 52
licensed lay ministry 90
life-long learning 24–5, 31,
   89–92, 140–1
Lilly Foundation 67
Lima Document, *see Baptism,
   Eucharist and Ministry*
local church as learning
   community x–xi, 4, 59–60,
   62, 66, 81, 91, 94–8, 102, 106,
   133–4, 138
locally based training 94–8, 101,
   106, 133–4, 136, 139
love 21–2, 47–8
Luther, Martin 4
Lyon, Stephen 56

MacIntyre, Alasdair 42, 47, 68

Mayer, John D. 108
McIntosh, Mark 54
Melbourne College of Divinity 62
Messy Church 100
Methodist Church 119–21
Mezirow, Jack 62–3
Miller-McLemore, Bonnie 69
Ministerial Development Review 134–5, 160
ministry or mission areas 97, 122, 136, 148
mission ix, 1, 3, 31, 59–62, 66, 68, 89, 91, 92, 95, 96, 97, 104, 106, 126, 131, 132, 134, 136, 148, 151
Mission-shaped Church 153
Mission-shaped Ministry course 95
Monmouth, Diocese of 24

Newbigin, Lesslie 34 n3, 68
Nixon, Naomi 121–2

online learning 97, 106–7, 134, 138, 143–4
ordinary theology xiii, 75–6, 80, 97
Origen 48
oversight 24, 90, 91, 99–100, 107, 136–7, 140, 147–9, 151–3
Oxford, Diocese of 7–14

paideia 41, 48, 50, 81
Paris, University of 39
pastoral equipping contract 93–4
pastoral imagination 67–72, 73–4, 81, 88, 89, 97, 101, 102, 103, 111, 117, 141
Paterson, Michael 119

PC3 programme 102–3
Personal Discipleship Plans 90, 92–4, 95, 98, 106, 133
phronesis, see practical wisdom
Pickard, Stephen 22
pioneer ministry 2, 61, 90, 96, 100–1, 124–6, 147, 149, 151, 153
Polanyi, Michael 40, 69
potential theological educators 117
practical wisdom 70–1, 73–4, 88, 110, 141
practices, concept of 15, 26, 42–8, 49–50, 57, 60, 79–81, 88
preaching 42–3, 46, 90, 97, 114
Proctor, Brigid 119

Quality Assurance Agency for Higher Education (QAA) 115–16
Quinlan, Kathleen 39

'recognized' ministry 99
reflective practice, *see* theological reflection
Reimagining Ministry ix, x, 5, 33
residential training 2, 16, 101, 103–7, 142–4
Resourcing Ministerial Education 135
Ripon College Cuddesdon 112, 142
Rogers, Jenny 45
Roman Catholic Church 28
Ross, Cathy 124
Ruddick, Anna 125
Runcie, Robert 38
Russell, Anthony 23

safeguarding 90, 97, 99–100, 120
St John's, Nottingham 90
St Padarn's Institute 122–4
Salovey, Peter 108
Samaritans 28
Scharen, Christian 71–2
Schleiermacher, Friedrich 48–9,
    51
scholarly guild mentality 60, 116
Schön, Donald 41, 59, 73
Schwarz, Christian 65
Senge, Peter xi, 132
Servant of the Lord 33–4, 144–5
'Setting God's People Free' x–xi,
    3–7, 12, 75–6, 92, 93, 94, 132,
    133
SHAPE course 90, 106, 134
Shaping the Future 112
Shaw, Perry 65–7
Shepherd, Bridget 94
Shepherd, Nick 94, 121–2
small group leadership 44–5
Soul of Britain research 29
Southwark Ordained Local
    Ministry Scheme 55–7, 113
Southwark Ordination Course
    54–5
Spencer, Stephen 107
spiritual direction 90
spiritual practices 8–9
St Albans, Diocese of 6
Street Pastors 97, 100
supervision 16, 90, 118–21,
    136–7, 156, 157, 158

tacit knowledge 40–1, 56, 69–70
Taylor, Charles 27, 51
teamwork 96, 137, 148, 160, 161

Tearfund 29
Theological Educators Network
    112
theological reflection ix–x, 2, 7,
    9–10, 11, 15, 24–7, 59, 66, 70,
    72–9, 80–1, 87 n92, 89, 97,
    100, 103, 105, 113, 123, 125,
    134, 139, 156, 159
threshold concepts 8, 77–8,
    121–2
training incumbents 107, 137–8,
    147–54
transformative learning 62–4,
    121–2
Trinity 21, 58

unconscious bias 156
university accreditation 20,
    38–42, 63–5, 70, 79–80

Volf, Miroslav 4, 47–8
Volland, Michael 102–3
von Ranke, Leopold 52

Ward, Frances 119
Warren, Robert 5
Wenger, Etienne 47, 109–10
West, Michael 122–4
Wilkie Collinson, Sylvia 59
Williams, Rowan 4–5, 72
Wilson Carlile Centre 112
Wilton, Gary 112
Wood, Charles 50
Woodward, Linda 36 n22
Wright, Tom 53–4
Wycliffe Hall 90

Xplore course 95